# THE COMPLETE GUIDE TO BUYING AND SELLING APARTMENT BUILDINGS

# The Complete Guide to Buying and Selling Apartment Buildings

## Second Edition

**STEVE BERGES**

WILEY

John Wiley & Sons, Inc.

Published by John Wiley & Sons, Inc., Hoboken, New Jersey.
Published simultaneously in Canada.

*Library of Congress Cataloging-in-Publication Data:*

Berges, Steve, 1959–
    The complete guide to buying and selling apartment buildings / Steve Berges.
       p.     cm.
    Includes index.
       ISBN 0-471-68405-8 (pbk.)
     1. Apartment houses—United States. 2. Real estate investment—United States. 3. Apartmetn houses—
Purchasing—United States. 4. Residential real estate—Purchasing—United States. I. Title: Guide to buying
and selling apartment buildings. II. Title: Buying and selling apartment buildings. III. Title.

HD259.B47 2004
333.33'8—dc22                                                                                                   2004042246

Printed in the United States of America

10 9 8 7 6 5 4 3 2 1

It has been said that behind every good man is a good woman. This statement holds true for me, except that in my case, there have been two good women. This book is dedicated to the two women who have had a most profound influence on my life. They are my mother, Eleanor May Miller Berges, and my wife, Nancy Anne Thompson Berges.

In memory of my mother, thank you for your kind words of encouragement throughout my childhood years. I will always remember your example of dedication and perseverance to attain your goals. It was you who convinced me of my self-worth, and it was you who taught me to believe in myself. Your example will forever live in my heart.

To my beloved wife, thank you for your continued support over the years. While my mother laid down the torch of life, you have picked it up in her stead. You are now the driving force in my life. It is you who carries on her tradition of love, confidence, and inspiration. It is you who gives me strength when I need it most. Of all the things God created, truly you are the most beautiful.

## ACKNOWLEDGMENT

I wish to express my sincere thanks to my wife, Nancy, for her editorial support during the production of this manuscript. Her wisdom and insight have contributed significantly to the successful completion of this book.

# CONTENTS

**CHAPTER 1**    Introduction to Multifamily Ownership         1
                 Introduction                                  1
                 Holistic Approach                             2
                 Background                                    4
                 Market Outlook                                6
                 Regional Trends                               9

**CHAPTER 2**    Advantages of Multifamily Ownership          13
                 Time and Efficiency                          14
                 Market Liquidity                             15
                 Transaction Costs                            16
                 Concentration of Units                       17
                 Management and Labor Considerations          17
                 Tax and Record Keeping Considerations        18
                 Divestiture of Property                      18

**CHAPTER 3**    Bridging the Gap                             21
                 Strategies                                   22
                 Leverage—The OPM Principle                   23
                 Clearly Defined Objectives                   24
                 Maslow's Hierarchy of Needs                  27
                 Conquering Your Fears                        29

**CHAPTER 4**    The Value-Play Strategy                      35
                 Buy and Hold versus Buy and Sell             36
                 Ten Ways to Create Value                     39
                 Diamonds in the Rough                        47
                 How to Tell a Diamond from a Lump of Coal    61

**CHAPTER 5**    Establishing Your Niche and Locating Properties  69
                 Establishing Your Niche                      70
                 Availability of Resources                    70
                 Property Size                                71
                 Property Age                                 74
                 Holding Period                               79

# Contents

**CHAPTER 6**   Six Ways to Locate Properties                                  85
      Real Estate Brokers                                        86
      Classified Advertisements                                  87
      Industry-Specific Real Estate Publications                 88
      Local and National Web Sites                               88
      Associations and Real Estate Investment Clubs              89
      Banks                                                      89

**CHAPTER 7**   Financial Analysis                                             91
      Valuation—How Much is That Property Really Worth?          92
      Two Crucial Principles That Saved Me $345,000              93
      Valuation Methodologies                                    95
      Financial Statements                                      102
      Five Key Ratios You Must Know                             117
      The One-Minute Assessment                                 124
      How to Read Between the Lines                             125

**CHAPTER 8**   Case Study Analysis                                           129
      Case Study 1: 52 Units in Flint—My Way or the Highway     129
      Case Study 2: 12 Units in Saginaw—Below-Market Rents      142
      Case Study 3: 16 Units in Beaumont—A Banker's REO         151
      Case Study 4: 98 Units in Houston—Creating Synergism
          through Consolidation                              162

**CHAPTER 9**   Negotiation Strategies and the Due Diligence Process          175
      Five Cardinal Rules of Successful Negotiation             176
      The Due Diligence Process                                 185

**CHAPTER 10**   Financing Your Acquisition                                   191
      Traditional Financing Alternatives                        192
      Secondary Financing Alternatives                          203
      Additional Financing Considerations                       206

**CHAPTER 11**   Closing the Deal                                             215
      Closing Fundamentals                                      216
      Closing Credits Can Add Up                                219

**CHAPTER 12**   Managing Your Property                                       223
      Hiring a Professional Property Management Firm            224
      Your Role as a Strategic Manager                          227
      Expect the Unexpected                                     228

# Contents

**CHAPTER 13**    Four Effective Exit Strategies    233
Outright Sale    234
Refinancing    235
Equity Partnership    245
Exchange of Properties    248
Combining Methods    249

**CHAPTER 14**    Five Keys to Your Success    255
Understanding Risk    256
Overcoming Fear of Failure    259
Accepting Responsibility    261
Willingness to Persevere    264
Defining Your Sense of Purpose    267

**APPENDIX A: WWW.THEVALUEPLAY.COM**    273

**APPENDIX B: WWW.SYMPHONY-HOMES.COM**    275

**GLOSSARY**    277

**INDEX**    297

# THE COMPLETE GUIDE TO BUYING AND SELLING APARTMENT BUILDINGS

## CHAPTER 1

**The Light of Integrity**
*The soul is dyed the color of its thoughts. Think only on those things that are in line with your principles and can bear the full light of day. The content of your character is your choice. Day by day, what you choose, what you think, and what you do is who you become. Your integrity is your destiny . . . it is the light that guides your way.*
**—HERACLITUS**

# Introduction to Multifamily Ownership

## Introduction

The systematic acquisition of real estate properties over time is unquestionably one of the surest means of accumulating wealth. While building a respectable real estate portfolio is a process that can take months, or even years, the patient and diligent investor enjoys a high probability of earning above-average returns for his or her efforts. Careful analysis, however, is required for each and every property considered. Proper analysis is not limited to a simple review of the property's condition and location. To be successful in this business requires a more exhaustive approach.

This book is intended as a guide to developing a format for a thorough examination of each and every property you are considering. This format, when properly applied, will provide you with a significant competitive edge. It is my intent that by following the guidelines in this book, you will no

1

SFH   34%
2~4   19%
5+    43%

longer arbitrarily determine value as it applies to real estate; rather, you will truly understand it. By the time you are finished reading this book, you will know why a multifamily complex, for example, is worth only $700,000 instead of the $950,000 the seller is asking. Proper understanding of this single principle can be the difference between success and failure.

While readers of this book are likely to have broad and diverse backgrounds, you do share one thing in common—your interest in real estate. I will attempt to be as thorough as possible, because some readers are likely to have little to no experience, while others are seasoned professionals searching for that edge. This being the case, those readers who have a great deal of experience may find some of the material to be a bit basic. It is crucial, however, to lay the proper foundation for those who are not as experienced. Many readers have most likely purchased single-family houses at one time or another and have at least a minimal degree of rental property experience.

## Holistic Approach

In addition to providing a comprehensive approach to analyzing, buying, and selling apartments, this book also offers a holistic approach that will enable you to more fully achieve your true potential. Personal examples, inspiring stories, anecdotes, and quotes are used throughout to stir your mental faculties and encourage you to reach deep within yourself to fulfill your dreams, whatever they may be. While understanding the mechanics of multifamily transactions plays an important role in the level of your success, it is my personal belief that the stories and examples used throughout the book are what will truly enable you to become successful, not only in real estate, but in life as well.

I cannot help but feel that the hand of Providence guides my writing from time to time, as thoughts flow freely from my heart and mind with little or no effort. After the first edition of this book was published, I received overwhelmingly positive responses from readers who were inspired for one reason or another by portions of it. For example, one kind lady named Melinda was so inspired, she felt compelled to contact me, which she did only a month ago. Melinda, who is from New York, had just suffered the loss of her husband a few short weeks before. I listened to Melinda's story for well over an hour with empathy as she described how despondent she had felt after her husband died. Not sure where to turn, she happened across my book and after reading it thoroughly, felt a renewed sense of hope, knowing that somehow everything would be all right. Melinda's kind words of gratitude left me feeling appreciative that in some small way, I had been instrumental in lifting her spirit, even if only for a moment.

Recently, I received a call from a gracious gentleman named Lambis who lives in Athens, Greece. Like Melinda, he, too, had just finished reading this book and felt compelled to contact me. Lambis explained how he had been in one of the largest bookstores in Athens searching for a book on real estate investing. When he asked one of the employees where the real estate section was, he was told the bookstore did not have one. Lambis explained to me this was due to the fact that there really is no real estate market in Athens because families rarely move. In other words, once a family purchases a house, they stay there for most of their lives and often pass the house down from one generation to the next. As Lambis was perusing the economics section of the bookstore, however, he came across a single real estate book, which just happened to be this one.

Lambis then proceeded to tell me that he would be flying to the States in two weeks and would like to meet with me. Feeling honored at such a request, I readily agreed. While Lambis arranged his flight schedule, I arranged my work schedule to set aside an entire day for him. In fact, it was just last Friday that the two of us met. Lambis, a most remarkable man, shared many fascinating stories with me over the course of the day. He told me of his grandfather, a prominent engineer, well-known for his numerous contributions to major projects throughout the city of Athens. He told me of his father, another distinguished engineer, who built one of the most respected companies in Athens employing over 4,000 men and women. He also told me of the devastating setbacks his father experienced due to the oil embargo during the late 1970s.

Lambis explained that although his father had built a vast empire, there was one primary flaw that contributed to the ultimate demise of the family's business. His father's management style was extreme control in every facet of the organization. It was this unwillingness to relinquish control and delegate responsibility to his senior managers that set the stage for the inevitable collapse of the business. When the oil crisis occurred, it was as if one leg, and then another, was knocked out from underneath a three-legged stool. When one leg is removed, the stool becomes very unstable, and when the second leg is removed, the stool has no choice but to fall. Rather than declaring bankruptcy, Lambis' father spent the next decade liquidating the company's assets in an effort to repay as many of the debts as possible. During that period, his father, once a Greek icon of monumental stature, suffered a series of no less than 10 heart attacks. He passed away in 1991 with his majestic honor, his noble character, and his impeccable integrity fully intact. Saddened by this tragic loss, Lambis vowed not to repeat his father's mistakes in his own business affairs. It was apparent to me that he had indeed learned from his father, as Lambis is today a successful businessman in his own right, with a management team in place that allows him to freely come and go without the day-to-day oversight required by most business owners.

# Background

A confluence of events from my own life experiences over the past 20-plus years has provided me with unique insights on the real estate market. Three primary components have contributed to my experience.

First and foremost, like many of you, I have bought and sold a number of both single-family and multifamily properties over the years. As principal of Symphony Homes (www.symphony-homes.com), a residential construction company, I am a current and active investor.

Second, my experience as a financial analyst at one of the largest banks in Texas has provided me with a comprehensive understanding of cash-flow analysis. Working in the bank's mergers and acquisitions group, I reviewed virtually every line item of the financial statements of related income and expenses for numerous banks that were potential acquisition candidates. I spent 8 to 10 hours a day using a fairly complex and sophisticated model to determine the proper value of these banks, given a specific set of assumptions. Since leaving the bank some years ago, I have developed my own proprietary model, which I now use to assist me in determining the value of multifamily properties. The beauty of understanding cash-flow analysis is that once you grasp the concept, it can be applied to anything that generates some type of cash flow, whether it be banks, apartment complexes, manufacturing businesses, or fast-food restaurants.

Finally, my experience as a commercial mortgage broker has provided me with an inside look at the lending process—more specifically, what the lenders' underwriting departments typically look for. This book devotes an entire chapter to this subject, and I am confident that it will enable you to present a property in its most favorable light when you are seeking funding.

Although I had bought and sold real estate for a number of years prior to my experience at the bank in Texas, it was after I gained a more complete understanding of the principles of finance learned during my graduate studies at Rice University and my tenure at the bank that I was able to significantly accelerate my investment goals. I developed my own proprietary financial models that enabled me to more fully analyze an asset's value based on its cash flows and price relationship to similar assets. The combination of these financial analysis tools and a sound understanding of valuation principles has allowed me to increase my personal real estate investment activities from a meager $25,000 in volume a year to a projected $8 to $10 million this year alone. I am confident that the culmination of my own skill sets and life experiences will be of great benefit to you as you seek to enlarge and develop your own real estate holdings.

## Market Outlook

With interest rates at 40-year record lows, more people than ever are enjoying the benefits of home ownership. On the surface, this would seem to have a negative impact on the apartment industry. After all, if a greater number of families are purchasing homes, then surely there must be a fewer number of families who are renting houses and apartments, right? The answer is, not necessarily. In fact, research conducted by several leading analysts of the multifamily industry suggests the market outlook for apartments is actually quite favorable for several reasons. According to a report by the chief economist of the National Multi Housing Council, Mark Obrinsky, changes in population, demographics, and household composition will each have a positive impact on the apartment industry (January 29, 2004 issue). Obrinsky supports his assertions in the following excerpt.

When John F. Kennedy famously said "a rising tide lifts all boats," he wasn't talking about the apartment industry. He wasn't even talking about housing. Yet, his sentiments apply very nicely to our industry today. Conventional wisdom tells us that low interest rates and government incentives are driving home ownership rates up, and that those increases are bad news for apartments. Not so, according to NMHC analysis. The rising tide in this case is our country's rising population, which will raise demand for both owner- and renter-occupied housing. Housing, in other words, is not a zero-sum game, and home ownership's gains are not the apartment sector's losses thanks to demographics, immigration and population gain.

While banking changes and the investment climate drove home ownership rates up in the 1990s, the key factor driving housing demand in the next decade is demographics. Population growth—through natural population increase, continued high levels of immigration, and increased life spans—will increase demand for owner- and renter-occupied housing.

And some demographic trends will clearly favor rental housing, especially the swell of echo boomers and the continuing shift toward single-person households. After declining for two decades, the population in the traditional renting years (ages 20–29) is expected to increase 11 percent between now and 2010. Eventually more than 80 million "echo boomers" (ages 8–27) will move into the housing market, most likely as renters first. And there is no "baby bust" expected behind this generation, just a plateau.

Then there are the changes in household composition underway. The households most likely to own—married couples with children— are declining in number and now account for less than one-quarter of all households. Meanwhile, two-thirds of all new households in the past decade were non-family households, which have the lowest home ownership rates. This demographic shift alone would cause the overall home ownership rate to drop by 70 basis points by 2010.

Immigration will create even more new renters. Over two million legal immigrants have entered the U.S. since the beginning of this decade. In fact, fully 50 percent of the expected population growth in the U.S. will be immigrants, and half of all immigrants are renters.

Data taken from the United States Census Bureau also suggests that increases in the population are all but certain. Based on current growth projections, the population is expected to increase from its current level of 285 million people to a level of 315 million by 2010. This represents a phenomenal increase of 30 million residents over the next few years. The increase in growth will necessitate an increase in demand for housing, which is likely to place upward pressure on prices since the supply and demand ratio already remains fairly tight. Furthermore, with increasingly strict environmental and governmental regulations and concern over so-called "urban sprawl," supply will become increasingly constrained as builders find it more and more difficult to construct new housing. This, too, will place upward pressure on prices for housing.

Obrinsky also makes a convincing argument that addresses the issue of low interest rates. Although a low-interest-rate environment will initially have a negative impact on the rental market due to a shift of renters opting to become homeowners, this shift will eventually taper off as home prices increase, thereby making them less affordable, and as rental prices soften, thereby making them more affordable. Evidence of the balance between home ownership and the rental market moving into equilibrium is already apparent as new home sales have begun to moderate while rental occupancy rates are strengthening. In the following excerpt, Obrinsky contends:

> What if interest rates remain low? Won't that draw renters out of apartments? Our research mirrors the findings of a study by two professors at the University of California: interest rates play no discernible role in increasing home ownership rates in the short- or long-run. Housing affordability can worsen even with low interest rates if house prices are appreciating faster than household income, a situation that describes many current markets.
>
> Many analysts believe the pressure on apartments from home ownership is moderating. As rising house prices make them less affordable, renting becomes a more competitive option. According to the Harvard University's 2003 State of the Nation's Housing report, if the recent run up in housing prices makes home ownership too expensive, the number of new renters expected in the next decade could easily grow from one million to five or six million.
>
> Interest rate changes and home ownership incentives aside, housing is not the win-lose game many analysts would have you believe it is. The rising tide

created by population growth and demographic changes will lift all boats—regardless of whether they are docked at a single-family or a multifamily residence.

In the meantime, apartment firms are successfully competing with single-family houses by offering better locations, larger apartments, more user-friendly floor plans, cutting edge technologies, new amenities and abundant conveniences. The multifamily sector will continue down the path of offering not just a housing alternative, but a lifestyle alternative that many young professionals and empty nesters find attractive.

So there you have it. Obrinsky makes a convincing case for the apartment industry over the coming decade. The culmination of an increase in population of over 30 million residents, changes in demographic trends and household composition, a tight supply and demand ratio, and equilibrium between affordability of home ownership and the rental market all contribute to the positive outlook for multifamily property owners.

# Regional Trends

In order to maximize the return on invested capital, investors also should be aware of regional trends. On a national level, as Obrinsky claims, the rising tide will lift all boats. Not all boats will be lifted as high, however, since the gravitational pull of some regions is much stronger than that of others. For example, coastal regions in the West, South, and East are all experiencing positive growth for various reasons, while parts of the Midwest and the Northeast are actually experiencing negative growth.

According to the 2004 "National Apartment Research Report" published by Marcus & Millichap, changes in job growth combined with changes in the new construction of multifamily apartments will directly impact the performance of each market. Marcus & Millichap monitor and analyze different markets throughout the United States and have devised a measurement guide known as the National Apartment Index (NAI). Research analysts assert the following in the report.

> The NAI is a snapshot analysis that ranks 40 apartment markets based on a series of 12-month forward-looking supply and demand indicators. Markets are ranked based on their cumulative weighted-average scores for various indicators, including forecasted employment growth, vacancy, construction, housing affordability and rent growth. Taking into account both the forecasted level and the degree of change over the forecast period, the index is designed to indicate the relative supply and demand conditions at the market level.

Investors with limited capital interested in purchasing multifamily properties may find it more difficult to participate in regional opportunities than investors with a larger capital base due primarily to management requirements. A smaller 12-unit apartment building, for example, is likely to be managed out of necessity by an owner who lives within a close proximity to the property. Owners of smaller properties typically take more of a hands-on approach and are much more involved in the day-to-day operations of running an apartment than owners of larger apartments. Larger multifamily properties, such as those with 100 units or more, are typically operated by a full-time manager with additional oversight provided by a management company. An investor living in New York, for instance, can easily own and operate a 250-unit apartment building in Florida since he or she is not likely to be involved in the day-to-day operations of running it. On the other hand, an investor living in New York would likely find it difficult to own and operate a fourplex located in Florida, unless responsibility for its management had been turned over to a reputable property management firm.

Research conducted by Marcus & Millichap as reported in the 2004 NAI highlights important changes occurring in the top 40 regional markets.

These changes, which include forecasted employment growth, vacancy, construction, housing affordability, and rent growth have had a positive impact on some markets and a negative impact on others. Analysts report the following findings in the top 10 supply-constrained high-growth areas:

Orange County, CA, topped this year's index, rising four places on the back of top-five marks in every category except employment growth, where it ranked in the top 10. Job growth of 2.2 percent and low single-family home affordability will push vacancy down to 3.5 percent, allowing owners to raise rents by 4.6 percent. San Diego was this year's runner-up, with high scores for low vacancy, strong rent growth, and the lowest single-family home affordability in our coverage universe. Rounding out a Southern California sweep of the top four spots are Los Angeles (#3) and Riverside-San Bernardino (#4). The former is expected to post the lowest year-end 2004 vacancy among the 40 markets we survey, while the latter is forecast to register the highest rent growth this year. Fort Lauderdale (#5) rose 10 places on its sanguine outlooks for job and rent growth, while Las Vegas (#6) gained eight places amid expectations for increased tourist traffic and a 50 percent drop in completions. Oakland (#7), Washington, D.C., (#8), and San Francisco (#9) share similar employment outlooks and all three benefit from low levels of completions in relation to the size of their respective markets. Boston rounds out the top 10. While its employment base will grow for the first time in three years, the gain in jobs will be insufficient to stem its rising vacancy, resulting in a drop of six places from its 2003 rank.

According to the NAI, Orange County, California is the number one spot in the nation for investing in apartments in 2004. The National Apartment Index is a comprehensive report that can be of great value to those investors seeking to deploy their capital in one or more of the nation's top markets. It also serves as a useful tool to individuals who intend to invest in their own local markets by providing relevant data specific to that market. This type of data is essential to help investors identify trends in various markets. For example, is a particular region experiencing rising, declining, or stable rental rates? Identifying the proper trend will then enable individuals to implement the most appropriate investment strategy. For example, if rental rates are expected to rise significantly in a given market over a three-year time horizon, it may make sense to adopt an intermediate to long-term holding strategy. On the other hand, if rental rates are expected to decline in a given market, investors should likely adopt a short-term, buy-and-sell strategy.

The focus of this book, in fact, centers on using a short-term, buy-and-sell approach, which I refer to as the *value play.* The value-play strategy is equivalent to *flipping* or *rehabbing* single-family houses, but on a larger scale. Investing in an asset such as real estate is similar to investing in another type of asset—stocks. Some investors prefer the buy-and-hold approach, while other investors prefer the buy-and-sell approach. The holding period for a stock can be as little as a few seconds, as the rapid-fire day trader prefers, or as long as several years, or even several decades, as the investor who is in it for the long haul prefers. Each strategy has its advantages and disadvantages, which investors should consider before making decisions that affect their capital. The day trader, for example, will have considerably higher transaction costs and a potentially higher tax rate structure than will the long-term investor. The skilled day trader, however, has the opportunity to earn significantly higher returns than the average 6 to 12 percent the long-term investor may expect. Both of these approaches are explored in much greater detail in subsequent chapters. Regardless of which strategy you adopt, the market outlook for the multifamily industry over the coming decade remains positive.

## CHAPTER 2

*Successful and unsuccessful people do not vary greatly in their abilities.*
*They vary in their desires to reach their potential.*
**—JOHN MAXWELL**

# Advantages of Multifamily Ownership

Ownership of multifamily properties offers investors a number of advantages over ownership of single-family properties. One of the chief elements all investors are constrained by is time. The deployment of investment capital into larger assets such as multifamily properties affords investors the opportunity to make more efficient use of their time. Another key advantage is the liquidity of the multifamily market, which has a steady supply of inventory offset by a constant demand for that inventory. Additional advantages of multifamily ownership include reduced transaction costs, the concentration of units, more efficient use of management and labor, improved tax and record keeping, and the divestiture of the property.

# Time and Efficiency

One of the most valuable commodities we possess is our time. Each one of us has the same 24 hours available in a day, no more and no less. It stands to reason then that we want to make the best possible use of our time. From a purely practical standpoint, it only makes sense that if you can identify and subsequently purchase a group of units in a single transaction, this process is by its very nature more efficient and requires less time than purchasing several units in multiple transactions.

Say, for example, that you set a goal to acquire a total of 24 units over the course of the next 12 months. This means that if you were to focus solely on single-family housing, you would have to purchase an average of two units per month. Experience has taught me, and I am sure many readers as well, that before purchasing even one unit, you will probably look at as many as 10 units, or possibly even more. For the sake of simplicity, we will assume that in some form or another, you will review an average of 10 properties for every one that you purchase. This means that each and every month for the next 12 months, you will review approximately 20 properties, or a total of 240, to achieve your goal of purchasing 24 units. I am assuming that many readers have full-time jobs and invest in real estate to supplement their existing income in an effort to build long-term wealth. If you have a full-time job, the amount of time and effort required to review this many properties simply is not practical. Even if you are available to invest and manage your real estate holdings on a full-time basis, if you spend all of your time looking at potentially suitable properties, there is little time left for anything else. The exception to this might be if you are an active investor with a well-established and finely tuned network in place and a steady supply of prospective properties in your pipeline. This type of operation would likely be assisted by a support staff, as well. If you are just getting started, however, you will be largely dependent on your own efforts and therefore will be somewhat limited in the amount of time you can spend reviewing properties.

Now let us take those same 24 units and shift our focus to multifamily properties. You could choose to acquire the 24 units in any number of ways. For example, you could purchase all 24 units at once, or you could buy two 12-unit properties, three 8-unit properties, six fourplexes, or some combination of properties. Let's assume that for your 24 units, you were able to locate a 12-unit, an 8-unit, and a fourplex. This would give you a total of 3 transactions over the course of the year as opposed to 24. Using the same assumption as we did for single-family housing, you would have identified and reviewed a total of 30 properties rather than 240. Although it may be argued that it takes longer to identify multifamily properties, once they are located your time is spent much more efficiently than on the arduous task of purchasing 24 units individually. Even if you took your time and finally purchased a 24-unit property in Month 12, you still would come out much further ahead.

# Market Liquidity

Another key advantage of owning multifamily properties is that the market for them is fairly liquid. The availability of both single-family and multifamily properties will vary widely from area to area. Supply and demand, as well as proximity to a major metropolitan area, are the primary determinants of inventory availability. For the benefit of newer or less experienced investors, the term *inventory* can be and is applied to real estate just as it is to any other product that is marketed. Inventory is the supply of goods or products that are available to the customer, whether it is groceries in a supermarket, chemicals in a refinery, or housing in the real estate industry. The number of readily available single-family units on any given day far exceeds the number of available multifamily properties. You may initially think this is an advantage. Further observation, however, would suggest that while the physical supply of single-family houses may be greater, this is largely offset by greater demand. While literally thousands of people are in the market every day searching for a home to live in, the number of real estate investors such as yourself is much more limited. This is not to say that you will be the only one looking at a prospective multifamily property. Certainly there is competition in the marketplace. In summary, it can be said that supply and demand for both single-family and multifamily properties are generally in equilibrium at any given time.

## Transaction Costs

With each and every purchase, some type of transaction costs will be incurred. These costs include lender and attorney fees; third-party reports such as appraisals, surveys, and possibly environmental and engineering inspections; title fees; and the like. Consider the earlier example of the 24 units. Imagine the time, energy, and expense of purchasing 24 separate single-family units, each having its own closing. That's 24 separate sets of loan documents that must be prepared by 24 respective loan departments, 24 sets of documents for attorneys to review, 24 sets of third-party reports that will be required, and on and on and on. Now compare this to the purchase of the 12-unit, the 8-unit, and the fourplex. Instead of 24 closings, you now have only three. It is true that some of the fees are based on the size of the loan or the property value, but this actually works to your advantage. On larger deals, the parties involved can afford to be more competitive. They want your business and will often be somewhat flexible in the fees they assess. The smaller single-family deals will require almost as much work, and therefore there is not as much room for negotiation. If you have ever been through the closing process, I think you will agree that 3 closings as opposed to 24 represents a much more efficient use of your time.

# Concentration of Units

Having your units concentrated in a specific area will also enable you to make more efficient use of your time. Once again, consider the 24 units as an example. If you live in a small town or community, chances are your rentals will be in close proximity to one another, so this will not make much difference. However, if you live in a major metropolitan area, and you are not careful, you may find yourself buying property on the other side of town because it represents a fair value. Do this two or three times and you will be endlessly zig-zagging back and forth across town, through traffic, sometimes in adverse weather, and at who knows what time of day or night. Maintaining your focus in a specific area will once again allow you to make more efficient use of your time. This is not to say, however, that you cannot own apartment complexes located in different parts of the city. If you own, for example, a 52-unit complex on the south side of town and a 98-unit complex on the north side of town, you will most likely have on-site staff to assist you—and in this case, you are simply commuting between 2 properties, not 24.

# Management and Labor Considerations

The same principles apply to the most efficient use of your property manager's time, as well as that of any additional staff you may have, such as full- or part-time maintenance personnel. If you are managing only the 24 units we have been using for an example, chances are you are doing much of the work yourself. With 50 or more units, however, you will want to have someone who is capable of helping you operate your property. Depending on its size, your assistant may serve a dual role by not only functioning as a property manager, but also performing some of the light maintenance. If the units are all situated at a common location, this will greatly simplify things for your staff. Materials, supplies, and equipment can all be kept readily available and easily accessible for your personnel's use.

## Tax and Record Keeping Considerations

At the risk of sounding redundant, record keeping will be much easier for a multifamily property with 24 units as opposed to 24 single-family houses. If you have ever filed an Internal Revenue Service (IRS) Schedule E form (or any other tax-related form for that matter), you know that it can be a very tedious and time-consuming process. With 24 single-family houses, you will need to track each property separately. This includes all expenses such as labor, maintenance, supplies, materials, and utilities. It also means tracking depreciation and interest expense separately for each property. Even with the advent of tax software programs, a great deal of effort will be required on your part, and on the part of your accountant if you use one. With the multifamily apartment complex, you still have these same items to track, but for a single property, and the work is therefore much easier to keep up with.

## Divestiture of Property

There are advantages and disadvantages to both single-family and multifamily housing when it comes to selling your property. One clear advantage of selling single-family units is that you are free to choose how much or how little to divest. You can sell one or two houses, or you can sell them all. If, for example, you wanted to accelerate your program of wealth accumulation by continuing to enlarge your holdings, you might want to consider selling the unit or units in which you had built up the most equity. If you had a large amount of equity in a unit built up over time, or recently created through a value-added process, you could choose to dispose of that unit and that unit only. This would enable you to then turn around and acquire two or three additional properties while retaining your other holdings. An obvious disadvantage of selling single-family units, of course, is the difficulty involved if you should decide to sell all 24 units at once. You could offer them to other investors as a package deal, but there are no guarantees. More than likely, you would end up primarily with individual sales, and, just as when you acquired the units, disposal of each unit would be a separate transaction, with separate closings, and third-party reports, and all related fees and expenses.

With the 24-unit apartment building, it is either all or none. You do not have the advantage of breaking out single units to sell if you need to raise some cash. If you have substantial equity in the property and would like to leverage yourself up to a larger complex, your existing 24-unit property should be fairly easy to sell. This will depend on several factors such as interest rates, local market conditions, and the strength of the economy in your particular region. There are generally ample buyers for smaller properties like these. Finally, if you decide to divest your apartment building, you will need to concern yourself with only a single closing rather than the numerous closings required for the single-family houses in our example.

I believe that after reviewing the various elements just discussed you will agree that, as a whole, the advantages of multifamily property ownership far outweigh those of single-family property ownership. Probably the most limiting factor for most investors will be the level of resources available to work with. Given adequate capital or other assets, the prudent real estate investor will recognize that it is far more efficient to engage in a systematic process of acquiring multifamily properties for the accumulation of long-term wealth than it is to purchase single-family houses.

## CHAPTER 3

*Character cannot be developed in ease and quiet. Only through experience
of trial and suffering can the soul be strengthened,
ambition inspired, and success achieved.*
**—HELEN KELLER**

# Bridging the Gap

Now that you are sold on the advantages of multifamily property ownership, you may be wondering how to get from here to there, or how to bridge the gap between single-family and multifamily units. Unless you already have a substantial capital base to work from, you will probably want to start with a smaller multifamily complex, such as an 8-unit or a 12-unit. You may want to begin even smaller, with a duplex or a fourplex. If you have limited experience in the real estate market, starting with a smaller building will give you just the experience you need without overwhelming you. This will provide you with an excellent opportunity to get your feet wet and to get some real hands-on experience.

# Strategies

In my experience working with other investors and previous clients, I have frequently heard statements like, "Yes, Mr. Berges, I prefer the buy-and-hold approach. My idea is to buy a property, pay it off, and live off of the income." Sound familiar? While this method of building a real estate portfolio is a valid one, it is in my estimation certainly not the best method. If you have another source of income that is fairly substantial and therefore allows you to make large investments in real estate on a periodic basis, then this may be the method for you, or at least the one that you are most comfortable with. This approach, however, prevents you from maximizing the utility of your resources.

An alternative approach, one that I prefer, is what I call the *value play*. This method involves buying a smaller multifamily property, such as an 8-unit or a 12-unit, that requires limited repairs, most of which should be cosmetic. In other words, it is the classic fixer-upper. Your mission, should you decide to accept it, is to initiate a series of improvements immediately after acquiring the apartment complex. This will include things like painting, landscaping, trimming the trees, making minor parking lot repairs, and just giving the site a good overall cleanup. This will enable you to increase the rents—which, in turn, adds value to the property—within the first few months of ownership. Assuming you are on an aggressive fast track to wealth accumulation, you will want to unlock that newly created value by the twelfth month of ownership, either by selling the property or by refinancing it. The validity of this methodology proves itself by permitting you to take your original equity, plus the additional equity created by adding value, and leveraging yourself up to the next level, which would be a property approximately twice the size of the one you just sold or refinanced.

This process will allow you to bridge the gap from single-family to multi-family property ownership at a greatly accelerated pace. Chapter 4 discusses the merits of the value play in much greater detail.

## Leverage–The OPM Principle

You are quite likely to be already familiar with the *OPM* principle—*other people's money*. Your objective is to control as much real estate as possible while using as little of your own capital as possible, and this means that you have to use other people's money. This money can be from a traditional source such as a bank, or it can be from a family member, a partner, or even the seller, who may carry back a note in the form of a second mortgage. Whatever the source, you want to use as little of your own money as possible, because this is what your returns are based on. Your return on investment, or cash on cash return, is derived from the simple ratio of the net cash remaining after all expenses have been paid over the amount of your original investment plus any out-of-pocket improvements or expenses that require an additional owner's contribution. So, in a very simple example, if you pay all cash for a $100,000 building that generates $5,000 of income, your return on investment is 5 percent. You might as well leave your money in the bank and save yourself the time and energy that an apartment building will require. On the other hand, if you invest only $20,000 in the deal and borrow, or leverage, the remaining $80,000, assuming the same $5,000 of income, your return on investment now jumps to 25 percent. As previously stated, this is a very simplified example and does not take into account the debt service for the mortgage.

# Clearly Defined Objectives

If you are serious about being successful in the real estate industry, you will need to establish clearly defined objectives. This business is like any other business in that regard. You must have a business plan in place. Taking the time to do so will help you to stay the course. If you do not know where you are going, how will you know when you get there? Think of a ship about to embark on a journey across the ocean. Imagine if that ship had no rudder. It would be tossed to and fro, wandering aimlessly, and would be carried off its course by strong oceanic currents. In short, a ship without a rudder would never reach its destination.

Like the ship, you, too, must have a rudder, and that rudder will be your plan of attack, your clearly defined objectives, your business plan. And like the captain on the ship, who must occasionally adjust the ship's course, so will you, too, occasionally have to adjust your course. You cannot afford to undertake a journey in your real estate profession without having some idea of where you want to go. Many people go through their entire lives in a rather haphazard fashion with no sense of direction; hence, they end up precisely where they set out to go—nowhere.

The process of proper planning is crucial to your success in this business. Yes, you may have to think a little bit, and it will require some effort on your part to formalize your plans, but I can assure you that any time spent developing a plan will greatly contribute to your success. By mapping out your strategy in advance, like the ship traveling across the ocean with its rudder intact, you will eventually reach your destination. You may run into a few storms along the way, but, like the ship, you will ultimately reach your safe harbor.

In the original *Chicken Soup for the Soul* (Deerfield, FL: Health Communications, 1993), Jack Canfield relates the story of how a good friend of his, Monty Roberts, set a clearly defined goal while he was a senior in high school. Monty was required by one of his teachers to write a paper about what he wanted to be and do when he grew up. Because Monty was the son of a horse trainer and had been working with horses most of his life, he dreamed of owning a horse ranch. Canfield writes of Monty as follows:

> That night he wrote a seven-page paper describing his goal of someday owning a horse ranch. He wrote about his dream in great detail and he even drew a diagram of a 200-acre ranch, showing the location of all the buildings, the stables, and the track. Then he drew a detailed floor plan for a 4,000 square foot house that would sit on the 200-acre dream ranch.
>
> He put a great deal of his heart into the project and the next day he handed it in to his teacher. Two days later he received his paper back. On the front of the page was a large red F with a note that read, "See me after class."
>
> The boy with the dream went to see the teacher after class and asked, "Why did I receive an F?"
>
> The teacher said, "This is an unrealistic dream for a young boy like you. You have no money. You come from an itinerant family. You have no resources. Owning a horse ranch requires a lot of money. You have to buy the land. You have to pay for the original breeding stock and later you'll have to pay large stud fees. There's no way you could ever do it." Then the teacher added, "If you will rewrite this paper with a more realistic goal, I will reconsider your grade."
>
> Monty took his paper home to confer with his father, who told him this was a decision he must make on his own. For the next week, Monty thought very carefully about what he should do. Finally, at the end of the week, he decided to leave the paper exactly as it was. He returned the paper to his teacher with no changes and told him, "You can keep the F and I'll keep my dream."

Canfield concludes the story by sharing his use of Monty's 4,000 square foot house situated in the middle of a 200-acre ranch to conduct fundraising events to raise money for youth-at-risk programs. Monty never lost sight of his clearly defined goals. In fact, he still keeps that school paper mounted in a frame where it hangs on the wall above the fireplace in his 4,000 square foot house. Monty had the courage to follow his heart and pursue his dream and refused to let anyone steal it from him. Like Monty, you may encounter any number of friends or acquaintances who may attempt to steal your dreams. Also like Monty, have the unrelenting courage to follow the dreams of your heart. Stay the course and adjust your rudder as necessary, but follow the dreams of your heart.

Three basic components must be considered when defining your objectives: your entry, postentry, and exit strategies. For example, to define your *entry strategy* you will need to start by determining what type of property you are looking for, the price range you are considering, and the holding period. Are you going to buy an apartment complex, fix it up, and turn around and sell it, or are you going to hold it for a number of years? Your *postentry agenda* should include things such as management changes, property improvements, and rental increases. Your *exit strategy* is probably the most important of the three components. You should specifically define your intentions before you even purchase a property. Whether you are going to hold it short term or long term, you must determine in advance how you will eventually unwind your position in the property. If you are a short-term investor and are going to "flip" the property, you want to be certain the market is conducive to your plan. In other words, is there sufficient demand, and are interest rates going up, going down, or stable? If you are going to hold the property for a number of years, these factors are not as crucial. If you elect to maintain your interest in the property and choose not to sell, an alternative to consider is refinancing. This will allow you to unlock some of the equity that has accumulated over the years to invest in additional apartment buildings. An advantage of accessing your equity in this manner is that you avoid paying any capital gains taxes.

# Maslow's Hierarchy of Needs

We have discussed the principle of long-term wealth accumulation, but without fully understanding why this concept should be important to you, you may find yourself feeling dissatisfied when you do eventually achieve your goals. In short, it is just as important to know *why* you are going where you are going as it is to know *where* you are going. It is again like the captain of a ship—sailing across a great ocean with a specific destination in mind, the captain also has a specific mission or objective to achieve. It may be that the ship is taking passengers abroad to enjoy a cruise, or perhaps the ship is delivering cargo. Whatever the reason, the captain is not just out on a joyride, but is traveling with a very specific purpose.

If you have taken any organizational behavior classes in college, you may remember Maslow's hierarchy of needs. In 1935, Abraham Maslow outlined his needs theory in a work entitled *Motivation and Personality* (New York: Harper & Row, 1987). Maslow stated that we have a hierarchy of five needs. From the most basic to the highest, they are as follows:

1. Physiological.
2. Safety and security.
3. Belongingness and love.
4. Esteem.
5. Self-actualization.

Maslow asserted that with a proper understanding of these principles, we can have a better grasp on what motivates us as humans. If we understand the underlying behavioral motivation factors, we can more fully understand the *why* of achieving our goals. On the surface, you might state in general terms that wealth accumulation is important to you because you want a new car, or a bigger house, or a new boat for your new cabin on the lake. Although these are honorable goals, there lies within each of us much greater potential than perhaps we may realize. While new toys can certainly be a lot of fun, they are largely self-serving and superficial at best. The proper understanding of some fundamental concepts will enable us to achieve much more than we ever thought ourselves capable of.

Let us examine Maslow's theory in greater detail. The first and most basic needs we have are *physiological*. This includes our individual needs for food, water, and shelter, to name a few. They are fundamental to our ability to sustain ourselves.

After our physiological needs are met, we then seek *safety*. Safety includes a need for physical safety, security, and protection, as well as for things like job security.

Maslow's third behavioral need is for *belongingness and love*. We all want to feel a sense of belonging, love, and acceptance, whether it is at home within one's own family, or perhaps at work, or within some other social organization, such as church or a baseball team.

*Esteem* needs extend beyond belongingness and love in that we desire to feel a sense of self-esteem as we grow and progress in proficiency at our jobs or within the community.

Once these four needs have been met, the highest need is for *self-actualization*. This concept includes our need to reach and achieve the fullest extent of our potential. It is a higher need than all of the others in that it is at this point that individuals begin to look outside of themselves. This is why, for example, many successful businesspeople go into politics. Their other four basic needs have already been met, they have built at least a minimal degree of wealth, and now it is time to make a lasting and meaningful difference in society. This is, of course, not just restricted to politics. Opportunities present themselves in many different forms, and may include one's desire to provide better housing, for example—or, as in the case of Bill Gates, cofounder of Microsoft, to literally change the way we conduct business and to improve almost every facet of our lives.

Okay, so what does all of this have to do with you? If you can understand the simple concept that within each one us is the seed of excellence and that we have a higher purpose in life, then you can use these principles to drive yourself far beyond what you ever thought possible. The *why* of the accumulation of wealth can serve as the catalyst to propel you to excellence— and along the way, as you are successful, there is certainly no harm in enjoying some of the new toys that you have always dreamed about. Perhaps the greatest thing that the wealth-accumulation principle can provide is *freedom*. When you get to a point in your life where you have accumulated sufficient wealth, you can choose a greater level of freedom than otherwise might be possible. It is this autonomy that allows you to reach the higher plane of self-actualization, and to ultimately reach your greatest potential.

## Conquering Your Fears

Conquering your fears may not seem like an appropriate topic to some readers, but if you are new to multifamily property ownership, I believe it is one that should be given proper consideration. Without the self-confidence to move forward in your pursuit of wealth accumulation, you will likely deprive yourself of many opportunities.

One of the best ways to develop confidence in your abilities is through experience. Here is an example. Well-known comedian Jerry Seinfeld once told a joke about public speaking being high on the list of factors causing the most anxiety. He said that given a choice, most people attending a funeral would rather be the one in the casket than the one giving the eulogy. As a general rule, this is probably true. However, if you make presentations on a regular basis, you become accustomed to what is required each time you speak. Yes, there may be a little nervous energy just before the presentation, but you have experienced this before and you now know how to properly channel that energy to use it to your advantage. With each presentation or speaking engagement, you grow a little more confident. As your confidence grows, you become more and more comfortable with your ability to communicate effectively. You develop specific skills along the way. You know how to use various voice inflections to deliver a powerful and dynamic message and to keep your audience acutely attuned to your every word. It is this process of experience that allows you to overcome your predisposition to fear of public speaking.

Just as public speakers develop confidence in their abilities with each and every presentation made, so, too, will your confidence grow with each and every transaction. If you are reading this book, you have most likely at some time already purchased a single-family house to be used as rental property. Purchasing multifamily apartments is simply the next logical step in the process. You don't have to start with a 100-unit complex if you are not comfortable with that. Start with a 10- or 20-unit property or whatever level you are comfortable with. As you gain experience with this property, you will be preparing yourself to make progressively larger and larger deals.

For some, this process will come more naturally than for others. I believe that for a variety of reasons, some people are naturally more comfortable with risk than others. The upbringing one receives within the family is one of the most significant factors that contributes to self-esteem and self-confidence. When I reflect back on my own childhood, it is with great fondness that I remember my mother's encouraging words. She reminded me many, many times over the years that God had given me talents and that they were to be used, not wasted. She often told me that I could do anything that I set my mind to. During my adolescent years, unfortunately, my mind was not set to much of anything worthwhile. It was not until later that I heard her inspiring words over and over in my mind, prodding me along, and it was not until then that I finally began to believe her. If you have children (or remember your childhood), you may be familiar with the story of *The Little Engine That Could*. The Little Engine struggles mightily to pull a heavy load of toys up a steep hill. As the Little Engine struggles up the hill, he says, "I think I can, I think I can, I think I can. . . ." Whenever my five-year-old and three-year-old sons tell me, "Daddy, I can't do it," I gently remind them of the Little Engine. As I remember the lessons from my mother, who sang the songs of praise and encouragement at every opportunity, I strive to carry on this legacy in her memory within my own family.

Regardless of whether you received guidance from a parent, family member, or friend, establishing an acceptable level of comfort with risk is a process that can be developed one step at a time through your life experiences. While this process may come more naturally for some, everyone has the ability to assume risk in varying degrees. Sometimes you may have to push yourself to take that initial step, but you must be willing to step outside of your comfort zone, to push the boundaries a little bit. This is the only way you can learn and progress. With each and every step, you will gain confidence in your abilities. It is this confidence that will ultimately enable you to achieve your goals and reach your full potential.

Respected author and religious leader David O. McKay, in *Secrets of a Happy Life* (Englewood Cliffs, N.J.: Prentice Hall, 1960), describes differences among youth by their degree of ambition into three different classes. Although the text is directed toward youth, it is certainly apropos to all of us.

The author writes:

Let us consider youth as grouped into three classes according to their degree of aspiration.

1. First in their degree of aspiration: The "Infusoria" class in which falls the listless, drifting youth. Down among the lowest types of living creatures, there is a little animal that moves about randomly and aimlessly. . . . The Infusoria enter upon life aimlessly, and ninety-nine out of one hundred of these animals perish in consequence. . . .

2. Higher in the scale of intelligence and uplift, there are those who may be classed as the "firefly men." Often on a summer's evening you perhaps observed as children what we used to call the lightning bug. These flying creatures seemed most active just before a shower. The light from each would shine but for an instant, then the thing would be absorbed in the darkness. Another momentary flash, then blackness again. Such is the "Firefly" youth with respect to noble aspiration. He has luminous hours in which his soul ardently desires to rise above all things mean and sordid, and to bask in the realm of enlightenment and beauty. He would be valiant and courageous in defending virtue and right under all circumstances. If he could only obtain strength and power, he would use them to help his fellowmen and make the world better! But when a few hours later he associates with his companions unfired by such noble ideals, the light of his aspiration fades, the fires of enthusiasm die, and his soul is absorbed in the darkness of indifference. However, it is better to have hoped and yearned for better things and had the hopes fade, than never to have yearned at all. The flicker at least shows the presence of a light that might be fanned into a constant flame. That is better than damp driftwood from which will come not even a spark.

3. Then there is the third group, which I call the "Conifer" youth. In using this term, I have in mind not just the ordinary cone-bearing tree of the Conifer group, but particularly, the Giant Sequoia. . . . Among them is

one, "The General Sherman," which is estimated to be 3,500 years old. It has withstood lightning, floods, fire and still lives on. It has survived because in it is the power of resistance. The "Conifer" youth senses the fact that man is not just a mere animal, but is rather a spiritual being. He realizes that he is more than a physical object that is tossed for a short time from bank to bank, only to be submerged in the ever flowing stream of life. There is something within him which urges him to rise above himself, to control his environment, to master the body and all things physical, and to live in a higher and more beautiful world. (pp. 30–31)

And so let us, too, strive to become more like the Conifer youth, and in particular, the General Sherman tree. Life has a way of challenging each of us with our own set of unique storms. Lightning will strike when we least expect it, floods will follow, and fires will rage. Just as a blade of steel is tempered by a hot fire, so also are our souls tempered by the trials and challenges life presents us. Let us respond with courage in our hearts and resist the adversarial powers that may attempt to thwart our progress, and, in so doing, become more like the giant sequoia, able to rise above ourselves, to control our environment, to master all things physical, and to live in a higher and more beautiful world.

## CHAPTER 4

*Go as far as you can see, and when you get there you can always see farther.*
**—ZIG ZIGLAR**

# The Value-Play Strategy

An aggressive real estate acquisition campaign based on what I refer to as *the value play* is undeniably one of the quickest and surest strategies available to investors. Many real estate books espouse the buy-and-hold strategy of building long-term wealth. Proponents of this approach claim that to retire with a leisurely lifestyle, all an individual has to do is buy one property a year for, say, 10 years, rent the units out, and pay down the debt. At the end of 25 years, all of the debt will be paid off and the investor can live off of the rents. It may be that this strategy works fine for many investors, and this may be all that some are comfortable with, but as this chapter demonstrates, investors who maximize their efforts through utilization of the value-play concept will end up with far greater wealth than those who implement a simple buy-and-hold strategy.

As previously suggested, to achieve our maximum potential and what Maslow refers to as the process of *self-actualization,* we must be willing to step outside of our comfort zone. Some years ago, my wife bought me a plaque for my birthday, and I now keep it in my office. In large letters across the side, it has the word *RISK*. The caption reads, "Don't be afraid to go out on a limb . . . that's where the fruit is." This serves as a constant reminder to me that I, too, must be willing to step outside of my comfort zone. The primary reason we are reluctant to do so is our fear of the unknown. Uncertainty about what lies outside the scope of our experience creates fear, and it is this fear that is perhaps the greatest of all impediments to success. Will we make mistakes along the way? Of course we will. Will we experience some setbacks in the pursuit of our goals? Most likely, but this is how we learn. I'm sure you have heard the expression that experience is the best teacher. Our failures and our successes give us experience, and it is through our experiences that we learn. To be truly successful, you must be willing to assume risk. Conquer your fears, and in doing so, you will be able to achieve all that you are capable of.

## Buy and Hold versus Buy and Sell

The financial implications of value-added measures can be quite significant. The examples of investor strategies shown in Tables 4.1 and 4.2 illustrate just how powerful the value play can be. Investor A implements a simple buy-and-hold strategy of acquiring one property a year for 10 years and holds all 10 properties through Year 25 (Table 4.1). He chooses not to sell any of them, but ensures that all mortgages are fully paid by the end of the 25-year period. Investor B implements the value-play methodology over the same 25-year period. She elects to buy and sell one property each year for 10 years, with the exception of the last property, Property 10, which she will keep through Year 25 (Table 4.2). Like Investor A, she will ensure that the mortgage is fully paid by Year 25.

**Table 4.1** Investor A: Buy-and-Hold Strategy

| Year | Unit 1 | Unit 2 | Unit 3 | Unit 4 | Unit 5 | Unit 6 | Unit 7 | Unit 8 | Unit 9 | Unit 10 | Combined Values |
|---|---|---|---|---|---|---|---|---|---|---|---|
| 1 | 100,000 | | | | | | | | | | 100,000 |
| 2 | 104,000 | 100,000 | | | | | | | | | 204,000 |
| 3 | 108,160 | 104,000 | 100,000 | | | | | | | | 312,160 |
| 4 | 112,486 | 108,160 | 104,000 | 100,000 | | | | | | | 424,646 |
| 5 | 116,986 | 112,486 | 108,160 | 104,000 | 100,000 | | | | | | 541,632 |
| 6 | 121,665 | 116,986 | 112,486 | 108,160 | 104,000 | 100,000 | | | | | 663,298 |
| 7 | 126,532 | 121,665 | 116,986 | 112,486 | 108,160 | 104,000 | 100,000 | | | | 789,829 |
| 8 | 131,593 | 126,532 | 121,665 | 116,986 | 112,486 | 108,160 | 104,000 | 100,000 | | | 921,423 |
| 9 | 136,857 | 131,593 | 126,532 | 121,665 | 116,986 | 112,486 | 108,160 | 104,000 | 100,000 | | 1,058,280 |
| 10 | 142,331 | 136,857 | 131,593 | 126,532 | 121,665 | 116,986 | 112,486 | 108,160 | 104,000 | 100,000 | 1,200,611 |
| 11 | 148,024 | 142,331 | 136,857 | 131,593 | 126,532 | 121,665 | 116,986 | 112,486 | 108,160 | 104,000 | 1,248,635 |
| 12 | 153,945 | 148,024 | 142,331 | 136,857 | 131,593 | 126,532 | 121,665 | 116,986 | 112,486 | 108,160 | 1,298,581 |
| 13 | 160,103 | 153,945 | 148,024 | 142,331 | 136,857 | 131,593 | 126,532 | 121,665 | 116,986 | 112,486 | 1,350,524 |
| 14 | 166,507 | 160,103 | 153,945 | 148,024 | 142,331 | 136,857 | 131,593 | 126,532 | 121,665 | 116,986 | 1,404,545 |
| 15 | 173,168 | 166,507 | 160,103 | 153,945 | 148,024 | 142,331 | 136,857 | 131,593 | 126,532 | 121,665 | 1,460,727 |
| 16 | 180,094 | 173,168 | 166,507 | 160,103 | 153,945 | 148,024 | 142,331 | 136,857 | 131,593 | 126,532 | 1,519,156 |
| 17 | 187,298 | 180,094 | 173,168 | 166,507 | 160,103 | 153,945 | 148,024 | 142,331 | 136,857 | 131,593 | 1,579,922 |
| 18 | 194,790 | 187,298 | 180,094 | 173,168 | 166,507 | 160,103 | 153,945 | 148,024 | 142,331 | 136,857 | 1,643,119 |
| 19 | 202,582 | 194,790 | 187,298 | 180,094 | 173,168 | 166,507 | 160,103 | 153,945 | 148,024 | 142,331 | 1,708,843 |
| 20 | 210,685 | 202,582 | 194,790 | 187,298 | 180,094 | 173,168 | 166,507 | 160,103 | 153,945 | 148,024 | 1,777,197 |
| 21 | 219,112 | 210,685 | 202,582 | 194,790 | 187,298 | 180,094 | 173,168 | 166,507 | 160,103 | 153,945 | 1,848,285 |
| 22 | 227,877 | 219,112 | 210,685 | 202,582 | 194,790 | 187,298 | 180,094 | 173,168 | 166,507 | 160,103 | 1,922,216 |
| 23 | 236,992 | 227,877 | 219,112 | 210,685 | 202,582 | 194,790 | 187,298 | 180,094 | 173,168 | 166,507 | 1,999,105 |
| 24 | 246,472 | 236,992 | 227,877 | 219,112 | 210,685 | 202,582 | 194,790 | 187,298 | 180,094 | 173,168 | 2,079,069 |
| 25 | 256,330 | 246,472 | 236,992 | 227,877 | 219,112 | 210,685 | 202,582 | 194,790 | 187,298 | 180,094 | 2,162,232 |

Assumptions for Investor A:

1. Purchases one house each year for 10 years
2. Holds each property through Year 25
3. Arranges mortgage payments so all units are owned free and clear by Year 25
4. Assumes annual growth rate of 4%

## Table 4.2  Investor B: The Value Play

| Year | Apartment 1 | Apartment 2 | Apartment 3 | Apartment 4 | Apartment 5 | Apartment 6 | Apartment 7 | Apartment 8 | Apartment 9 | Apartment 10 | Combined Values |
|---|---|---|---|---|---|---|---|---|---|---|---|
| 1 | 100,000 | | | | | | | | | | 100,000 |
| 2 | 20% | 200,000 | | | | | | | | | 200,000 |
| 3 | 20,000 | 20% | 400,000 | | | | | | | | 400,000 |
| 4 | 20,000 | 40,000 | 20% | 800,000 | | | | | | | 800,000 |
| 5 | 40,000 | 40,000 | 80,000 | 20% | 1,600,000 | | | | | | 1,600,000 |
| 6 | 20% | 80,000 | 80,000 | 160,000 | 20% | 3,200,000 | | | | | 3,200,000 |
| 7 | 200,000 | 20% | 160,000 | 160,000 | 320,000 | 20% | 6,400,000 | | | | 6,400,000 |
| 8 | | 400,000 | 20% | 320,000 | 320,000 | 640,000 | 20% | 12,800,000 | | | 12,800,000 |
| 9 | | | 800,000 | 20% | 640,000 | 640,000 | 1,280,000 | 20% | 25,600,000 | | 25,600,000 |
| 10 | | | | 1,600,000 | 20% | 1,280,000 | 1,280,000 | 2,560,000 | 20% | 51,200,000 | 51,200,000 |
| 11 | | | | | 3,200,000 | 20% | 2,560,000 | 2,560,000 | 5,120,000 | 53,248,000 | 53,248,000 |
| 12 | | | | | | 6,400,000 | 20% | 5,120,000 | 5,120,000 | 55,377,920 | 55,377,920 |
| 13 | | | | | | | 12,800,000 | 20% | 10,240,000 | 57,593,037 | 57,593,037 |
| 14 | | | | | | | | 25,600,000 | 20% | 59,896,758 | 59,896,758 |
| 15 | | | | | | | | | 51,200,000 | 62,292,629 | 62,292,629 |
| 16 | | | | | | | | | | 64,784,334 | 64,784,334 |
| 17 | | | | | | | | | | 67,375,707 | 67,375,707 |
| 18 | | | | | | | | | | 70,070,735 | 70,070,735 |
| 19 | | | | | | | | | | 72,873,565 | 72,873,565 |
| 20 | | | | | | | | | | 75,788,507 | 75,788,507 |
| 21 | | | | | | | | | | 78,820,048 | 78,820,048 |
| 22 | | | | | | | | | | 81,972,850 | 81,972,850 |
| 23 | | | | | | | | | | 85,251,764 | 85,251,764 |
| 24 | | | | | | | | | | 88,661,834 | 88,661,834 |
| 25 | | | | | | | | | | 92,208,307 | 92,208,307 |

### Example

| | |
|---|---|
| Purchase price | 100,000 |
| Value created % | 20% |
| Value created $ | 20,000 |
| Original equity | 20,000 |
| Accumulated equity | 40,000 |
| LTV ratio | 20% |
| Next purchase | 200,000 |

Assumptions for Investor B:

1. Starts with initial $20,000 equity
2. Buys and sells one value-play apartment building each year for 10 years, but holds the last building purchased in Year 10 through Year 25
3. Creates value on each deal of 20%
4. Maximizes leverage on each new property purchased using a loan-to-value (LTV) ratio of 80% (or 20% down on each deal)
5. Assumes annual growth rate of 4%

I think that after reviewing Tables 4.1 and 4.2, you will agree that the difference between the two methodologies is quite significant. Using the assumptions as outlined in Table 4.1, Investor A's equity in the combined properties is $2,162,232. Not bad. All he has to do is buy one property a year for 10 years and hold them for 25 years, and he can retire with a very comfortable nest egg. Not bad, that is, until you compare his value with Investor B's (Table 4.2). Investor B has managed to amass a fortune of $92,208,307. What a remarkable difference! To fully exploit the value-play methodology, you must have a well-defined plan and adhere to it rigorously, and you must be willing to execute it, that is, to take action. This kind of wealth accumulation does not happen merely by chance, but only by design.

It could be argued that the assumption of 20 percent appreciation is not reasonable, but I can tell you from my own experience that not only is it reasonable, but it is conservative. A 22-unit property I purchased, for example, was subsequently sold within a year for a price that represented approximately 80 percent more than I paid for it. I will concede that in the latter years of the plan, when much larger properties are acquired, value creation of 20 percent will be more difficult to achieve. If we were to take Table 4.2 and reduce Assumption 3 for Investor B from 20 percent down to 15 percent, the resulting value at the end of Year 25 would be $27,723,147. This still represents a value of wealth roughly equal to 13 times that of Investor A. Clearly, the value-play strategy warrants every investor's consideration.

## Ten Ways to Create Value

Before you even make an offer on a multifamily property, you will want to know the potential value that can be unlocked from it. Creating value in multifamily apartment buildings can be accomplished in any one of several ways. Your review of a prospective apartment complex will consist of examining all of the variable components of an income-producing property—in other words, anything at all about the property that can be changed. This would include, for example, the income, expenses, and physical condition of the property, but not its location. While the property's location is certainly important, it is not a variable that can be changed to add value. Let us examine each of these 10 variable components in greater detail.

### The 10 Ways to Create Value

1. Increase rents.
2. Convert a master-metered property to a submetered property.
3. Add vending services including laundry, pay phones, and soft drinks.
4. Offer exclusive rights to cable TV service with revenue sharing.
5. Offer exclusive rights to satellite service with revenue sharing.
6. Provide access to building rooftops for cellular companies.
7. Consolidate two or more apartment complexes to achieve synergies.
8. Convert excess storage space into rentable living area.
9. Install water-saving devices in showers and bathrooms.
10. Protest assessed tax valuations to have them lowered.

## Income

There are many ways to enhance the income stream from an apartment complex. The most obvious of these is to raise rents. Generally, in order to justify a substantial rent increase in the minds of your tenants, you must give them something in return, such as improvements to the building. Smaller rent increases may not necessarily require improvements. Part of your initial analysis will include researching comparable properties in the area and their respective rates. This can be done by simply calling several of the apartments in the market you are considering and asking, for example, what the rates are for a one-bedroom, a two-bedroom, and so on. You will also want to know what your competitors are offering in the way of move-in specials, deposit requirements, and amenities. If your property has a pool and covered parking, and the one a few blocks down the street does not, then an adjustment should be made to reflect this. Most competent brokers who deal primarily with commercial or multifamily real estate (as opposed to single-family properties) will be able to help you with your market analysis by providing data such as the average rent per square foot. If the average rate in the area is, for example, $0.67 per square foot and the apartment you are considering is charging only $0.57 per square foot, you need to know why. The current owner, for any number of reasons, has not kept up with the market. A qualified and capable broker can also provide historical data regarding occupancy rates so you can determine whether an area has a stable, declining, or increasing level of occupancy. You will also want to note differences between the overall market's occupancy rate and that of the apartment you are considering.

Increasing rents is only one way to improve the revenue stream. Another way is to determine whether the property rent plan is "all bills paid," or the utilities have been submetered. Most newer apartments have been built with individual meters so that the tenants are responsible for their own electric bills. Many older buildings, however, have not. If the building has not been submetered, converting it from an all-bills-paid environment is an excellent way of enhancing income. Converting a property is not that difficult and can be done very cost effectively. Passing the cost of the electric bill directly on to the tenants will likely necessitate an offsetting decrease in rents by approximately 70 percent of the average electric bill on a per-unit basis. After making the tenants responsible for their own utility bills, they will become more conservative in utility usage by about 30 percent on average.

Consider an example. If the average electric bill per unit is $50, you will reduce the tenant's rent by 70 percent of $50, or $35. This will result in an immediate savings of $15 per unit per month. On a 50-unit building, this represents an annual improvement of $9,000. Using a capitalization rate of 10 percent, this is the equivalent of creating $90,000 in value.

You need to be aware that this conversion process will most likely create some tenant turnover, because some people simply prefer to have all bills paid with the rent. There are effective ways to minimize turnover, and most companies in the electrical submetering business can assist you with this process.

If you may be questioning the validity of the 30 percent savings, I can assure you from personal experience that in an all-bills-paid environment, the majority of tenants are not cost conscious. They are thinking about maximizing personal comfort, not about conserving energy. During a scorching-hot Texas summer, I once did an inspection of an apartment building that had not yet been converted to individual meters. One tenant was literally sitting on his couch watching television wrapped up in a blanket! I checked the setting on his thermostat during the course of my inspection. It was set at 58 degrees! Further inspection revealed that many of the tenants worked all day long, but left their thermostats adjusted down to about 65 degrees so their apartments would be nice and cool when they arrived home from work. I am sure they reasoned, "Why not? I'm not paying for it."

You may also be able to generate additional income by providing vending services. Most apartment buildings of 20 units or larger will offer some type of laundromat services. If the current owner or manager is servicing the equipment and collecting the money, it may be time for a change, especially if the machines are older. You can eliminate the headache of having to service this equipment by turning the entire process over to a professional company specializing in this business.

The best way to illustrate this is by sharing an example. I had a 25-unit building under contract to purchase, and I knew that the owner was servicing the washers and dryers himself. He repaired the machines when they broke down, collected the money from them, and had to deal with the tenants when they didn't work properly. The building was approximately 30 years old at the time, and judging by the way those machines looked, I believe they had probably been there since Day 1. You may be surprised to know that this is exactly the kind of thing that excites me, because I see an immediate opportunity for improvement.

As soon as I had purchased the building, I arranged to contract the laundromat services out. The company providing the services replaced the old equipment with brand-new washers and dryers and completely redecorated the laundry facility at its own expense. I signed a seven-year contract with the company. It would receive one-half of all moneys collected in exchange for servicing the equipment. In addition, the company gave me an immediate up-front advance of $5,000 for allowing it the privilege of providing these services. Not a bad deal. I got a check for $5,000 and a brand-new laundry room complete with equipment within 30 days of closing, and the company got to take care of my laundry facility!

There are other techniques for generating additional income that are generally not as well known. For example, just as a laundry service will pay you for the right to offer its services on your property, so will cable TV and satellite services. You can negotiate with the local cable and satellite companies to determine who will give you the best deal for the right to provide your tenants with television services. These companies may or may not be interested in providing your tenants with their services. Factors such as the number of apartment units you have, the proximity of existing services to your specific location, and the feasibility of installing the necessary equipment at the site will all impact their decisions.

You might also want to consider whether your apartment building is located in an area where the local cellular phone company might need a repeater tower. With the advent of cellular phones, phone companies are constantly seeking to rent space to place their equipment on building rooftops. The equipment need not always be visible, either. A minister was known to have received $1,200 per month for allowing the phone company to install a repeater tower inside the church steeple.

Finally, you might think about any excess storage space that can be converted into rentable living area, or other space that is currently not generating income. On the 25-unit building previously mentioned, the owner occupied one very large unit, which was not producing any rent. I had initially decided to convert the large unit into two smaller units, because the owner would be moving shortly after closing. Cost projections proved to be too high to justify the conversion, so I decided to rent the apartment as one large unit to be shared by two families. Since the seller of the apartment building accounted for rents on only 24 of the units, I had effectively created rents equivalent to those for an additional two units, for a total of 26, without any additional costs.

## Expenses

There are numerous ways to trim the operating expenses of a prospective apartment building. Each line item on the operating statement should be examined for the possibility of cost cutting. Over time, you will come to know what it costs to operate a property, and you will develop a feel for the average expenses on a per-unit basis, on an average-cost-per-square-foot basis, and on a percentage basis. The proprietary model I developed for analyzing my own properties makes these calculations automatically. Following are just some of the many points you will want to consider in your cost-cutting analysis.

- *Management fees.* Fees paid to a professional property management firm will generally range from about 3 percent of total revenues collected on the low end to 10 percent on the high end. If you are using or intend to use a management company, you should be able to procure competent and professional services for no more than 5 percent on 50 units or more. If you have a smaller apartment building, you may end up paying more.

- *Repairs and maintenance.*   The cost of building repairs will vary with the age and condition of the building. Allow 10 to 20 percent of budgeted revenues in your analysis. It may be that after an initial injection of capital for property improvements you can scale back your budget to the 10 percent range.

- *Salaries and payroll.*   Salary expenses can vary widely as a percentage of revenues. They will be determined by factors such as your level of involvement and the total number of units in your complex. If you are going to self-manage the property and assume many of the management and maintenance duties yourself, then 5 percent or less should be adequate. To justify a full-time manager, I recommend a minimum of 50 units. Since a competent manager should be able to manage up to 100 units, you can achieve greater efficiency through better economies of scale. For example, with a manager earning an annual salary of $25,000 operating 50 units, your cost per unit is $500. Using the same manager earning the same salary operating 100 units, however, your cost per unit drops to $250.

- *Utilities.*   I have already described in considerable detail how a master-metered apartment complex can be converted into an individually metered property and the cost savings that can result. While the majority of existing-construction apartment properties have master-metered gas and water utilities, new-construction properties are moving more and more toward individual meters. The responsibility for conserving our resources is being shifted to the end users, the individuals who have direct control over where the thermostat will be set and how long showers will run. Most of the apartment buildings you will be considering, however, will have master-metered gas and water systems in place. Although they can be converted to individually metered systems, it is generally not cost-effective to do so. Individual metering of gas and water is much more costly than it is for electricity. With the installation of electric meters, the electrician generally just has to install the meters and run a few wires to them. With gas and water utilities, however, a good deal of piping and plumbing is required, which may result in the temporary disruption of services. Since this process is much more labor and time intensive, your resulting costs will be considerably higher.

A fairly simple and low-cost way to help control water expenses is to implement a program whereby faucets, fittings, and toilets are inspected with every make-ready. Every time a tenant moves out, all faucets and toilets should be checked for leaks and promptly repaired as necessary. This is so simple that it almost sounds naive to mention it, but I know from experience that many owners and managers simply don't take the time to control leaks. I have inspected apartment buildings where I have seen leaks in no less than 4 out of 5 units. Another simple cost-savings measure is to replace the flush mechanisms inside the toilet tanks. Many older toilets use 2 to 5 gallons per flush, while all new toilets are mandated by law not to exceed 1 gallon per flush. Rather than replacing the entire commode, simply replace the flush mechanism with one equipped with a water-saving feature. You can shave 20 to 30 percent off your water bill almost immediately by implementing this one simple strategy.

- *Real estate taxes.* More than likely, you will have little control over the amount of taxes you pay on your property. There are tax advisors, however, who can be instrumental in getting the assessed value of your property lowered, which will result in a reduction of your annual tax payment. This is achieved by analyzing neighboring apartment buildings and comparing their respective tax rates with those on your building. If a significant difference exists, the advisors can represent you in arguing for a reduction in the assessed value of your building. These types of tax advisors will generally charge a fee based on a percentage of the cost savings to you.

- *Insurance.* The cost of insurance will vary widely among agents. You should look for an insurance agent who specializes in commercial real estate. While there are many agents who provide auto insurance, home owners' policies, and life and health insurance, there are also those who specialize in providing commercial services. Let us look at an example of what the difference between these types can mean to you. The owner of a 22-unit property I had under contract was paying about $4,500 per year for property and liability insurance. I got a quote from an agent who had been providing my auto and home owner's insurance for years. She offered the same coverage to me for $5,200. The mortgage broker I was working with at the time suggested I call another agent who specialized in commercial insurance. When he quoted me $2,400 for the exact same coverage, I had difficulty containing my enthusiasm over the phone. While I thought this was an exceptional deal, I did not want to let him know that. I have been using this particular agent ever since and have been quite satisfied. Depending on the level of coverage your lender requires, you should be able to insure your property for about $100 per unit per year on average.

# Diamonds in the Rough

Searching for the right property can be like looking for a diamond in the rough, that unpolished gem that just takes a little bit of work to make it shine. The level of deterioration you are willing to accept should be reflected in the price of the project. If the prospective property requires a total rehabilitation to bring its condition up to a standard that is livable, then there should be considerable upside in the deal for you as the buyer. In other words, there should be sufficient reward for the additional risk you will have to assume. I prefer looking for properties that are more than 90 percent occupied and that just look a little rough from the outside due to poor management and neglect. Rents for this type of apartment building will generally be below market. Because the price of an income-producing property is derived from its *net operating income* (NOI), the property should be priced accordingly. Do not let a broker attempt to convince you that the property is worth anything more than a multiple of its existing NOI. Less experienced brokers who do not fully understand value really do not know what a property is worth. I have dealt with many real estate brokers, and I can assure you that their level of experience varies widely. I have seen apartment deals priced at $500,000 that were really worth only $350,000. Some brokers will try to persuade you to buy at the higher price based on the upside potential, but that is not the way you make money in this business. There is much greater detail on valuation analysis in Chapter 7.

Finding an apartment building with an occupancy rate of more than 90 percent will help to ensure that you can service the debt on it—in other words, make your monthly payment to the lender. Many lenders have minimum occupancy standards and will not provide financing if the building is not adequately inhabited. Lenders are by their nature risk averse and will therefore attempt to make every effort to minimize their risk on every loan. You want as much in your favor as possible going into a deal. Ensuring that you have adequate rental income sufficient to meet all of your obligations associated with the property will allow you to focus on the task of creating value rather than having to worry about monthly expenses.

In your search for that diamond in the rough, I recommend concentrating your efforts on the type of building that *appears* to be in disrepair but, in reality, just needs a little tender loving care. This is the classic fixer-upper. The apartment building will probably need a fresh coat of paint, a thorough cleaning of the grounds, and some general sprucing up. Unless you are prepared to incur greater investments of your capital, avoid buying properties needing major repairs. This would include things like foundation problems, completely replacing the roof, and replacing the boiler or air-conditioning equipment. Doing a cost-benefit analysis will help you determine the maximum amount you can spend on capital improvements and still achieve an acceptable rate of return on your investment.

Here is an example. A few years ago, I came across a 22-unit multifamily property that at first glance appeared to be very reasonably priced. The seller was asking $350,000. The 22 units consisted of a row of 11 duplex buildings that were side by side. Also included in the sale was an empty lot, which was located adjacent to the units. The apartments enjoyed an occupancy rate of more than 95 percent, with minimal turnover. A drive-by of the property revealed that the buildings had not seen any new paint since their construction, approximately 17 years earlier. The lawn was not kept up and was in need of attention. Shrubs and hedges lined each building, but had not been trimmed for years. There were trees planted next to each driveway that offered nice shade for the tenants, but they were all seriously overgrown. Each unit had its own private fenced-in yard, but, like the worn paint, the fences also appeared to be original and in need of repair. So far, so good. Paint, landscaping, and fencing are all fairly inexpensive improvements and, in addition, are short-term improvements, meaning they can be made in a short amount of time.

While the $350,000 asking price sounded very reasonable, I needed something to compare it to so as to provide an idea of the potential value that could be created once they were cleaned up. As I drove around the neighborhood, I came across an entire street lined with duplexes very similar to the ones I was looking at. One of them had a For Sale sign out front, so I jotted down the number and returned to my office to inquire about the property. I visited with the seller at length; as it turned out, he represented the owner, who had at one time owned all 36 duplex buildings on the street, which was a total of 72 units. The owner had initially maintained them as rentals, but over the past three years had begun selling them off to the individuals who lived in them, or to other investors who rented them out. Of his original inventory of 72 units, he had sold 68 and now had only 4 left. His asking price was $39,000 per unit or $77,000 for two units. This information was crucial in that it told me two important things. First, the owner had sold 68 units over a three-year period. This meant there was a market for these properties. Second, the price of $77,000 per building had been established and could be used as valuable comparables for appraisal purposes. The 22 units I was looking at suddenly began to look very attractive, as the owner was asking only $31,818 per building. The seller of the 72 units told me that a couple of the investors who had bought duplexes from him were renting them out for $575 to $595. A quick phone call confirmed this. The 22 units I was considering were being rented for only $425 to $440. Since the units in both properties all had two bedrooms and two baths and were comparable in size, I knew immediately what the potential upside was. This also explained in part the relatively low turnover. The tenants had found cheap housing and they knew it.

At this point, I need to share a few things with you about the seller of the 22-unit building. He was a partner in a surveying and engineering company that kept him quite busy. He was not in the apartment business, nor did he care to be. He had an elderly couple as full-time caretakers, who occupied one of the units and were responsible for collecting the rents and performing some light maintenance. The seller also paid the couple a salary. His objective was to completely minimize his involvement in dealing with tenants, upkeep, and pretty much anything to do with the property. In short, the seller was a true "don't wanter." While he was an intelligent man, he just did not want to be in the apartment business. Fortunately for me, he was not aware of the fact that he had a genuine diamond in the rough. Where he saw nothing but headaches, I saw nothing but opportunities. I would be relieving him of his problems related to the duplexes, and by assuming this risk, would be entitled to the potential rewards resulting from any additional value created.

After brief negotiations with the seller through my real estate broker, I put the duplexes under contract for an agreed price of $333,000. This included all 22 units as well as the vacant tract of land adjacent to them.

One unique attribute of this transaction was that all 11 duplex buildings were separately platted and surveyed. This meant that as long as the right type of financing was in place going into the deal, the buildings could all be sold separately or parceled out in any number of ways. For example, an individual could purchase one unit (half or one side of a duplex), two units (all of a duplex), or any combination of units he or she wanted.

Proper financing on this type of purchase is a key factor. Most lenders financing multifamily apartments will place a single loan on the entire property and use all of it as collateral. Then when you are ready to sell, it is either all or none. In other words, you cannot sell off individual units or buildings because the entire purchase is being used to secure the loan or mortgage.

After numerous phone calls, I finally found a local bank that was willing to work with me and structure the purchase in a manner that would facilitate my objectives. I can assure you that the bankers did not just immediately get out their checkbook and write out a check to me. It was only after presenting them with a full business plan outlining my objectives in detail that they decided to approve the financing. The loan was set up so that each time I sold a unit, building, or group of buildings, a portion of the loan was paid off and the respective collateral was released to the new lender. If you have ever been through a condominium conversion, the financing arrangements are very similar.

As mentioned in Chapter 1, clearly defining your objectives is crucial to your success in this business. An effective way to do this is to develop a business plan. Embodied within your plan are the entry, postentry, and exit strategies. Formalizing your plan in this manner may require a good deal of time and effort, but it will be time and effort well spent. This process will benefit you in two primary ways. First, it will force you to think about every step of your plan and commit those plans to writing. This will solidify your objectives in your own mind and help you to evaluate their soundness. Second, presenting your business plan to the lender (in person if possible) will demonstrate to the lender that you are a serious investor and are not taking your acquisition lightly. By following the step-by-step process you have outlined in your business plan, the lender will also be able to evaluate the soundness of your plan. In short, it will enable the lender to establish a level of comfort with you and your transaction that may not otherwise be possible.

Following is a sample list of some points you will want to include in your business plan. These can all be organized in a very professional manner in a notebook that includes tabs.

- *Executive summary.*   Include a one- or two-page summary of your plan.
- *Mission statement.*   Include one or two paragraphs that succinctly state your purpose.
- *Background.*   Present information about yourself and your experience.
- *Financial statement.*   List your assets, liabilities, and net worth.
- *Site location.*   Include a list of benefits, maps, and proximity to shopping and schools.
- *Demographics.*   Present information about the people living in the area (income, education, etc.).

- *Competitor analysis.* Determine who your competitors are and present average rents and sales comparisons.
- *Marketing strategy.* Define your target market (tenants, buyers, etc.).
- *Financial analysis.* Include historical and pro forma operating statements.
- *Improvements.* Define capital improvements to be made to the property.
- *Purchase agreement.* Include your sales contract with the seller.
- *Exhibits.* Include photographs of the property, tax returns, sample floor plans, and the like.

As soon as I had the duplexes under contract, I performed the usual due diligence. This included an examination of the seller's records of income collected and expenses such as taxes, utilities, and repairs. The next step was a thorough physical inspection of each unit, inside and out. After carefully examining the property, I was able to assess more precisely the amount of repairs needed to bring the apartments up to a level I thought was suitable. The drive-by of the property I did before entering into the contract proved to be representative of the interiors as well. Just as for the exterior, the needed interior repairs were largely cosmetic. There was the usual wear and tear—worn carpets, leaky faucets, and old paint, but nothing of major significance.

After I was satisfied with the due diligence, the next step was to order the required third-party reports. This particular lender required a survey, an appraisal, an inspection, and a Phase I environmental report. All reports came in satisfactory. An added bonus was the appraised value—$520,000, with the property in its "as-is" or existing condition. I was of course pleased with the report, because it served to validate my beliefs about the upside potential that existed in this deal.

After all reports were sent to the lender, a final review of the loan package was completed and subsequently approved. The seller and I closed a few days later. It was truly a win-win-win situation for all the parties involved. The seller was relieved of his headache, I had just purchased a diamond in the rough, and the banker had made a sound loan. Now the real fun was about to begin. It was time to get to work and unlock the hidden value in this little gem!

I have already described at length the entry strategy implemented to acquire the 22 units. Now let us take a look at the postentry process. During the period when I had the duplexes under contract, I procured several estimates from contractors on all of the work I wanted done. Before the deal ever closed, I had most of them lined up to begin working on the Monday following the closing. The tenants were notified that the property was under new management and that they would begin seeing some much-needed improvements. The flurry of activity actually created some excitement among them, and they were genuinely enthusiastic that someone was finally taking an interest in their community.

The property was a real eyesore when I bought it. My intent was to clean it up and make it as aesthetically appealing as I could for the least amount of money possible. This is not to imply that I am cheap. As an investor, my goal was to maximize the utility of each and every dollar spent on the project. I took the time to get several bids from contractors on all work performed, and did not hesitate to spend as necessary within the budget I had established prior to the purchase.

Over the next 60 to 90 days, the contractors stayed busy cleaning up the property. The very first people sent to work were a professional landscaping crew. You would be amazed at what a difference simply mowing down the weeds can make. They did not stop there, though. They trimmed all of the hedges, edged along the sidewalks, and cleaned up the grounds. I also had the landscaping crew bring in several truckloads of fresh mulch to place around all the bushes and hedges. Upon signing an annual contract with them, they assumed responsibility for all mowing, hedging, and edging on a weekly basis and at a very reasonable rate. There were large, beautiful trees planted next to each of the driveways, but they were so overgrown that they, too, had become an eyesore. A tree-trimming service promptly alleviated that problem. Within a single day, the crew had all of the trees trimmed and most of the branches hauled away.

While the landscapers and tree trimmers were busy with their work, I had also engaged the services of a painting crew. The painters did an excellent job of painting the exteriors of all 11 buildings. Each building was given two coats of paint by brush or roller. They used a combination of four different color schemes so as to give each building its own unique look while still maintaining a standard of uniformity throughout the community. The painters had the most work to do, and, consequently, their job took the longest.

As previously mentioned, all 11 buildings were side-by-side duplexes. Each one had a fence to separate the units' backyards. This gave each tenant a small private yard with a gate that could be locked for privacy. Most of the fences were dilapidated, and the gates were barely functional. I had another crew replace all of the worn-out fencing with brand-new cedar fencing. Each unit also got a new entry gate for the backyards.

Meanwhile, I employed the services of a sign maker to build signs for the two entryways into the community. There were no signs up at all when I acquired the duplexes, so there was no way for prospective tenants to call for information. The sign maker built two professional signs out of 2-inch-thick redwood and installed one at each entryway, prominently displaying the name of the community and the telephone number.

Since the community was family oriented, I thought a nice amenity to offer the tenants would be a playground where they could bring their children. As it was, there was no playground equipment close by. I had determined that the vacant lot included in the purchase, which was immediately adjacent to the buildings, would be the perfect place for such a playground. I started off by having a concrete crew pour a large 20- by 30-foot slab of concrete, complete with goalposts. This gave the tenants a new basketball court. I also had a company that made professional playground equipment install a swing set, monkey bars, and two ride-on animals that were mounted on springs and anchored in concrete. For the parents, new vinyl-coated park benches were installed. The new management at the duplexes (namely me) was rapidly gaining favor in the eyes of the tenants. The children were especially happy—after all, they had a new park to play in. By the time all of the work had been completed, the 22 units looked like new, and the complex as a whole looked like a breath of fresh air. The tenants now lived in a community they could truly take pride in.

I knew before I ever bought the duplexes that my exit strategy would be either to sell or to refinance the property within 12 months of the time of purchase. To justify the additional value, I needed to increase the net operating income. In this particular case, expenses were already fairly minimal because the tenants were responsible for all of their utilities, including gas and water. As previously mentioned, an evaluation of rents at nearby properties had revealed market rents of $575 to $595, compared to the $425 to $440 I was collecting. As my tenants' leases began expiring, I offered to renew them at $475 to $495. The stable tenant base the previous owner had enjoyed was suddenly not as stable. I had anticipated this, however, and when some tenants elected not to renew, I was able to rent the units out to others promptly.

With the first vacancy, I have to admit I was a little gun-shy. Even though I knew that similar properties in the neighborhood were being rented for much more than mine, the jump from $425 to $595 seemed like a lot to me at the time, psychologically. So I offered the first vacancy at $540 and had it rented within a week.

"Okay," I was thinking, "that wasn't so hard."

The next vacancy was offered at $570 and again was promptly leased. The next went for $585, and the one after that went for $595, both with no problem. I had tested the water a little bit at a time, and it was starting to feel pretty good.

The next vacancy was offered at $625. It was at this point that I met some resistance, so I lowered the rent back down to $595, and again had it rented in no time. The market research I had done before I even purchased the duplexes proved to be right on target.

One key factor contributing to my easy success in renting the units at the higher rates was the fact that I had just spent considerable time and money on improving the overall condition of the property. I now had a very attractive apartment community to offer to prospective families. The positive changes I had made were both welcomed and appreciated.

I considered several approaches to unlock the newly created value in the duplexes. The first was to sell the units either individually or as a package deal to an investor. My original intent was to sell the units individually for $77,000 per building or $38,500 per unit, just as the other seller with the 72 units that were similar to mine had done. With this in mind, I decided to set up one unit as an office that would also double as a model. The initial response from my existing tenants as well as others was quite favorable. Within the first 90 days, I had commitments for 17 of the units. What I was not prepared for was the poor credit quality of most of the prospective buyers. I was working through a mortgage company that could provide financing for A-, B-, or C-quality paper, but the majority of those who expressed an interest could not even come up with the necessary down payment, which was minimal. Of those 17, only one made it all the way to closing.

Fortunately for me, I always have a contingency plan, or a Plan B as I like to call it. (Actually, I usually have a Plan C and a Plan D, too.) Okay, so on to Plan B.

I had learned that going through the mechanics of dealing with individual buyers for the units was very time consuming and did not represent the best use of my time. I decided to advertise the units in the classified section of the newspaper. I offered them as a package deal to investors. The ad generated quite a bit of interest. I had the remaining 21 units under contract with one investor who assured me he could close the deal in 30 days. As it turned out, he could not, and the deal fell out of contract. At this point, I began thinking seriously about Plan C.

Plan C was to get a new appraisal of the property that would reflect the newly created value, and subsequently refinance it. The only drawback to this approach was that most lenders require a seasoning period, usually a minimum of 12 months. I had owned the duplexes barely four months, so I was not having much success. If it came down to it, I had located a lender who expressed a strong interest in refinancing all 21 remaining units at 90 percent of whatever the new appraisal was, but I would have to wait for the 12-month seasoning period to do so.

As I was mulling my options over in my mind, I received a call from two investors who were partners. They stated that they were interested in all 21 units and wanted to meet me at the property. I agreed to meet with them, but really did not take them too seriously, as I had already had a number of prospective buyers come by and kick the tires. I initially met with one of the two partners and later met with the second one. They said they wanted to buy the property. At the time, I was still thinking about just keeping the property and refinancing it, so I was not sure. Also, I had not been told no by enough lenders to discourage me. The two partners began to press me to sell the duplexes to them. This was a good sign, because if they wanted it that badly, then chances were they would see the deal all the way through to the closing.

I knew that each building would easily be appraised for a minimum of $77,000 because I had an entire neighborhood of comparables right down the street. Because the investors agreed to buy all 21 remaining units in a package deal, I agreed to what was an attractive discount for them, but also left plenty of profit for me. After all, I was not doing this for free.

Here is how the deal played out. I agreed to sell each building at a net discounted price of $66,364. Because the buyers were receiving a discount of a little over $10,000 per building, they agreed to pay all closing costs. Over the next six to eight months, the buyers followed through and purchased all 21 remaining units from me. It took that long because they used several lenders for their financing. They could have gotten a commercial loan to cover all 21 units, but they would have had to put down 20 percent. Instead, they placed several single-family housing loans on the property which provided 90 percent financing rather than the 80 percent a commercial lender would have offered them. The buyers had to use several lenders because the lenders' underwriting guidelines did not permit them to loan on more than a maximum of four units to any one individual. Although their decision to use this type of financing prolonged the sell, they did follow through, and within a year of purchasing the property myself, I had sold all 22 units.

Following is a recap of the numbers on this transaction (rounded estimates):

| | | |
|---|---|---|
| Purchase price | $333,000 | |
| Closing costs | 17,000 | |
| Total purchase price | $350,000 | |
| | | |
| Capital Improvements | | |
| Painting | $12,000 | |
| Landscaping | 8,000 | |
| Playground equipment | 15,000 | |
| Fencing | 7,000 | |
| Signage | 5,000 | |
| General improvements | 13,000 | |
| Total improvements | $60,000 | |
| Total purchase price | $350,000 | |
| Total cost basis | $410,000 | |
| | | |
| Contract sales price | $696,818 | [For 21 units (66,364/2) × 21] |
| Contract sales price | 39,500 | [For the first unit] |
| Total sales | $736,318 | |
| Total cost basis | $410,000 | |
| Net proceeds | $326,318 | |

This example demonstrates the potential of the value play. As you can see, it can be quite effective. In this particular instance, my out-of-pocket capital was approximately $100,000, or about 25 percent of the total cost basis. The return on investment (ROI) was roughly 326 percent ($326,000/ $100,000). The total increase in value of the property was almost 80 percent [($736,318 − $410,000)/$410,000]. So, you can see that the assumptions outlined in Tables 4.1 and 4.2 are reasonable. If we used the 20 percent assumption used in Tables 4.1 and 4.2, I would have needed to create only $82,000 in additional value. By employing some relatively basic techniques, I was able to achieve almost four times that amount. I do not mean to imply that you can create value of this magnitude in every case; however, I do want you to be aware that such opportunities exist and that the assumption of 20 percent is conservatively feasible.

# How to Tell a Diamond from a Lump of Coal

Now that we have explored how to recognize a diamond in the rough, let us consider how to distinguish it from a lump of coal. Here is a personal example.

Through contacts in the Texas market, I had identified two separate apartment buildings available for sale by the same owner. One was a 25-unit complex, and the other was a 36-unit complex. The two properties were located about a mile apart and could be operated by the same manager. On the surface, the deal appeared to be priced right and to offer some upside potential. I was very knowledgeable about that specific market, because I owned a 98-unit building approximately five minutes away from these two. Both buildings were rented out as all-bills-paid (master-metered); but, surprisingly, both buildings had been wired with individual meters. The current owner was absorbing that unnecessary expense out of his income. That was fine with me, however, because it represented an opportunity to create value. In addition, rents were below market, and I knew from experience that occupancy in that market was very high. This was a Class C building in a Class C neighborhood with strong demand. The thing I love about Class C properties (in the right market) is that their supply is finite. In other words, they don't make Class C buildings anymore. All new-construction apartments are by definition Class A. When the supply of available units is fixed and the demand for these types of units continues to increase, it can mean only one thing. That's right, you guessed it: continued upward pressure on rents.

So far, things were looking pretty good. The two apartment complexes had all the makings of a good value play. According to the real estate broker representing the seller, both buildings were in fair condition, but did need a little work. That was okay with me, because I am used to buying them that way. As I have already described, that is one of the key ways to create value. Because I lived out of state, I could only go by what the broker told me over the phone, and also by a couple of photos he sent me. The photos looked good, and the broker assured me the properties were in fair condition, so I put the deal under contract. I had a 30-day feasibility period for due diligence and property inspections, so that gave me ample time to arrange a flight to Texas to view the properties.

Before I go any further with my story, let me say a word or two about real estate brokers. Their job is to sell, and part of that selling process includes presenting a property in its most favorable light. The real estate broker in this case was not dishonest with me; he simply presented the deal to me in the best possible light. This is certainly not to imply that all brokers are the same; it is just to say that some are more forthcoming than others.

Now, on with the story. I had already seen the 25-unit building on a previous trip, and knew it needed quite a bit of work. It needed to be painted, which wasn't a big deal, but it also needed a new roof and extensive interior repairs, and the parking lot needed to be resurfaced. I was aware of these facts before ever entering into an agreement with the seller, and an offsetting adjustment was reflected in the contract price.

Because I had already seen the first building, I met the broker at the second building, which was the 36-unit. I also had an associate of mine, Richard, who was a property manager, meet us there. His experience from an operational and maintenance standpoint have proven to be invaluable to me.

My first impression of the apartments from the outside was somewhat favorable. They obviously needed to be painted, they looked a little dumpy, and there was definitely room for improvement with the lawn care and landscaping. That was all fine with me because those are the kinds of deals I like—the ones that need aesthetic improvements, just a little face-lift. A closer inspection of the interiors was about to reveal much, much more than I had bargained for.

We started with some of the downstairs units. A kind old lady invited us into the first unit. One of the things I noticed almost immediately, besides the overall relatively poor condition of the unit, was its lack of central air and heat. Not only did it not have *central* heat—it did not have *any* heat!

Not one of the 36 units was equipped with heat. Some of them had window air-conditioners, but not one of them had a furnace. Now, I used to live in Texas, and I know it does not get that cold, but when it is 40 degrees outside, you expect to be able to come in and turn the heat on.

I asked the lady in the apartment what she did for heat. She replied, "Well, I have a little electric space heater I use sometimes, but usually I just turn on all the burners on the stove, turn the oven on high, and open the oven door."

After hearing that, I almost went into cardiac arrest right on the spot. All of the stoves were natural gas. So, that came to 36 stoves with all the burners lit and the oven doors wide open 24 hours a day during the winter. I was truly amazed the building had not already burned to the ground, or that a tenant had not died from asphyxiation. Maybe one had and I just did not know about it. What I did know, however, was that this kind of situation was a major liability I was not willing to assume. Okay, so my associate Richard jotted down "no heaters" on his notepad.

On to the next unit. The broker knocked on the tenant's door, and a young lady of about 20 or so answered. We told her we were there to do a quick walk-through inspection and would only be a minute. She was very accommodating and invited us in.

When I first stepped into the apartment, I could not believe my eyes: parked right in the middle of the living room was an old, broken-down Harley-Davidson motorcycle! Somewhat jokingly, I asked the lady if the motorcycle came with the apartment. She replied, "No, it's just my boyfriend's." I wanted to ask her if the oil dripping out of the bottom of it and all over the carpet was her boyfriend's, too, but I held my tongue.

Even though I had not seen a truly representative sample yet, I was already beginning to get a good feel for the tenant mix, as well as the property's management. Richard scribbled another note on his pad: "motorcycle in living room, oil on carpet."

As we continued our inspection, every apartment had its own unique way of contributing to what was beginning to look more and more like a lump of coal, rather than a diamond in the rough. The young man living in one particular unit had to remove his wild-eyed, raving-mad pit bulldog before we could enter. I did not have a lot of confidence in the leash the man used to lead his pit bull out the door. That dog looked as if he would take your leg off in one bite if you got too close to him. Just what I needed, another liability. Another note: "pit bull in #24."

Our inspection revealed major problems throughout the building. Most of the units were in disrepair and needed quite a bit of work. The appliances were old, the carpets were old, and most of the bathrooms showed evidence of leaky faucets and pipes. In several cases in the upstairs units, this had caused damage to the flooring in the bathrooms, and also to the ceilings in the apartments below. Sagging ceilings in the upstairs units also suggested strong evidence of major roof problems. In one of the units we inspected, the entire front portion of the apartment was sloping downward. Hmmm. What do you suppose could have caused that? You are exactly right, of course—foundation problems. Richard could barely write fast enough: "floor damage, plumbing problems, roof leaking, foundation settling."

Well, by that time, I had seen enough. In fact, what I saw was a large siphon sucking money right out of my pocket. I thanked the broker for his time and told him I would get back to him after discussing my assessment of the property with my associate. He pressed me for feedback, so I gave it to him. I told him the apartments required a lot more work than I had anticipated (actually, than he had led me to believe) and that I would need to review my findings in greater detail with Richard, whose opinion I greatly respected. I also told the broker I would not be prepared to move forward with the contract unless some concessions were made by the seller to cover the cost of the badly needed repairs.

Afterward, Richard and I reviewed our notes and both determined the 36-unit would require considerable work to bring it up to our standards. Richard agreed to get repair estimates over the next week or so. Once we had those, I would be in a better position to make a final decision. About a week later, Richard faxed the following itemized estimates for the necessary repairs we had discussed.

| | |
|---|---:|
| ■ 36 new breaker boxes and rewire for 220 V | $ 9,940 |
| ■ 36 A/C units with electric heat | 20,615 |
| ■ Installation of 36 A/C units | 1,800 |
| ■ Replace rotted wood | 12,100 |
| ■ Scrape, prime, and paint exterior | 12,800 |
| ■ Replace roof | 28,200 |
| ■ Replace carpet | 10,800 |
| ■ Replace floor tile | 8,640 |
| ■ Replace 20 refrigerators @ $400 each | 8,000 |
| ■ Replace 16 stoves @ $350 each | 5,600 |
| ■ Repair ceramic tile | 2,000 |
| ■ Redo bad Sheetrock repair in apartments | 7,200 |
| ■ Replace 36 porch lights at $25 each | 900 |
| Total | $128,595 |

So there you have it, only $128,595 to bring the 36-unit building up to acceptable standards. This figure did not even allow for the tenant turnover that would surely occur. For a project like this, I would estimate a turnover ratio of 75 percent, or 27 out of the 36 units. For every tenant that moved, I would incur a make-ready expense and also a loss of rents. On average, this would be about $1,000. This number was higher than normal because of the extensive work required on the interiors of the units. So I could add another $27,000 to the cost of the project, bringing the total up to $155,595, or $4,322 per unit. At the price I was paying for the apartment complex, there would be very little upside potential left, if any, by the time I invested the additional money for the required capital improvements.

I faxed the list of repairs to the broker back in Texas and explained to him that the price we had initially agreed on no longer made sense from an investment standpoint. I was about to exercise my right to terminate my interest in both properties when the broker persuaded me to make one last counteroffer. Quite frankly, I was ready to be through with this deal, but I agreed to make one final counter, thinking what the heck, with the right terms and conditions in place, it could still prove to be profitable. My counteroffer was to leave the sales price exactly as it was, but to receive a credit for repairs of $125,000 at closing. This way I would not have to come up with the capital for the repairs out of pocket. If the sales price were adjusted downward by $125,000, I would have had to put up the 15 percent down payment and also come up with an additional $125,000 for the capital improvements. Since I was not at all interested in tying up my money in such a deal, I requested the credit at closing. That way I would have the money immediately available to begin making the improvements. As it turned out, the seller rejected my counteroffer, which was fine with me, and both of the agreements were terminated.

Remember these examples when searching for your own value-play opportunities. You should limit your selection to those properties that need minimal work, primarily aesthetic in nature, as was illustrated in the example of the 22-unit complex. I would suggest avoiding properties like the 25- and 36-unit buildings that require extensive and costly repairs. If you do decide to assume the additional risk associated with such properties, it should be reflected in the price. As a value player, you are seeking to maximize the return on your investment. You are not in the charity business. Do not allow yourself to be persuaded into buying these kinds of deals unless the seller is willing to offer you additional incentives.

You probably remember your mother telling you at one time or another that "patience is a virtue." Well, guess what? She was right. I point out this subtle fact because in your search for your very first value-play opportunity, you are likely to be excited and anxious. Do not allow your enthusiasm to blur your rational thinking. Look at the numbers. Review every item carefully, and then ask yourself, "Does this deal make sense?" If you have some reservations that are not induced by fear, then you should probably do as your mother suggested and be patient. There will be another opportunity. However, if you determine that the deal does make sense, then by all means, charge ahead!

## CHAPTER 5

*Success is not measured by what a man accomplishes, but by the opposition
he has encountered and the courage with which he has maintained
the struggle against overwhelming odds.*
**—CHARLES LINDBERGH**

# Establishing Your Niche and Locating Properties

The preceding chapter discusses the merits of the value play. This chapter examines some important concepts to consider prior to the deployment of your acquisition campaign. You must first determine your niche in the marketplace by analyzing key factors regarding the type of property you are seeking. Once you have defined exactly what type of property you are looking for, you will be ready to embark on locating the property best suited to your needs.

# Establishing Your Niche

Before you begin your search for an apartment complex, you must first define your niche in the marketplace. There are four crucial factors to consider:

1. The resources available to work with.
2. The size of the property.
3. The age of the property.
4. Your holding period.

It goes without saying that there is some crossover among these factors. For instance, the more capital you have to work with, the larger and more expensive a property you can acquire. One is not necessarily a function of the other, though. Just because you have a large pool of capital to draw from does not mean that you have to buy a larger property. Let us examine each factor in more detail.

# Availability of Resources

Obviously, the amount of capital you have available for real estate investments is a key factor in establishing your niche. The more you have to work with, the greater your choices are. In general, loan-to-value (LTV) financing of 80 percent is readily obtainable. If you had $100,000 to invest and procured an 80 percent loan, you could buy a $500,000 apartment building. With that same $100,000, you could acquire a $750,000 complex with an 85 percent loan or a $1 million building with a 90 percent loan. In my experience, "nothing-down deals" do not exist when it comes to buying larger properties. You may be able to find them for single-family homes, but for multifamily properties, be prepared to come to the closing table with your checkbook. I am not suggesting that it is *impossible* to find a nothing-down deal for apartments; I am just saying that I have never seen one. I suppose you could structure a deal on an 80/10/10 basis, meaning 80 percent bank financing, 10 percent seller carry-back, and 10 percent from a partner, friend, or relative. The bottom line is that the capital you have to work with will be a constraint and a determining factor in establishing where you will fit into the multifamily marketplace. Define your limits before conducting your search.

## Property Size

While the number of units you can acquire is in part a function of the capital you have to invest, there is a wide range of prices per unit available. Some older apartment complexes may sell for as little as $5,000 per unit, while newer properties may sell for as much as $75,000 to $100,000 per unit or more, depending on the region you choose to invest in. I recommend that newer investors get their feet wet with a smaller property of 50 units or less. A smaller apartment building will provide you with the opportunity to be directly involved in the operations of the property. In short, it will give you some hands-on experience. As your expertise and knowledge grows, so will your confidence. This self-assurance will manifest itself through your ability to graduate to larger and larger multifamily properties.

Midsized apartments typically range in size from 50 to 150 units. As you move up the scale in size and magnitude of the properties in your portfolio, you will most assuredly want to employ full-time managers and mainte-nance personnel. Furthermore, unless you plan to keep up with all of the accounting functions, such as the accounts receivables, payables, and collections, you should seriously consider engaging a reputable property management firm. An effective management company will handle all of the day-to-day operations such as managing the staff, collecting the rents, and paying all of the bills. It will also generate month-end financial reports from its accounting programs, which will provide you with all of the details of revenue and expenses. Depending on the size of the company, management firms generally use field supervisors, adding a level of supervision that would not otherwise exist. These supervisors will usually oversee and be responsible for 5 to 10 different apartment complexes. If your on-site manager runs into a problem outside of the normal day-to-day operations, he or she can call the field supervisor for help. A competent supervisor should be able to resolve most issues.

Larger multifamily complexes are typically those with 150 units or more. Larger properties allow the owner to achieve a higher degree of efficiency through economies of scale. Depending on the size, instead of having one all-purpose maintenance person, you would be able to hire one maintenance person who is also qualified in air-conditioning and another who has plumbing skills, in addition to a groundskeeper and perhaps a porter. Employing individuals with these types of skill sets can be a very effective cost-savings measure because you do not have to call in an outside contractor every time an air-conditioning unit goes out, for example. With maintenance personnel on-site and readily available, your tenants will benefit, too. They will appreciate the better service. Satisfied tenants mean lower turnover, resulting in additional cost savings to you. Larger complexes generally mean larger budgets, which can give you greater flexibility in the way you operate your property. You can afford to have a professionally trained sales staff that will ensure that things run as smoothly as possible. A skilled manager will know how to address issues as they arise and how to deal with them effectively. This, too, will result in lower turnover. Trust me: a qualified manager can make all the difference in the world in how profitable your apartments are. Don't be afraid to spend a little more on the individual overseeing the day-to-day operations. An increase in salary expense of $5,000 for a competent manager will be more than offset by an increase in revenues.

Regardless of the size of apartment building you purchase, the use of a professional property management company can be extremely important to you as an owner. You and you alone must determine what the best use of your time is. Where do you add the most value to the process? In the early stages of building wealth through real estate, the day-to-day, hands-on involvement will give you invaluable experience not available from any other source. As your level of expertise increases, however, it will be time to shift some of those responsibilities to others. Why burden yourself with trying to personally manage and oversee every detail of a 100-unit complex, for example, when you can pay someone $20,000 to $30,000 a year to assume those duties for you? This frees up your time to focus on more important things, such as preparing to implement your exit strategy for your existing building and beginning to identify potential acquisition targets for your next value-play opportunity.

If you allow yourself to get bogged down in the day-to-day management, you will soon discover there is little time left for anything else. I am not, of course, suggesting that you remove yourself completely from the process. Your role is to manage the managers by defining your objectives for the property. You provide the leadership, and then get out of the way and let them do their jobs. Do *not* micromanage. You will continue to maintain close contact and make yourself available for questions. In addition, you will scrutinize every detail of the financial reports every month to ensure that you are on track to meet your stated objectives.

In summary, whether you own a small, midsized, or large apartment complex, you must decide as the owner what the best use of your time will be and how you personally can add the most value to maximize the return on your investment.

# Property Age

Depending on their age and physical condition, apartment complexes are commonly classified as *A, B, C,* or *D properties.* As a general rule, the newer a property is, the more expensive it will be on a per-unit basis. You might pay, for example, as much as $75,000 to $100,000 per unit for a newly constructed building, or you might pay as little as $5,000 per unit for a much older building.

*Class A apartments* will typically be newer properties, less than 10 years old and in excellent condition. They may even be newly constructed buildings that are still being leased up. This type of apartment will command the highest price per unit for several reasons, one of which is the cost of new construction, building materials, and labor. Due to an inflation-driven economy (even at 3 to 4 percent per annum), it is a simple fact of life that it costs more to build today than it did a year ago, 5 years ago, or 10 years ago. Before developers and builders begin a project, they will perform a feasibility study to determine whether the project makes sense. They will estimate all of the costs that go into the project, examine the potential market rents, calculate the pro forma net operating income, and extrapolate the value of the completed project based on a range of capitalization rates. If the rate of return on the developer's invested capital meets the threshold, the project is deemed viable and they move forward with it. All of these factors drive the value of the property and result in a higher per-unit cost compared to older buildings. Class A apartments are often held by a group of investors that owns a portfolio of properties, possibly in a real estate investment trust (REIT).

Advantages of Class A buildings include higher rents, lower maintenance costs, and numerous amenities such as swimming pools and weight rooms to attract tenants. Disadvantages include a much higher per-unit cost to you as the investor and, usually, a lower initial rate of return. Another disadvantage you must be aware of is that in the event of a downturn in the economy, this will be the first group to get hit, especially if the downturn is followed by a strong upward cycle. This is due to the fact that as interest rates decline, more and more product comes on line, and as rates start to go back up, there are still a number of projects in the pipeline yet to be completed. In a very strong upward cycle, the housing market may become oversaturated with supply. If the economy softens, Class A properties may be affected because of (1) the oversupply of new product and (2) tenants' tendency to migrate toward less expensive housing in an effort to save money and conserve their own resources. Instead of paying $1,500 a month to live in a nice Class A complex with all of the amenities, they will likely look to move down to a Class B property for only $900 per month. I remember that the Texas economy, and Houston in particular, got hit hard with a situation very similar to this in the mid-1980s. There was an oversupply of Class A buildings available; oil prices turned downward, and layoffs followed. Almost overnight, vacancy rates increased significantly, and prices came down hard and fast. Many, many bank loans went bad as investors walked away from their properties.

In summary, for the value-play investor, Class A apartments offer the least upside potential because there is no additional value to create. The properties are newer, the utilities are already submetered, and they offer many amenities to their tenants. Furthermore, not only is there no additional value to create, but investors will often pay a premium for these higher-quality assets.

*Class B apartments* are slightly older than Class A buildings, usually between 10 and 20 years old, and are still in relatively good condition. Class B properties will generally range from $25,000 to $75,000 per unit, depending on the market. These properties are often located in solid middle-income areas and are likely to be the most stable among the various property classes. This is due to the fact that the surrounding neighborhoods are well established and are in relatively good condition, with little or no deterioration. The apartments are still new enough to offer many attractive amenities, and old enough to be affordable for many families. As air-conditioning units and other equipment begins to fail, Class B properties will experience higher maintenance costs than the newer Class A apartments.

Opportunities to create value acquiring Class B apartments are available to the patient investor who takes the necessary time to conduct a diligent search. They are not as readily available as Class C apartments, however. The example cited in Chapter 4, the 22-unit building, was a solid B property that had not been kept up. As previously mentioned, most of the deterioration was aesthetic and was therefore not that costly to bring back into good condition.

*Class C apartments* are those that range in age from 20 to 30 years and in price from $10,000 to $30,000 per unit, depending on the relative market values, rents, and property condition. Value-play opportunities are abundant in the Class C category for a variety of reasons. Many of these older units are still in fairly good condition, but may not offer some of the amenities that newer ones do. Cosmetic improvements can do wonders for Class C buildings, as can the addition of a few of the amenities that newer apartments offer. Modernizing the individual units with updated appliances and cabinets is an affordable way to add value. In addition, many of the Class C buildings were built before the notion of submetering became popular. As energy costs rose, investors in newly constructed units began more and more often to pass these costs on to the tenants. Also, many investors in existing buildings have retrofitted their apartments with individual meters to provide the tenants with direct control of the comfort in their respective units, as well as the responsibility for the bills. The all-bills-paid properties are quickly becoming a dying breed as investors move to shift these costs to tenants, especially in the face of ever-higher energy costs.

Class C buildings are usually in fairly stable neighborhoods that are well established and have not suffered from deteriorating conditions in the surrounding area. As an investor, however, you must be careful in your selection of Class C apartments—some buildings may qualify as Class C units, but the immediately surrounding area may be suffering from declining values due to high crime, an influx of low-income families who may not have the resources to properly care for their homes, or any other number of contributing factors. Conversely, you might find a C property in a B neighborhood, which would likely present an excellent opportunity to add value by bringing that building up to the standard of the community in which it is located.

The migration in and out of neighborhoods is sometimes cyclical in nature, with the cycles lasting many years, perhaps even decades. An example of this has occurred in many larger cities over the past 100 years or so. At first, homes sprang up all around these cities. As the cities began to grow and mature, many people left the inner-city areas and moved to the surrounding suburbs. The decline in demand for inner-city areas led to lower rents and, ultimately, deteriorating conditions in many cases. The growth in suburban America created a whole new set of problems, most of them related to heavy traffic conditions. In an effort to avoid lengthy daily commutes, younger couples and singles have begun to return to inner-city areas in recent years. Neighborhoods that just a few years ago attracted only low-income families now find themselves in vogue and have undergone dramatic transformations. In many cases, older buildings have been completely razed and replaced with new, upscale apartments that attract affluent professionals who work in the downtown area. Simply put, it is crucial to note the trends that are occurring in the community where you are considering putting your investment capital to work. Acquiring a Class C apartment complex in a neighborhood that has reversed in trend and is enjoying an increase in popularity and demand may very well prove to be a perfect value-play opportunity.

*Class D apartments* are generally those in excess of 30 years of age; they range in value from $5,000 to $10,000 per unit, depending on the relative market values, rents, and property condition. Value-play opportunities do exist in this category. The caveat, however, is that they tend to be more capital intensive. Older buildings may require repair or replacement of heating and cooling equipment, boiler equipment for hot water, roofs, parking lot surfaces, and the like. Depending on the age of the building, it may even be time to replace the electrical wiring. This can be very costly. Furthermore, you will want to know whether the wiring is copper or aluminum. This may sound trivial, but believe me, it is not—for the simple reason that a number of lenders who specialize in financing multifamily properties will not even *consider* loaning money on an apartment with aluminum wiring. The risk of fire is supposedly higher in a building with aluminum wiring than in one with copper wiring, so they do not loan money on them. (Copper versus aluminum wiring may or may not be an issue in Class B and C apartments as well, so you will want to consider this when conducting your research.) I am not suggesting not to buy an apartment complex just because it has aluminum wiring; I just want you to be aware of the potential issue from your lender's perspective.

Class D buildings are likely to be found in declining neighborhoods, so improvements to the property may not result in that much added value, because people who can afford higher rents will likely choose a similar property in a nicer community at comparable rates. This is not to say that opportunities do not exist in the Class D category. Quite the contrary is true, but as an investor putting your hard-earned capital to work, you must go in with your eyes open. A thorough analysis of similar apartment buildings within a 1- to 3-mile radius of the building you are considering will give you an idea of the potential upside in the property you have targeted. I have seen an 800-unit apartment complex in a solid Class B to B+ neighborhood that was for all practical purposes abandoned. A group of investors came in and gutted the buildings and completely renovated the apartment complex. What was once a D to D– property is now a very attractive B+ to A– complex that enjoys high occupancy and was much welcomed by the surrounding community. This group of investors was obviously well capitalized, judging from the extensive renovations required to bring the apartment complex up to this new higher standard. I do not know personally what they paid for the property, but I am certain it is worth considerably more today than it was before they bought it. This value-play example probably falls outside the scope of most investors, but it does represent the breadth of opportunities available, from those that require only a minor face-lift to those that require extensive surgery.

# Holding Period

For value-play investors, the quicker the turnover, the better. Remember, you are attempting to maximize your wealth by going in, creating value, and getting out. Depending on the size of the property you are acquiring and the extent of work being done, your turnaround time may vary from three months to two or more years. Among the most important factors to consider when determining your optimum holding period are the tax implications and how they will impact your bottom line.

The holding period can be broken into two primary categories for tax purposes. Capital gains are treated as either short term or long term. *Short-term capital gains* are defined as gains on properties that are bought, held for a duration of less than 12 months, and subsequently sold, while long-term capital gains are defined as gains on properties that are bought, held for a duration of greater than 12 months, and subsequently sold. Selling an apartment building in less than 12 months should be a last resort, so as to avoid short-term capital gains treatment. Short-term capital gains are treated as ordinary income, which means there are essentially no tax advantages and that the income is taxed at your normal, or ordinary, tax rate. Furthermore, it may be subject to other taxes as well. However, as of this writing, long-term capital gains are taxed at a flat rate of 15 percent. Here is a simple example:

|  | Short-Term Capital Gains | Long-Term Capital Gains |
|---|---|---|
| Purchase price | $1,000,000 | $1,000,000 |
| Sales price | $1,250,000 | $1,250,000 |
| Capital gain | $250,000 | $250,000 |
| Tax rate | 33% | 15% |
| Taxes due | $82,500 | $37,500 |

Difference = $82,500 − $37,500 = $45,000

Using this simplified example, the difference between selling after Month 12 and selling before Month 12 would be an additional tax savings of $45,000. For the aggressive investor seeking to maximize wealth over the shortest period of time, these additional tax savings must be given serious consideration, especially if you are in a position to wait for the twelfth month to sell.

An effective method many investors use to defer taxes on capital gains for years and years is referred to as a *1031 exchange*. The IRS allows buyers and sellers to exchange property that is defined as "like kind." According to the *Money Income Tax Handbook* by Mary L. Sprouse (New York: Time Warner, 1999), "this refers to the nature or character of the property, for example, real property being traded for real property, rather than to grade, quality, or use. Thus, new property may be traded for used, or land can be exchanged for a building. But land could not be traded for machinery (real property for personal property)."

Examples of like-kind exchanges cited by the *Money Income Tax Handbook* (Sections 26.711–26.715) include the following:

- An office building for an apartment building.
- A rental building for land on which a rental building is constructed within 180 days.
- Business automobile for a business computer.
- Real property you own for a real estate lease with a term of 30 years or more.
- Used business truck for a new business truck.
- Oil leasehold for a ranch.
- A remainder interest for a complete ownership interest.
- An easement for any type of real estate.
- A life insurance contract for a life insurance, endowment, or annuity contract.
- An endowment contract for an annuity contract (but not vice versa).

The goodwill and going-concern value of one business can never be of a like kind with another business. Depreciable business or investment property may be exchanged for property of a "like class."

Also, according to the *Money Income Tax Handbook:*

A tax-free exchange must generally be completed within a 180-day period, and the qualifying period may be even shorter. Property will not be considered like-kind property if received (1) 180 days after the date you transferred property, or (2) after the extended due date of your return for the year in which you made the transfer, whichever date is earlier. Moreover, the property you are to receive must be identified within 45 days after the date you transferred property. Under proposed regulations, this 45 day requirement may be met by describing the replacement property in a written document signed by you and hand delivered or otherwise sent before the end of the 45 day period to a third person (other than a relative) involved in the exchange. You may also identify the replacement property in a written agreement for the exchange of properties. Exchanges that fail the time tests are taxed as installment sales if there was a bona fide intent to make a tax-free exchange. If the exchange is begun in one year and the replacement property is received in the next, but not within the time limits, the swap is taxable as an installment sale in the year the replacement property is received. If an exchange was not intended, any gain is taxed in the first year. The replacement property must be clearly described. You may identify more than one property; however, the maximum number of properties you may identify is (1) three properties of any fair market value, or (2) any number of properties as long as their aggregate fair market value at the end of the 45 day period is not more than (a) 200% of the aggregate fair market value of all the properties you are giving up or (b) the properties you receive are worth at least 95% of the value of the properties you identified. A building to be constructed will qualify if it is completed within the 180-day period. But later construction is treated as cash received and is taxable. You can employ an unrelated person as a middleman to help in the exchange. Naturally, your family members do not qualify. Nor do (1) partnerships or corporations in which you have more than a 10% interest; (2) your agent, including your employees, attorneys, accountants, investment bankers, or real estate agents or brokers who worked for you in the two years before the exchange (except in connection with another exchange); or (3) anyone who is related to your agent. See Section 26.100 for more information on related parties. Sales proceeds must be kept in escrow. You will be taxed if you are able to keep too much control over or withdraw escrowed funds before the exchange is completed. These funds can earn interest or be enhanced by a growth factor.

The process of exchanging like properties can be an extremely effective technique for deferring taxes on capital gains; however, as is evident from the preceding paragraphs, the process can also be quite complex. My advice is to seek the counsel of a competent attorney or certified public accountant (CPA) who has extensive experience in this area.

## CHAPTER 6

*While we may surpass our goals, we can never surpass our dreams. The extent
to which we can achieve is therefore only limited by the breadth
of our vision and our capacity to follow through.*
—**R. DALE JEFFERY**

# Six Ways to Locate Properties

Finding just the right property can sometimes prove to be challenging. Utilizing a comprehensive approach will provide you with the greatest chances for success. You must be willing to exercise patience and diligence in your search. Doing so will enable you to minimize your risk and maximize the return on your hard-earned investment capital. The more sources you have available in your arsenal, the better your odds of locating the type of property most suited to your objectives. In my experience, the following have all proven to be useful at one time or another.

**Six Ways to Locate Properties**

1. Real estate brokers.
2. Classified advertisements.

3. Industry-specific real estate publications.

4. Local and national Web sites.

5. Associations and real estate investment clubs.

6. Banks.

# Real Estate Brokers

Having two or three real estate brokers scouting properties for you is one of the most effective ways to quickly and efficiently identify potential multifamily property acquisitions. I must stress that it is *crucial to your success* to ensure the competence of the brokerage team you put together. I have worked with many brokers; their range of expertise and experience varies greatly. There are residential brokers who focus primarily on single-family dwellings and occasionally sell a duplex or triplex and suddenly think they are qualified to represent you in a large multifamily property transaction; in truth, they will have no clue as to the intrinsic value of the apartment building you are considering because the valuation approaches are so different. Single-family property appraisals are largely based on comparable sales, while multifamily property valuations are driven primarily by income.

Then there are commercial real estate brokers who focus on a mix of income-producing properties. These will often include office buildings, retail strip centers, small businesses, hotels and motels, industrial sites, and, finally, apartment buildings. This group of brokers is certainly more qualified than the residential brokers, because they are used to valuing properties on an income basis rather than on comparable sales. To clarify, comparable sales are taken into account when valuing apartments, but the values are predominately derived from the income approach, which is discussed in much greater detail in the next chapter.

Finally, there are those brokers who focus solely on multifamily properties and nothing else. These are the people you want on your team! These brokers are generally experts in the multifamily property industry who have migrated from single-family or commercial sales for one reason or another. Their specialized knowledge can save you a great deal of time, energy, and money. Apartment brokers are well informed and are in direct contact with buyers and sellers every single day. They know which areas of town are hot and which are not. They also know when new properties are about to be made available for sale, so if they know what you are looking for, they can notify you immediately when an apartment building that meets your criteria hits the market. It is important to note that a Multiple Listing Service (MLS) such as the one used for single-family houses does not exist for apartment buildings, but apartment brokers are plugged into a network of similar brokers, and they will be among the first to know when a building becomes available. This can vary, however, because brokers will sometimes attempt to keep a listing in-house and offer it to their own lists of buyers to avoid splitting the commission with another agent.

An additional advantage apartment brokers can offer is that they often maintain an extensive database of apartment owners they can contact. Even if an apartment is not officially listed for sale, the broker may know from a prior conversation that if the right buyer comes along at the right price, the owner would consider an offer.

## Classified Advertisements

Most larger metropolitan newspapers carry an "Apartment" or "Multifamily" heading in the real estate section; this will often provide a handful of listings. Sometimes they may be found in the commercial property section. The information in these ads is usually fairly limited. They are designed to get you, the investor, to call the broker for more information. This can be an effective way to get to know apartment brokers.

## Industry-Specific Real Estate Publications

Companies and organizations in many areas periodically publish books or magazines that are specific to the commercial or multifamily real estate industry. Some of these are regional, while others are national. The national publications are often geared toward larger investors, as such investors tend to diversify by investing in many areas throughout the country. These publications can be a very good source for locating potential deals. You will also find many helpful real estate–related advertisers in these publications, such as apartment brokers, lenders, appraisers, environmental engineers, and surveyors.

## Local and National Web Sites

There are a number of Web sites that offer all kinds of information about apartment buildings. You can do a local search by keying in a phrase such as "multifamily listings Dallas," for example, and you should be able to find something. The most comprehensive and well-known Web site related to commercial properties is LoopNet. You can find it on the Web at www .loopnet.com. LoopNet boasts more than 130,000 listings for various income-producing properties, including office, retail, hotel and motel, industrial, multifamily, mobile home park, and land listings. With approximately 1.5 billion square feet, it also maintains the largest inventory of commercial space available for lease. It is essentially the Multiple Listing Service for income-producing properties. Unlike the MLS, you do not have to be a real estate agent to access LoopNet's listings. It is very much like a public MLS for commercial properties made available to anyone with a computer and access to the Web. You can search by property type, state, county, city, price range, and minimum and maximum square feet, as well as several other criteria. Most listings provide a descriptive overview of the property, photos, and limited financial and offering information.

## Associations and Real Estate Investment Clubs

Most cities have a number of real estate investment–related associations and clubs. These clubs provide an excellent opportunity for you to network with others who share similar interests. Members often include investors like yourself, real estate brokers, tax and real estate attorneys, engineers, appraisers, and other real estate professionals. Club and association members will usually meet on a periodic basis, such as monthly, to discuss current events and share information. In addition, they will frequently feature guest speakers who provide insight into a given area of expertise. Appendix A lists a number of active investor associations throughout the United States.

## Banks

Smaller local or regional banks can also be a good resource for locating properties. Lenders, of course, are not in the business of managing real estate, nor do they want to be. The very nature of their business, however, demands that they assume risk with every loan they extend to borrowers. Unfortunately for the banks, those borrowers sometimes default; when they do, the lender forecloses on the property, and the real estate is transferred into the lender's real estate owned (REO) portfolio. The last thing banks want to do is be in the business of collecting rents, so they will usually have property management firms manage their REO portfolios.

Lenders are often quite flexible in the terms and conditions they are willing to offer, which may result in an opportunity for you to reach an agreement that is acceptable to both of you. The basis for the lender's starting point will likely be determined by the hard costs the bank has sunk into the property. While the bank will no doubt make every effort to minimize its losses, if it is anxious to get the property off its books, there is a good chance it will be willing to negotiate in your favor by agreeing to write down a portion of the loan. If the deal does not make sense for you as an investor, you are better off letting the bank keep the property.

The best approach to identifying the property best suited to your specific needs will include using as many of these tools as possible. The most important thing to remember is to *be patient*. You will find the right property at the right price with the right terms. As the employer of your capital, your task is to have your employees (your capital) working as hard for you as possible. This means that your investment must offer an acceptable rate of return to you. Only you can determine what is acceptable. It is best to establish what is an acceptable rate of return early in the process, so you don't make the mistake of lowering your standard because you think you have found a property that is okay. Determine what your investment criteria and objectives are; implement them as an initial filtering device; and, when the time comes, be prepared to execute your acquisition strategy.

*Life is a series of cash flows. Learn to become their master, not their slave.*
**—STEVE BERGES**

# Financial Analysis

**T**his is probably the most crucial chapter in the entire book. Because the scope of this book is narrowly limited to multifamily properties, only one chapter is devoted to the principles of financial analysis. While an abundance of books are written on how to buy and sell real estate, the market is virtually devoid of any works that specifically address the principles of finance and value as they apply to real estate. These topics are, however, covered in *The Complete Guide to Real Estate Finance: How to Analyze Any Single-Family, Multifamily, or Commercial Property* (Hoboken, NJ: Wiley, 2004), which is written with an emphasis on the concepts of financial analysis as they pertain to real estate and is intended to help fill this current void. The book takes the theories of real estate finance discussed in other books and demonstrates how they can be used in real-world situations. In other words, it is the practical application of these theories that really matters to investors. An in-depth examination of a variety of case studies in *The Complete Guide to Real Estate Finance: How to Analyze Any Single-Family, Multifamily, or Commercial Property* provides the learning platform necessary for investors to make the transition from the theory of real estate finance to its practical application. For now, however, let us focus on buying and selling apartment buildings.

The key to your success in buying and selling apartment buildings is a thorough and comprehensive understanding of *value*. Proper valuation is the basis for all investment decisions, whether it be an investment in the stocks of various companies, precious metals, or real estate. You absolutely must be able to understand how value is derived in order to make prudent investment decisions. Without this vital skill, you will find yourself at a tremendous disadvantage.

## Valuation—How Much Is That Property Really Worth?

In this chapter, you will learn how to determine whether an apartment building a broker is listing at $800,000 is in fact worth the asking price. How do you know? It might really be worth only $600,000, or it could actually be underpriced and really be worth $1 million. The bottom line is that you need to know and understand the difference for yourself and not rely solely on what the broker and seller are telling you. I have seen many brokers who believe their client's property is worth more than it really is. I have also seen inexperienced investors, over and over again, attempt to justify the value the broker is asking. Somehow they think that if they can only buy the property, they will be able to unlock all that extra value. The truth, however, is that they will have overpaid. In a zero-sum game, it is their loss and the seller's gain.

The other side of this issue is that you, as the seller, must understand the correct value of your apartment complex when it comes time for you to sell. Just as I have seen brokers attempt to sell a property at a value that was excessive, I have also seen them list properties at prices that I believe were below market. This can, of course, work to your advantage if you are seeking to acquire an apartment building, but if you are the seller, look out! An incompetent broker can cost you thousands of dollars.

## Two Crucial Principles That Saved Me $345,000

Allow me to share a personal experience. I acquired a midsized Class C apartment complex that met all of my criteria for a value-play opportunity. I made a number of improvements to the buildings within the first six months, bringing it up to a Class C+ to B– range. I subsequently raised the rents, and the property was fairly stabilized by the ninth month. The complex was averaging 97 to 98 percent occupancy with minimal turnover. By the tenth month, it was time to begin implementing my exit strategy. I would do one of two things—either sell the property outright, or refinance it to pull as much of my equity out of it as possible. I already had a broker in mind whom I knew from a previous transaction. He happened to work for one of the nation's largest commercial real estate brokerage firms. He was a respected and active broker who knew the apartment market well, or so I thought.

My own analysis of the financial statements for my apartment complex suggested a value of approximately $2 to $2.1 million. For what I had into it, I thought I would probably list it at a price of $2.05 million and would be willing to settle for $1.9 to $1.95 million. To my utter dismay, the broker I was about to engage to represent me suggested a value of only $1.8 million on the high side and said I would be lucky to get $1.65 million. I must admit that I was temporarily devastated by his analysis. This was a broker I trusted and felt certain was competent. A sales price of $1.65 million was not at all what I had in mind. I began to question myself and wondered where I had gone wrong. After all, I had spent a great deal of time and energy, not to mention money, on this project. Was all of this for naught? My feelings of despair lasted for all of about 10 minutes.

I have been knocked down enough times to know that I have two choices— I can either stay down, or I can get back up. I chose the latter. It was time for a second opinion, and while I was at it, I thought I might as well get a third opinion, too. I quickly contacted two other brokers who I knew were active in that market and faxed my financials to them. I was careful not to prejudice their opinions with my own as related to the value. The first broker came back with a value of $2 to $2.1 million, while the second broker estimated the value to be $2 to $2.2 million. Bingo! Aahhh, life was good again. My analysis had proven to be right on target and was corroborated by two other brokers.

This story, by the way, has a happy ending. The property was subsequently sold for a price of $1,995,000. With new financing being secured, a full-blown appraisal was required. The appraisal report indicated a value of $2.15 million, which further served to validate my original analysis. If I had relied on the original broker's opinion, I would have been lucky to have sold the apartment complex for $1.65 million. His incompetence would have cost me $345,000. Yikes!

### Two Techniques That Can Save You Thousands

1. You must have a comprehensive understanding of value.
2. Exercise caution before engaging the services of a broker.

# Valuation Methodologies

Three traditional approaches are used in valuing and appraising property.

### The Three Traditional Valuation Approaches

1. Sales comparison approach.

2. Replacement cost approach.

3. Income capitalization approach.

Each approach has its place and serves a unique function in determining value. Depending on the type of property being appraised, more weight may be given to a particular approach as deemed appropriate.

## Sales Comparison Approach

Butler Burgher, LLC, a well-known appraisal firm based in Houston, Texas, defines the *sales comparison approach* as follows:*

> The sales comparison approach is founded upon the principle of substitution which holds that the cost to acquire an equally desirable substitute property without undue delay ordinarily sets the upper limit of value. At any given time, prices paid for comparable properties are construed by many to reflect the value of the property appraised. The validity of a value indication derived by this approach is heavily dependent upon the availability of data on recent sales of properties similar in location, size, and utility to the appraised property.
>
> The sales comparison approach is premised upon the principle of substitution—a valuation principle that states that a prudent purchaser would pay no more for real property than the cost of acquiring an equally desirable substi-

*Excerpts in this section are from a private annual appraisal report by Butler Burgher, LLC, Houston, Tex., July 2000. Reprinted here with permission.

tute on the open market. The principle of substitution presumes that the purchaser will consider the alternatives available to them, that they will act rationally or prudently on the basis of his information about those alternatives, and that time is not a significant factor. Substitution may assume the form of the purchase of an existing property with the same utility, or of acquiring an investment which will produce an income stream of the same size with the same risk as that involved in the property in question. . . . The actions of typical buyers and sellers are reflected in the comparison approach.

In short, the sales comparison approach examines like properties and adjusts value based on similarities and differences. This method is used most often in valuing single-family homes. Say, for example, you decide to sell your house. To help you determine what price you should list your house for, your broker will pull up all of the current listings in your neighborhood, as well as recent sales, and calculate a range of prices based on average sales per square foot. Then the broker will consider factors such as the overall condition and the various amenities of your home. Does it have a fireplace, or a swimming pool? Is it a two-car garage or a three-car garage? And so goes the process, adding and subtracting until a final value is determined.

The use of sales comparisons, or *sales comps,* as they are called, is an important factor to consider in the overall analysis to determine the value of multifamily properties; however, greater weight is usually given to the income approach. In fact, the income approach is what truly drives value. The sales comps are the result of that valuation approach and can be used as a basis to help gauge what the market will support. Table 7.1 illustrates several key factors found in a typical sales comparison chart.By comparing the subject property to recent like sales, you are better able to evaluate the reasonableness of the asking price of the subject property. An examination of the NOI per Unit column allows you to quickly compare the level of profitability on a per-unit basis. Because the average unit size will vary, a more accurate com-

**Table 7.1** Summary of Sales Comparables

| Property Name | Date of Sale | Sales Price | Number of Units | Price per Unit | Average Unit Size | Price per Foot | Year Built | NOI per Unit | Cap Rate |
|---|---|---|---|---|---|---|---|---|---|
| Grandview Gardens | Nov 01 | 1,600,000 | 70 | 22,857 | 800 | 28.57 | 1981 | 2,295 | 10.04% |
| North Pointe | Sep 01 | 9,800,000 | 448 | 21,875 | 795 | 27.52 | 1972 | 2,365 | 10.81% |
| Colonial Elms | Aug 01 | 1,600,000 | 80 | 20,000 | 735 | 27.21 | 1968 | 2,184 | 10.92% |
| Arlington Terrace | Apr 01 | 6,240,000 | 225 | 27,733 | 890 | 31.16 | 1970 | 2,465 | 8.89% |
| Queens Drive | Feb 01 | 2,575,000 | 116 | 22,198 | 925 | 24.00 | 1979 | 2,314 | 10.42% |
| | | | | | | | | | |
| Minimum | | 1,600,000 | 70 | 20,000 | 735 | 24.00 | 1968 | 2,184 | 8.89% |
| Mean | | 3,902,500 | 168 | 22,444 | 813 | 27.08 | 1973 | 2,301 | 10.00% |
| Maximum | | 9,800,000 | 448 | 27,733 | 925 | 31.16 | 1981 | 2,465 | 10.92% |
| | | | | | | | | | |
| Subject property | | 2,200,000 | 105 | 20,952 | 815 | 25.71 | 1971 | 2,245 | 10.71% |

parison of profitability can be made by measuring it on a per-square-foot basis, just as expenses are also often measured on a per-square-foot basis. Although not included in Table 7.1, other elements to take into account are the overall condition of the properties, the various amenities offered at each one (swimming pool, laundry facilities, covered parking, etc.), and what is included in the rent (cable TV, utilities, etc.).

## Replacement Cost Approach

Butler Burgher, LLC, defines the *replacement cost approach* as follows:

> The cost approach is based on the premise that the value of a property can be indicated by the current cost to construct a reproduction or replacement for the improvements minus the amount of depreciation evident in the structures from all causes plus the value of the land and entrepreneurial profit. This approach to value is particularly useful for appraising new or nearly new improvements.

The replacement cost approach is typically not used to value income-producing properties such as apartment complexes. It is most appropriately used when estimating the actual costs associated with replacing all of the physical assets. For example, if the building were to be completely destroyed by fire, the value established by the replacement cost approach would be useful in helping to determine exactly how much an insurance company would pay for the resulting damages. While not related to our valuation discussion, you should know that most insurance companies will include some compensation to you for the loss of income incurred as a direct result of the fire (or for any other reason as may be expressly stated in your policy). Check with your agent to ensure that your policy does in fact include coverage of this sort. The loss of rental income from some or all of your units resulting from some natural disaster does not absolve you of your responsibilities to your debtors. While they may empathize with you in your unfortunate circumstances, your debtors will nevertheless continue to demand payment.

## Income Capitalization Approach

Once again, I will rely on the appraisal firm of Butler Burgher, LLC, to define the *income capitalization approach,* or *income approach,* as it is also known.

The income capitalization approach is based on the principle of anticipation which recognizes the present value of the future income benefits to be derived from ownership of real property. The income approach is most applicable to properties that are considered for investment purposes, and is considered very reliable when adequate income/expense data are available. Since income producing real estate is most often purchased by investors, this approach is valid and is generally considered the most applicable.

The income capitalization approach is a process of estimating the value of real property based upon the principle that value is directly related to the present value of all future net income attributable to the property. The value of the real property is therefore derived by capitalizing net income either by direct capitalization or a discounted cash flow analysis. Regardless of the capitalization technique employed, one must attempt to estimate a reasonable net operating income based upon the best available market data. The derivation of this estimate requires the appraiser to (1) project potential gross income (PGI) based upon an analysis of the subject rent roll and a comparison of the subject to competing properties, (2) project income loss from vacancy and collections based on the subject's occupancy history and upon supply and demand relationships in the subject's market . . . , (3) derive effective gross income (EGI) by subtracting the vacancy and collection income loss from PGI, (4) project the operating expenses associated with the production of the income stream by analysis of the subject's operating history and comparison of the subject to similar competing properties, and (5) derive net operating income (NOI) by subtracting the operating expenses from EGI.

The technical description Butler Burgher uses to define the income approach may initially appear somewhat complex if you are not familiar with the methodologies used for the quantitative analysis of financial statements. Do not allow yourself to become discouraged by the technical nature of the income approach. Remember, proper and accurate valuation is the key to your success in this business. Without this very crucial key, the door will remain locked, and you will be left standing on the outside wondering why you cannot open the door. Take comfort in the fact that the case studies that follow in Chapter 8 outline in detail exactly how this valuation process works.

Let us break down the income approach to its most fundamental level by examining a basic financial instrument. For example, assuming a market interest rate of 5 percent, how much would you be willing to pay for an annuity yielding $10,000 per annum? The answer is easily solved by taking a simple ratio of the two values, as follows:

$$\text{Present value} = \frac{\text{income}}{\text{rate}} = \frac{\$10,000}{0.05} = \$200,000$$

In other words, if you purchased a certificate of deposit (CD) for $200,000 that yielded 5 percent annually, you could expect to earn an income stream of $10,000. It does not matter, by the way, whether the income continues indefinitely, or perpetually; the present value remains the same. If you changed the rate to 10 percent and the annuity generated the same $10,000 income stream, the instrument should be worth even more, right? After all, you are now earning a rate twice what you were receiving. Surely this must be worth more. Let us do the math:

$$\text{Present value} = \frac{\text{income}}{\text{rate}} = \frac{\$10,000}{0.10} = \$100,000$$

Okay, you ask, how can that be? Examining this equation as an investor, you know that if the market is paying 10 percent and the income generated remains constant at $10,000, the only other variable in the equation is the value of the investment, which in this case would be $100,000. If you add *time* to the equation, you then begin to enter the world of *discounted cash-flow analysis*. While I could delve into a lengthy dissertation on this subject, it really is not necessary for our analysis, because for all practical purposes we are primarily interested in the net operating income of an income-producing property as it exists today. Yes, we do want to know what the upside potential is, but in most cases we are willing to pay only what the property is worth today as it is currently operating.

Most everyone can grasp this very simple example of determining how much a financial instrument such as a CD is worth. So, if we know that a CD paying $10,000 per year at a yield of 5 percent is worth $200,000, how much would an apartment building yielding the same rate and generating the same level of income be worth? Right! The answer is exactly the same, $200,000! Any investment vehicle, whether it be stocks, CDs, or real estate, would have the exact same present value. As an investor, however, you will demand a higher rate of return to offset the increased risks assumed with some investments. In the case of CDs, you make your $200,000 deposit at what is referred to as the *risk-free rate*. There is essentially no risk as your investment is insured (with certain limitations and restrictions) by the Federal Deposit Insurance Corporation (FDIC). The bank makes monthly interest deposits in your account without your giving it a second thought, except to review your bank statement periodically. In the case of multifamily property investments, however, you, as the investor, will require a higher rate of return for assuming the additional risk associated with property ownership. If an investment in an apartment building yielded the same 5 percent, would you invest in a CD, or in the apartment building? Unless you just felt compelled to buy apartments, there would be no reason to invest in them. Clearly, you would invest in the CD, because it is a risk-free instrument with little to no effort required on your part. Why buy an apartment building, which requires a great deal of time and energy on your part, if it generates the same level of income as an instrument that requires virtually no effort? You would not buy it. There must be some additional incentive or premium paid to offset the additional risk, time, and energy required for ownership of a multifamily property.

In summary, each of the three traditional valuation approaches serves a unique function by using different methodologies to derive value. If a full and formalized appraisal were to be conducted, all three approaches would be employed, with varying weights applied to each one. Butler Burgher affirms, "The appraisal process is concluded by a reconciliation of the approaches. This aspect of the process gives consideration to the type and reliability of market data used, the applicability of each approach to the type of property appraised and the type of value sought." For our purposes, we will rely primarily on the income approach.

# Financial Statements

Financial statements represent the end product of the accounting process. There are a number of issues to consider, as well as various approaches employed, to report an entity's financial condition, most of which are covered under what are known as *generally accepted accounting principles* (GAAP). Financial accounting and reporting assumptions, standards, and practices that an entity uses in preparing its statements are all governed by GAAP. The standards for GAAP are prescribed by authoritative bodies such as the Financial Accounting Standards Board (FASB). These standards are based on practical and theoretical considerations that have evolved over the years in reaction to changes in the economic environment. The objective of this book is to consider these standards as they apply to multifamily properties, not to cover the entire scope of the accounting industry, so we will keep it simple and maintain a narrow focus on the issues as they apply to you, a multifamily property owner.

The financial statements for a multifamily property are primarily comprised of the income statement, balance sheet, and rent roll. Have the broker or seller furnish you, as a prospective buyer, with the most recent two to three years of historical operating statements; this will enable you to evaluate the performance of the apartment complex over an extended period of time. You should be able to detect any trends, such as a systematic increase in rents. Conversely, if you observe flat or declining rental rates, along with an increase in the vacancy rate, you might conclude that the market in that particular area has softened. This could also indicate management problems, which can be overcome much more easily than a softening market. Historical operating statements are not always readily available for one reason or another; however, the seller should be able to provide you with operating data for the most recent 12 months at minimum. The trailing-12-month period is the most crucial, as it will enable you to accurately assess the property's most recent performance, which is what your offering price should be based on. By examining each of the last 12 months in detail, you can evaluate the relative stability of the revenues, expenses, and net operating income.

## Income Statement

The income statement is the most important of all the financial statements. It reports the net income or net loss from operating activities and forms the basis for investment-related decisions. The income statement presents a summary of an apartment's earnings activities for a given period of time. It reports all of the revenues earned, as well as the expenses incurred to earn them. Operating revenues less operating expenses is equal to the apartment's net operating income. An in-depth analysis of the income statement will provide insight into the property's level of existing profitability, as well as an indication of future profitability. The income statement can be divided into five main categories.

**Five Essential Components of an Income Statement**

1. Operating revenues.
2. Operating expenses.
3. Net operating income.
4. Debt service.
5. Reserve requirements.

*Operating revenues* consist of all sources of revenue, such as gross scheduled income, vacancy loss, and other income. *Gross scheduled income* represents 100 percent of the potential income an apartment complex could produce if every single unit were occupied. In other words, if the vacancy rate were zero and all tenants paid 100 percent of their respective rent, the rental income for the property would be maximized. *Vacancy loss* represents the amount of income lost due to unleased units. Promotional discounts and concessions, as well as delinquencies, also fall under the vacancy loss category. *Other income* includes income from late fees, application fees, laundry rooms, vending machines, and any payments that may be collected for utilities.

Second, *operating expenses* include all of the expenses having to do with actually operating the property, such as general and administrative expenses, payroll, repairs and maintenance, utilities, and taxes and insurance. It does *not* include depreciation expenses, interest expenses, or any debt service. Depreciation and interest are of course expenses for tax purposes, but that is a separate issue. Our objective here is to analyze the income statement for *valuation* purposes. We are not concerned with the tax consequences at this juncture.

*General and administrative expenses* include disbursements for items such as office supplies, legal and accounting fees, advertising and marketing expenses, and property management fees. *Payroll expenses* consist of all expenses related to those personnel directly employed by the entity operating the apartment complex. Related expenses include payroll for office personnel, maintenance and grounds employees, payroll taxes, workman's compensation, state and federal employee taxes, and benefits such as insurance and 401(k) plans. Payroll expenses should *not* include any costs for work performed by subcontractors, even though you may furnish all of the materials and pay the subcontractor only for labor. These types of expenses fall under *repairs and maintenance*. Make-readies, contract services, security and patrol services, general repairs and related materials, and landscaping services should all be included in repairs and maintenance. *Utility expenses* consist of all disbursements related to the apartment's utility usage, such as electric, gas, water and sewer, trash removal, cable TV service, and telephone expenditures. *Taxes and insurance expenses* typically include outlays for real estate taxes and insurance premiums used to insure physical assets such as the building and any loss of income resulting from damage to the premises. Insurance premiums for boiler equipment and other machinery fall under this category as well.

The third category of the income statement is *net operating income*. While generally just a single line item, this is the most important element of the income statement. Net operating income is derived as follows:

Gross income – total operating expenses = net operating income

Net operating income is the remaining income after all operating expenses have been disbursed. It is also the amount of income available to service any associated debt—that is, to make any loan payments. Finally, net operating income is the numerator in the quotient used to calculate the capitalization rate, which is discussed in greater detail later in this chapter under Five Key Ratios You Must Know.

The fourth component of the income statement is *debt service,* which is fairly self-explanatory. It includes both the principal and interest portions of any debt payments being made on the property. In addition, it is the denominator in the quotient used to calculate the debt service coverage ratio, which is also discussed in greater detail under Five Key Ratios You Must Know.

Finally, the *reserve requirements* portion of the income statement is used to cover any capital improvements to the apartment complex. Lenders will often figure into their calculations a budgeted amount deemed appropriate to make necessary capital improvements. The reserve requirement is estimated on an annual basis, and often is broken down into a per-unit figure, such as $250 per unit per year. Under this scenario, on a 100-unit apartment complex, you would have a total of $25,000 budgeted for improvements.

Study Table 7.2 to better understand how the various components of an income statement work together. By examining as many income statements as possible, you will soon begin to get a feel for a property with just a quick perusal.

## Balance Sheet

The *balance sheet,* or *balance statement,* as it is sometimes known, reports a property's financial position at a specific point in time. In effect, it provides a snapshot of the apartment's position on a specific date, usually at

**Table 7.2** White House Apartments Income Statement, Fiscal Year 2000

Actual

| Operating Revenues | Qtr 1 | Qtr 2 | Qtr 3 | Qtr 4 | Annual |
|---|---|---|---|---|---|
| Gross scheduled income | 120,000 | 121,200 | 122,412 | 123,636 | 487,248 |
| Less vacancy | 6,233 | 2,850 | 4,624 | 5,112 | 18,819 |
| Net rental income | 113,767 | 115,681 | 117,788 | 118,524 | 465,760 |
| Utility income | 7,555 | 10,818 | 18,823 | 17,457 | 54,653 |
| Other income—laundry, misc. | 2,645 | 2,873 | 4,533 | 3,644 | 13,695 |
| Gross income | 123,967 | 130,337 | 141,144 | 139,625 | 535,073 |
| **Operating Expenses** | | | | | |
| General and administrative | | | | | |
| Management fees | 4,339 | 4,562 | 4,940 | 4,887 | 18,728 |
| Office supplies | 1,254 | 1,020 | 1,313 | 1,387 | 4,974 |
| Legal and accounting | 322 | 180 | 155 | 210 | 867 |
| Advertising | 114 | 245 | 385 | 283 | 1,027 |
| Total general and administrative | 6,029 | 6,005 | 6,793 | 6,767 | 25,594 |
| Repairs and maintenance | | | | | |
| Repairs, maintenance, make-readies | 10,212 | 9,987 | 8,715 | 9,268 | 38,182 |
| Contract services | 742 | 869 | 657 | 880 | 3,148 |
| Patrol services | 825 | 825 | 825 | 825 | 3,300 |
| Grounds and landscaping | 225 | 875 | 1,050 | 645 | 2,795 |
| Total repairs and maintenance | 12,004 | 12,667 | 11,247 | 11,618 | 47,536 |
| Salaries and payroll | | | | | |
| Office | 6,200 | 6,200 | 6,200 | 6,200 | 24,800 |
| Maintenance | 4,850 | 4,850 | 4,850 | 4,850 | 19,400 |
| Payroll taxes | 834 | 834 | 834 | 834 | 3,337 |
| Total salaries and payroll | 11,884 | 10,985 | 11,884 | 11,884 | 46,638 |
| Utilities | | | | | |
| Electric | 11,465 | 17,878 | 26,504 | 17,880 | 73,727 |
| Gas | 3,880 | 3,147 | 2,160 | 2,880 | 12,067 |
| Water and sewer | 9,222 | 9,910 | 11,879 | 11,546 | 42,557 |
| Trash | 1,425 | 1,425 | 1,425 | 1,425 | 5,700 |
| Telephone | 255 | 245 | 277 | 246 | 1,023 |
| Total utilities | 26,247 | 32,202 | 42,245 | 33,977 | 134,671 |
| Other | | | | | |
| Real Estate Taxes | 7,905 | 7,905 | 7,905 | 7,905 | 31,620 |
| Insurance | 2,556 | 2,556 | 2,556 | 2,556 | 10,224 |
| Total Other | 10,461 | 10,461 | 10,461 | 10,461 | 41,844 |
| Total Operating Expenses | 66,625 | 72,320 | 82,630 | 74,707 | 296,283 |
| Net Operating Income | 57,342 | 58,017 | 58,514 | 64,918 | 238,790 |
| Debt Service | 38,400 | 38,400 | 38,400 | 38,400 | 153,600 |

**Table 7.2** *(Continued)*

| Capital Improvements | | | | | |
|---|---|---|---|---|---|
| A/C and heating | 1,567 | 958 | 1,693 | 1,482 | 5,700 |
| Appliances | 0 | 800 | 420 | 850 | 2,070 |
| Building repairs | 1,807 | 0 | 0 | 5,686 | 7,493 |
| Carpet and tile | 1,310 | 615 | 1,335 | 1,995 | 5,255 |
| Driveways and parking lots | 0 | 0 | 0 | 2,395 | 2,395 |
| Drapes and blinds | 432 | 283 | 0 | 676 | 1,391 |
| Roof | 0 | 0 | 0 | 0 | 0 |
| Miscellaneous | 469 | 469 | 243 | 220 | 1,879 |
| Total capital improvements | 5,585 | 3,603 | 3,691 | 13,304 | 26,183 |
| Net Cash Flow | 32,815 | 34,797 | 34,709 | 25,096 | 127,417 |

monthly, quarterly, and annual intervals. The balance sheet can be instrumental in providing information about an entity's liquidity and its financial flexibility, which can at times be crucial in meeting unexpected short-term obligations. Examining the debt-to-equity ratio, for example, may indicate that the business is already highly leveraged and that no remaining borrowing capacity exists. The balance sheet is also useful in measuring profitability. For example, by relating a company's net income through the use of ratios to the owner's equity or to the total assets, returns can be calculated and used to assess the company's level of profitability relative to similar businesses. The balance sheet can be divided into three main categories.

**Three Essential Components of a Balance Sheet**

1. Assets.
2. Liabilities.
3. Equity.

**Balance Sheet Equation**

$$\text{Assets} = \text{liabilities} + \text{equity}$$
or
$$\text{Assets} - \text{liabilities} = \text{equity}$$

Observe that the two sides of the equation are equal; hence the name *balance sheet*. The two sides must always be equal, because one side shows the resources of the business while the other side shows who furnished the resources (i.e., the creditors). The difference between the two is the *equity*.

The *assets* of a business are the properties or economic resources owned by the business; they are often classified as current or noncurrent. *Current assets* are those that are expected to be converted into cash or used or consumed within a relatively short period of time, generally within one year of the operating cycle. *Noncurrent* or *fixed assets* are those whose benefits extend over periods longer than the one-year operating cycle. As related to a multifamily property, current assets include amounts owed but not yet collected (accounts receivable), cash, security deposits (with utility companies or suppliers, for example), prepaid items such as insurance premiums, and supplies. Fixed assets include items such as buildings, equipment, and land.

The *liabilities* of a business are its debts, or any claim another business or individual may have against the operating entity. Liabilities can also be classified as current or noncurrent. *Current liabilities* are those that will require the use of current assets or that will be discharged within a relatively short period of time, usually one year. *Noncurrent* or *long-term liabilities* are those longer than one year in duration. Current liabilities include amounts owed to creditors for goods and services bought on credit (accounts payable), salaries and wages owed to employees or contractors, security deposits (deposits made by the tenants prior to moving in), taxes payable, and notes payable. Long-term liabilities include mortgages payable and any kind of secondary financing secured against the property, such as loans for capital improvements or equipment financing.

The equity of a business represents that portion of value remaining after all obligations have been satisfied. In other words, if your position in an entity were to be liquidated by selling off all of the assets and subsequently satisfying all of the creditors, any remaining proceeds would represent your equity. Because the law gives creditors the right to force the sale of the assets of the business to meet their claims, your equity is considered to be subordinate to the debt. In the event a company declares bankruptcy, obligations to the creditors will be satisfied first, and obligations to owners or shareholders will be satisfied last.

The two primary categories of equity are (1) owner's contributions and (2) retained earnings. With respect to apartment ownership, the *owner's equity* represents the portion of capital that you, as the buyer, have personally invested. Assuming you put down $200,000 on a $1-million apartment complex, and then invested an additional $75,000 in capital improvements, your owner's equity would be $275,000. *Retained earnings* represent that portion of income left in or retained by the business. If the earnings were not left in the entity but were instead paid out to you as the owner, the equity decreases as a result of the owner's withdrawal.

In summary, the balance sheet represents an important segment of the financial statements and can provide you with valuable information. By studying Table 7.3, you will better understand how the various components of a balance sheet fit together.

## Rent Roll

The *rent roll,* or *rent schedule,* as it is sometimes known, provides information that is vital to you as a potential buyer. A good rent roll should provide most of the following data:

- *Unit number*—the apartment number
- *Tenant's name*—the name of your tenant
- *Type of apartment*—for example, two bedroom, two bath

**Table 7.3** White House Apartments Balance
Statement, Fiscal Year End 2000
(as of December 31, 2000)

| Assets | |
| --- | --- |
| Current | |
| Operating cash | 30,580 |
| Petty cash | 498 |
| Accounts receivable | 1,127 |
| Supplies | 588 |
| Prepaid insurance | 6,594 |
| Utility deposits | 17,885 |
| Total current assets | 57,272 |
| Fixed | |
| Buildings | 1,950,000 |
| Equipment | 46,500 |
| Land | 225,000 |
| Total fixed assets | 2,221,500 |
| Total Assets | 2,278,772 |
| Liabilities | |
| Current | |
| Accounts payable | 2,665 |
| Wages payable | 3,200 |
| Employee taxes payable | 496 |
| Property taxes payable | 22,300 |
| Security deposits | 15,600 |
| Total current liabilities | 44,261 |
| Long-term | |
| Mortgages payable | 1,422,558 |
| Notes payable—secondary financing | 156,452 |
| Notes payable—capital improvements | 95,545 |
| Total long-term liabilities | 1,674,555 |
| Total liabilities | 1,718,816 |
| Equity | |
| Capital | |
| Owner's contributions | 325,000 |
| Owner's withdrawals | (48,000) |
| Retained earnings | 282,956 |
| Total capital | 559,956 |
| Total Liabilities and Capital | 2,278,772 |

- *Scheduled rent*—the amount of rent your tenant was supposed to pay
- *Collected rent*—the amount of rent your tenant actually did pay
- *Other income*—any other income collected from utilities, application fees, late fees, and the like
- *Date paid*—the date or dates when rent payments were made
- *Comments section*—notes such as "new move-in" or "gave 30-day notice"

The seller should be able to provide you with rent schedules for no less than the previous three months. Ask for up to six months' worth if they are available. By closely studying the rent rolls, you should be able to assess the stability of the property, the efficiency of collections, and, probably most important, the occupancy rate (inverse of the vacancy rate).

The stability of an apartment complex is crucial for the smoothest possible operation, with minimal disruptions. A stable property is also an efficient property. Allow me to explain. First of all, *stable property* implies one where there is minimal or normal turnover. The turnover rate is calculated by dividing the number of units vacated over a given period of time by the total number of units:

$$\frac{26 \text{ move-outs}}{100 \text{ units}} = 26\% \text{ annual turnover rate}$$

In a 100-unit complex, for example, normal turnover might range from 1 to 5 move-outs per month, with 5 being on the high side, but allowing for some seasonality (more move-outs in the summer months). Low turnover suggests that the tenants are happy and content with their overall living accommodations. If they were not, they would move. If they moved, the turnover rate would be higher. If the turnover rate were higher, the property would not be as efficient, because higher turnover results in higher make-ready costs, higher maintenance costs, and higher advertising costs. A close examination of the rent roll will tell you exactly how many people are moving in and out each month. This is one case where less is more.

The rent roll should provide information about when the rents were collected. Most complexes collect rents at the beginning of the month. An inspection of the Date Paid column on the rent roll will quickly tell you whether rents are, on average, being collected when they are due. If they are not, this could very well be indicative of underlying problems within the management organization. The timely and efficient collection of rents is crucial in meeting your cash-flow needs. An effective manager will require strict enforcement of collections and be willing to proceed with the eviction process if necessary. Poor collection of rents may provide you with an opportunity to create value, but remember: the price you pay for the apartment complex should reflect the value of the property as it is *currently* operating, not what it would be if all of the rents were being collected. The value is created only after you have acquired the property and made the necessary changes to improve collections.

A high occupancy rate is usually, but not always, indicative of a well-managed property, a tight rental market, below market rents, or a combination of the three. A proficient manager will work hard to keep the units fully occupied. Such a manager knows when a tenant's lease is about to expire, how to effectively renew the lease so as to retain the tenant, how to point out all of the attributes of your apartment complex, and how to build a waiting list of prospective tenants in the event of a move-out. A good manager can save you thousands of dollars, so be sure to pay managers what they are worth. A tight rental market is obviously a strong plus, especially if it is in an area where only Class B or Class C units exist. Any new construction will by definition consist of Class A apartments and will therefore serve a different market, one that most likely will bear considerably higher rents than the

**Table 7.4**  White House Apartments Rent Schedule, January 2001

| Unit | Resident's Name | Apt Type | Appr Sq Ft | Scheduled Rent | Collected Rent | Utility Income | Other Income | Total Paid | Date Paid | Comments |
|------|-----------------|----------|------------|----------------|----------------|----------------|--------------|------------|-----------|----------|
| 101 | G. Washington | 2-2 | 850 | 950.00 | 950.00 | 75.00 | | 1,025.00 | 01/02 | Insists on using $1 bills to pay rent |
| 102 | J. Adams | 2-2 | 850 | 950.00 | 950.00 | 75.00 | | 1,025.00 | 01/03 | |
| 103 | T. Jefferson | 2-2 | 850 | 950.00 | 950.00 | 75.00 | | 1,025.00 | 01/04 | |
| 104 | J. Madison | 2-2 | 850 | 950.00 | 950.00 | 75.00 | | 1,025.00 | 01/03 | |
| 105 | J. Monroe | 2-2 | 850 | 950.00 | 950.00 | 75.00 | 25.00 | 1,050.00 | 01/06 | |
| 106 | J. Q. Adams | 2-2 | 850 | 950.00 | 950.00 | 75.00 | | 1,025.00 | 01/04 | |
| 107 | A. Jackson | 2-2 | 850 | 950.00 | 950.00 | 75.00 | | 1,025.00 | 01/02 | |
| 108 | M. Van Buren | 2-2 | 850 | 950.00 | 950.00 | 75.00 | 25.00 | 1,050.00 | 01/09 | |
| 109 | W. Harrison | 2-2 | 850 | 950.00 | 950.00 | 75.00 | | 1,025.00 | 01/02 | |
| 110 | J. Tyler | 2-2 | 850 | 950.00 | 950.00 | 75.00 | | 1,025.00 | 01/02 | |
| 111 | J. Polk | 2-2 | 850 | 950.00 | 950.00 | 75.00 | | 1,025.00 | 01/02 | |
| 112 | Z. Taylor | 2-2 | 850 | 950.00 | 950.00 | 75.00 | 25.00 | 1,050.00 | 01/07 | |
| 113 | M. Fillmore | 2-2 | 850 | 950.00 | 950.00 | 75.00 | | 1,025.00 | 01/02 | |
| 114 | F. Pierce | 2-2 | 850 | 950.00 | 950.00 | 75.00 | | 1,025.00 | 01/02 | |
| 115 | J. Buchanan | 2-2 | 850 | 950.00 | 950.00 | 75.00 | | 1,025.00 | 01/02 | |
| 116 | A. Lincoln | 2-2 | 850 | 950.00 | 950.00 | 75.00 | | 1,025.00 | 01/02 | Reported loose balcony railing |
| 117 | A. Johnson | 2-2 | 850 | 950.00 | 950.00 | 75.00 | | 1,025.00 | 01/05 | |
| 118 | U. Grant | 2-2 | 850 | 950.00 | 950.00 | 75.00 | 25.00 | 1,050.00 | 01/06 | |
| 119 | R. Hayes | 2-2 | 850 | 950.00 | 950.00 | 75.00 | | 1,025.00 | 01/05 | |
| 120 | J. Garfield | 2-2 | 850 | 950.00 | 950.00 | 75.00 | | 1,025.00 | 01/05 | |
| 121 | C. Arthur | 2-2 | 850 | 950.00 | 950.00 | 75.00 | | 1,025.00 | 01/04 | |
| 122 | G. Cleveland | 2-2 | 850 | 950.00 | 950.00 | 75.00 | | 1,025.00 | 01/02 | |
| 123 | B. Harrison | 2-2 | 850 | 950.00 | 950.00 | 75.00 | | 1,025.00 | 01/05 | |

| | | | | | | | | | |
|---|---|---|---|---|---|---|---|---|---|
| 124 | G. Cleveland | 2-2 | 850 | 950.00 | 75.00 | | 1,025.00 | 01/02 | |
| 125 | W. McKinley | 2-2 | 850 | 950.00 | 75.00 | | 1,025.00 | 01/04 | |
| 126 | T. Roosevelt | 2-2 | 850 | 950.00 | 75.00 | | 1,025.00 | 01/03 | |
| 127 | W. Taft | 2-2 | 850 | 950.00 | 75.00 | | 1,025.00 | 01/03 | |
| 128 | W. Wilson | 2-2 | 850 | 950.00 | 75.00 | | 1,025.00 | 01/03 | |
| 129 | W. Harding | 2-2 | 850 | 950.00 | 75.00 | | 1,025.00 | 01/02 | |
| 130 | C. Coolidge | 2-2 | 850 | 950.00 | 75.00 | | 1,025.00 | 01/02 | |
| 131 | H. Hoover | 2-2 | 850 | 950.00 | 75.00 | | 1,025.00 | 01/03 | |
| 132 | F. Roosevelt | 2-2 | 850 | 950.00 | 75.00 | | 1,025.00 | 01/04 | Asked to renew lease a 4th term; denied |
| 133 | H. Truman | 2-2 | 850 | 950.00 | 75.00 | 25.00 | 1,050.00 | 01/06 | |
| 134 | D. Eisenhower | 2-2 | 850 | 950.00 | 75.00 | 25.00 | 1,050.00 | 01/06 | Complained about inadequate security |
| 135 | J. Kennedy | 2-2 | 850 | 950.00 | 75.00 | | 1,025.00 | 01/05 | |
| 136 | L. Johnson | 2-2 | 850 | 950.00 | 75.00 | | 1,025.00 | 01/05 | |
| 137 | R. Nixon | 2-2 | 850 | 950.00 | 75.00 | | 1,025.00 | 01/04 | Work order to repair water, gate |
| 138 | G. Ford | 2-2 | 850 | 950.00 | 75.00 | 25.00 | 1,050.00 | 01/10 | Loose carpet—tripped on stairway |
| 139 | J. Carter | 2-2 | 850 | 950.00 | 75.00 | | 1,025.00 | 01/03 | |
| 140 | R. Reagan | 2-2 | 850 | 950.00 | 75.00 | 25.00 | 1,050.00 | 01/12 | |
| 141 | G. Bush Sr. | 2-2 | 850 | 950.00 | 75.00 | | 1,025.00 | 01/04 | |
| 142 | W. Clinton | 2-2 | 850 | 582.26 | 50.00 | | 632.26 | 01/02 | Job transfer—vacated 1/19/01 |
| 143 | G. W. Bush | 2-2 | 850 | 367.74 | 25.00 | 25.00 | 417.74 | 01/20 | New move-in—1/20/01 |

Other Income—laundry, vending, fund raisers, etc.                     1,465.00          1,465.00

| | | | | | | | | |
|---|---|---|---|---|---|---|---|---|
| Totals | 36,550 | 40,850.00 | 39,900.00 | 3,150.00 | 1,690.00 | 44,740.00 | | |
| Averages | 850 | 950.00 | 927.91 | 73.26 | 169.00 | 1,006.40 | 01/04 | |

Occupancy
97.67%

existing complexes can charge. To justify the higher costs of new construction, a developer will have to charge higher rents. One exception to this may be if the developer's project is being subsidized by some special low-cost government funding. If the rents are below market, you may be able to take advantage of one of the value-play techniques previously described. Here is a simple example. Say you have located a 50-unit apartment building that is charging on average $600 per month. Your research indicates the market will bear $640 per month. Using a capitalization rate of 10 percent, a bump in rental rates over a 12-month period of $40 per month would create $240,000 in additional value.

$$50 \text{ units} \times \$40/\text{unit} \times 12 \text{ months} = \$24,000$$

$$\frac{\$24,000}{0.10} = \$240,000$$

High occupancy is generally the result of a good manager, tight rental market, and underpriced rental units. The exception to this is when a property is operated by ineffective and inefficient managers. The units may be fully occupied, but there may be an "economic vacancy" factor of 20 percent or more. This can result when managers have poor collection and enforcement skills, as previously stated. In other words, the tenants' "aunt died," or "the car broke down," or "the baby is sick," and the managers allow them to postpone the rent indefinitely. Before the managers know it, they have an apartment complex full of deadbeats who do not pay their rent. Remember, find competent managers and hang on to them. Pay them what they are worth. Don't be penny wise and pound foolish.

In summary, the rent roll represents an equally important segment of the financial statements and can provide you with valuable information. By studying Table 7.4, you will better understand how the various components of the rent roll fit together.

# Five Key Ratios You Must Know

A *ratio* is a simple mathematical equation used to express a relationship between sets or groups of numbers. The use of ratios in analyzing multifamily properties is essential to properly and fully understanding their respective values. In addition, ratios provide a gauge or a general rule of thumb so that you can quickly determine how a given property is valued relative to the market. Five ratios are required in multifamily property analysis:

- The capitalization rate
- The cash return on investment
- The total return on investment
- The debt service coverage ratio
- The gross rent multiplier

Each of these elements plays an important role in helping you to determine whether the investment you are considering is worthy of your investment capital.

## Ratio 1: Capitalization Rate (Cap Rate)

The *capitalization rate,* or *cap rate,* is the ratio of net operating income to sales price:

$$\text{Capitalization rate} = \frac{\text{net operating income}}{\text{sales price}}$$

As you can see, this ratio is really a very simple calculation used to measure the relationship between the income generated by the property and the price it is being sold for. To help put this in a better perspective, refer back to the beginning of this chapter when we discussed certificates of deposits. We knew the value of a CD was calculated by its respective yield. The cap rate measures that exact same relationship!

$$\text{Present value of CD} = \frac{\text{income}}{\text{rate}} = \frac{\$10,000}{0.05} = \$200,000$$

Or, to look at it another way:

$$\text{Rate} = \frac{\text{income}}{\text{present value}} = \frac{\$10,000}{\$200,000} = 0.05 = 5\%$$

Buying an apartment building as related to this equation is really no different from buying a CD from your local bank. As an investor, you are willing to pay or invest a certain amount of capital in order to achieve a desired return. You know that the rates paid by banks for CDs will vary within a given range, say 4 to 6 percent, so you will most likely shop around a bit to find the most favorable rate. The same is true of apartment complexes. The rate paid, or yield on your investment, will vary within a given range, generally 8 to 12 percent, depending on a variety of market conditions including supply and demand issues, the current interest rate environment, and tax implications imposed by local, state, and federal authorities.

Here is an example. We know that net operating income (NOI) is derived by subtracting total operating expenses from gross income. If you were to pay all cash for an apartment building, NOI represents the portion of income that is yours to keep (before taxes and capital improvements), or the yield on your investment. If you were considering purchasing an apartment building that yielded $50,000 annually and the seller had an asking price of $800,000, should you buy it? Plug in the numbers and find out:

$$\text{Net operating income} = \$50,000$$
$$\text{Sales price} = \$800,000$$

$$\text{Cap rate} = \frac{\text{NOI}}{\text{Price}} = \frac{\$50,000}{\$800,000} = 0.0625 = 6.25\%$$

In this example, you can see that the asking price of $800,000 provides a yield of only 6.25 percent. Assume that comparable properties in this particular market are selling for cap rates of 10 percent. Armed with that knowledge, we can easily determine a more reasonable value for the property by solving for sales price, as follows:

$$\text{Cap rate} = \frac{\text{NOI}}{\text{Price}}$$

$$\text{Price} = \frac{\text{NOI}}{\text{Cap rate}} = \frac{\$50,000}{0.10} = \$500,000$$

So in this example, based on the limited information we have, we know the apartment is overpriced by $300,000. Understanding this simple yet powerful equation is fundamental to properly assessing value, allowing you to quickly determine whether the asking price of an apartment building is reasonable.

## Ratio 2: Cash Return on Investment (Cash ROI)

The *cash return on investment* is often referred to as the *cash on cash return*. It is the ratio of the remaining cash after debt service to invested capital:

$$\text{Cash ROI} = \frac{\text{remaining cash after debt service}}{\text{cash investment}}$$

The cash ROI is different from the NOI and the cap rate in that cash ROI is calculated after debt service, while the cap rate is calculated before debt service. Excluding tax implications, if you were to pay all cash for an apartment building, the cap rate and the cash ROI would be the same. Most investors, however, elect to utilize the other people's money (OPM) principle, which means that the cash return becomes a function of the return on your invested capital; hence, the name *cash on cash*. So while the cap rate is an important ratio used in determining relative property values, the cash ROI is an important ratio used to determine your cash rate of return on invested capital.

## Ratio 3: Total Return on Investment (Total ROI)

The *total return on investment* is similar to the cash ROI, with one important distinction—it accounts for that portion of return which is not cash, namely the principal reduction. In other words, it takes into account the portion of the loan that is reduced each year by payments that are applied to the remaining loan balance, or the principal portion of the loan payment. The total ROI is the ratio of the remaining cash after debt service plus principal payments to invested capital:

$$\text{Total ROI} = \frac{\text{remaining cash after debt service + principal reduction}}{\text{cash investment}}$$

The total ROI does exactly as its name implies: it provides a measurement of the total return on your invested capital by capturing both the cash and noncash portions. The noncash portion is similar to making a house payment for 10, 20, or 30 years. The value is there in the form of increased equity in your house as you reduce the loan balance a little at a time over a period of years. The gain is realized and converted to cash at the time of sale.

## Ratio 4: Debt Service Coverage Ratio (DSCR)

The *debt service coverage ratio,* also known as the *debt service ratio,* measures the relationship of the amount of cash available to service the debt payments, which is the net operating income, to the required debt payment:

$$\text{DSCR} = \frac{\text{net operating income}}{\text{debt payment}}$$

This ratio is especially important to lenders. Their primary concern is your ability to service the outstanding debt—in other words, your ability to make the payments. This ratio will vary among lenders, but a general range is from a minimum of 1.00 to a maximum of 1.35, with the most common ratio averaging 1.20. A number of factors influence the lender's DSCR requirement, including the age and condition of the property, the loan-to-value ratio, and your strength as a borrower.

While it is the lender who relies heavily on this ratio, it is equally important for you, as the investor, to understand its role in the financing equation. When you analyze a prospective property, you must be able to determine whether there is adequate cash flow to service the debt. Without it, you will never get a loan. If the deal does not provide sufficient cash flow to meet the DSCR requirements with a 20 percent down payment, chances are you will want to take a pass on the deal and go on to the next one.

One final thought here: please do not make the mistake of saying, "Oh, I'll just put more money down to lower my monthly payments." True, this would help to bring your DSCR into line, but guess what? By putting more money down, you are reducing the cash and total ROIs. If you have had some finance classes in your college days, go back to Finance 101.

QUESTION: What is the number-one objective for most corporations and businesses?
ANSWER: To maximize shareholders' wealth.

In the case of investing in apartment buildings, *you* are the shareholder, and do not forget it!

To summarize these concepts and tie all five key ratios together, consider the example in Table 7.5. Say you acquire a $2-million apartment building and are able to structure the deal so that you get in with a 15 percent down pay-

**Table 7.5**  Key Ratios

| Cost and Financing Assumptions | | |
| --- | --- | --- |
| Land | | 200,000 |
| Building | | 1,800,000 |
| Improvements | | 75,000 |
| Closing costs | | 25,000 |
| Total Investment | | 2,100,000 |
| Purchase price | 100.00% | 2,000,000 |
| Down payment | 15.00% | 300,000 |
| Balance to finance | 85.00% | 1,700,000 |
| | Annual | Monthly |
| Interest rate | 7.375% | 0.615% |
| Term | 25 | 300 |
| Payment | 149,099 | 12,425 |
| Down payment | | 300,000 |
| Improvements | | 75,000 |
| Closing costs | | 25,000 |
| Total cash outlay | | 400,000 |
| **Operating Revenue and Expense Assumptions** | | |
| Number of units | | 68 |
| Average monthly rent | | 605 |
| Gross annual revenues | 100% | 493,680 |
| Operating expenses | 55% | 271,524 |
| Net operating income | 45% | 222,156 |
| Debt service | | 149,099 |
| Cash flow from operations | | 73,057 |
| Principal reduction | | 24,543 |
| Total Return | | 97,600 |
| **Key Ratios** | | |
| Capitalization rate | 10.58% | |
| Return on investment | 18.26% | |
| Total return on investment | 24.40% | |
| Debt service coverage ratio | 149.00% | |
| Gross Rent Multiplier | 425.38% | |

ment plus $25,000 in closing costs. You budget another $75,000 for capital improvements for a total capital outlay of $400,000.

Examining the ratios in Table 7.5, you can see that they appear to be quite favorable. The cap rate calculation in this example takes into consideration the total investment of $2.1 million, as opposed to just the listed purchase price of $2 million. At 10.58 percent, it appears quite reasonable. Both the cash and total ROIs would meet most investors' threshold for an acceptable rate of return, and the DSCR certainly meets or exceeds most lenders' requirements.

## Ratio 5: Gross Rent Multiplier

The *gross rent multiplier,* or GRM, measures the relationship between the total purchase price of a property and its gross scheduled income. It is the ratio of price to income. The GRM calculation is made as follows:

$$\text{Gross Rent Multiplier} = \frac{\text{purchase price}}{\text{gross scheduled income}} = \text{GRM}$$

The GRM is similar to the cap rate in that it captures the relationship between revenues and price; however, there are two primary differences. The first is that while the GRM measures the relationship between gross revenues and price, the cap rate measures the relationship between net revenues, or NOI, and price. The second difference is that one ratio is inverted when compared to the other. For example, purchase price is the numerator in the GRM quotient, but the denominator in the cap rate. So while a higher cap rate is preferred to a lower cap rate, a lower GRM is preferred to a higher GRM. This is true because the ratio will decrease the lower the purchase price is relative to income. It will also decrease the higher the income is relative to the purchase price. Take a moment to review the GRM ratio illustrated in Table 7.5.

In Table 7.5, the GRM of 4.2538 measures the relationship between the total purchase price and the gross scheduled income.

$$\text{GRM} = \frac{\$2,100,000}{\$493,680} = 4.2538$$

In the model used to make the calculation, both improvements and closing costs have been factored into the analysis. If the improvements are expected to increase the gross revenues, that, too, should be taken into consideration. The GRM can be calculated on either an "as is" basis with no changes or improvements to the property, or on a pro forma basis, which includes both improvements and the expected increase in revenues that will result from the improvements.

# The One-Minute Assessment

You can learn to quickly do an initial assessment of a prospective property in less than a minute with just three easy steps. This initial assessment will help you determine whether you want to proceed with a more in-depth analysis.

Here is how it works. Sellers or brokers use "setup sheets," which provide minimal information about a property being offered for sale, such as the asking price, number of units, location, gross revenues, and terms. After reviewing the setup sheet for a given property, you can contact the seller or broker directly to ask for a full offering package, which they will gladly furnish. As a general rule of thumb, total operating expenses will average between 40 and 60 percent of gross income, depending on a variety of factors. If you split the difference, you end up with 50 percent on average. Take the gross income as reported on the setup sheet and multiply it by 0.50 (or simply divide by 2). The result is a reasonable estimate of net operating income, which can then be divided into the asking price, giving you an estimate of the cap rate. You know that cap rates are usually between 8 and 12 percent, with 10 percent being the average. Compare your result to the 10 percent average. Are you high, or low, or somewhere in the ballpark?

**The One-Minute Assessment in Three Easy Steps**

1. Divide gross income by 2; the result is an estimate of NOI.
2. Calculate the cap rate by dividing NOI by the asking price.
3. Determine whether the resulting cap rate is in line with the market.

*50% expense SFH lower (utilities)*

I frequently use this quick and dirty approach. If the offering price appears to be completely out of line, which it sometimes does, I move on to the next deal. Conversely, if it appears to be in line with my expectations, I may then decide to proceed with a more thorough analysis.

# How to Read Between the Lines

After analyzing dozens of financial statements for apartment buildings, you will begin to get a feel for every line item on the income statement. You will know, for example, that on average repairs and maintenance will run between 10 and 15 percent, property taxes will run about 5 percent, insurance will run about 2 percent, and management fees will run about 5 percent. These averages will obviously vary from area to area, but if you are focusing on properties in a particular city or county, you will have a good idea of what costs should be on average. By comparing the expenses as reported on the income statement with your expectations, anything outside of the norm will begin to jump out at you. If repairs and maintenance are reported at 4 percent, for example, you will want to investigate further. Something is out of line, and there is a good chance that not all of the repairs and maintenance items are being reported. Although unlikely, it could be an indication that management is operating the property extremely efficiently and that there is relatively low turnover.

Another benchmark you can use to determine relative income and expenses is to break everything down on a per-unit basis. You know, for example, that on average total operating expenses per unit run about $3,200 in your market. If you examine an income statement for a particular property that reports total operating expenses at $3,800 per unit, you will want to know why. This may be an indication of poor management and high turnover. If this proves to be the case, experience has taught you that with the right management team in place, you can significantly reduce costs and turnover and thereby create value.

Relative income and expenses can further be measured on a per-square-foot basis. Again, if you know that total operating expenses are averaging $3.25 per square foot in your area and the income statement you are analyzing reflects something outside of the normal scope, then you will want to investigate further to determine why. The bottom line is, be aware of red flags when you see them.

Appraisers and brokers who specialize in multifamily properties can be good sources to draw from in helping you with your initial assessments. Another good source is the Institute of Real Estate Management (IREM). Each year it publishes a comprehensive book entitled *Income and Expense Analysis: Conventional Apartments* (Chicago: IREM/National Realtors Association), which provides data on more than 3,700 apartment buildings in over 150 different major metropolitan areas. The book also includes the following features:

- Detailed analysis of financial operations
- Subdivisions by property age, size, and rental range
- Analysis of direction of vacancy rates and operating ratios
- Various other historical trend reports

The book retails for about $300, but if you become a member of IREM, you can buy it for half of that. Check out the IREM Web site at www.irem.org (note: *.org,* not *.com*). IREM provides a lot of other valuable resources, as well.

This chapter focuses primarily on the concepts and principles related to financial analysis. We have examined the three traditional methodologies used in valuing and appraising property—the sales comparison approach, the cost approach, and the income capitalization approach, and have discussed the appropriateness of their respective roles. We have also studied three primary financial statements used in analyzing apartments—the income statement, the balance sheet, and the rent roll. Each of these provides information vital to an investor who is looking to put hard-earned capital to work. Finally, we have examined five key ratios that are also crucial to your analysis—the capitalization rate, the cash ROI, the total ROI, the debt service coverage ratio, and the gross rent multiplier. The more acquainted you become with each of these concepts, the better you will be at analyzing possible acquisition candidates. Remember, your proficiency in valuing apartment complexes can potentially save you tens of thousands of dollars!

## CHAPTER 8

*Preparation + Opportunity = Success*
**—DON MAHONEY**

# Case Study Analysis

The preceding chapter discusses several isolated examples related to each of the financial analysis principles outlined. This chapter explores the practical application of the principles discussed in greater detail, by closely examining four live case studies in which real accept or reject decisions were made based on the information presented.

## Case Study 1: 52 Units in Flint— My Way or the Highway

One particular multifamily property I located was an older, but fairly well maintained 52-unit apartment building. The seller's asking price was

$1,150,000. Before ever going to look at a property, I first review the related financial statements. If the deal makes sense after running it through my model on the first pass, it may be worth looking at further. In this case, the output from my model indicated that the returns were acceptable, but that there was also room for improvement. I decided it was worth taking a look at to see if perhaps there was a way that I could add or create value. It also had been awhile since I had found any deals even close to being worth looking at, so with this in mind, I arranged to meet with the broker to see the property.

Table 8.1 contains the data in our model, *The Value Play Income Analyzer,* which was used to analyze this property. Take a moment now to review it.

In the upper left-hand corner of Table 8.1 is a box labeled "Cost and Revenue Assumptions." This box is used to input the basic assumptions by which much of the model's output will be determined. In this example, the total purchase price of the apartments was $1,150,000. I estimated the value of land at $325,000 and the value of the building at $825,000. The values attributed to the Land and Building inputs affect a depreciation calculation made in the model, but are essentially irrelevant if the Tax Rate further down in the model is set to zero. My initial value for the Improvements input was zero since the property was in relatively good condition and I did not antici-pate making any major capital improvements within the first year. Closing costs in this example were estimated to be $20,000. These values are then summed to provide a total cost assumption of $1,170,000. Following the cost assumptions are the revenue assumptions. This apartment building consisted of 52 units and, according to the seller, were rented at an average rate of $405 per month. The product of these two values is calculated by the model to determine the Gross Monthly Revenues, which in this example are $21,060.

Now take a look at the box labeled "Financing Assumptions." We know that the Total Purchase Price is $1,170,000 based on the inputs from our cost

**Table 8.1**  Property Analysis Worksheet—The Value-Play Income Analyzer

| Cost and Revenue Assumptions | | Financing Assumptions | | | Key Ratios | |
|---|---|---|---|---|---|---|
| Land | 325,000 | Total Purchase | 100.00% | 1,170,000 | Total Square Feet | 47,220.00 |
| Building | 825,000 | Owner's Equity | 15.00% | 175,500 | Avg Sq Ft/Unit | 908.08 |
| Improvements | 0 | Balance to Finc | 85.00% | 994,500 | Avg Rent/Sq Ft | 0.45 |
| Closing Costs | 20,000 | | | | Avg Cost/Sq Ft | 24.78 |
| Total | 1,170,000 | | | | Avg Unit Cost | 22,500.00 |
| | | | Annual | Monthly | Capitalization Rate | 9.71% |
| Number of Units | 52 | Interest Rate | 7.750% | 0.646% | Gross Rent Multiplier | 4.63 |
| Average Monthly Rent | 405 | Amort Period | 25 | 300 | Expense/Unit | 2,485.38 |
| Gross Monthly Revenues | 21,060 | Payment | 90,141 | 7,512 | Expense/Foot | 2.74 |
| Rental Increase Projections | | | 0.00% | 3.00% | 2.50% | 2.50% | 2.50% |
| Average Monthly Rent | | | 405 | 417 | 428 | 438 | 449 |
| Operating Expense Projections | | | 0.00% | −2.50% | 0.00% | 1.50% | 2.00% |

| Operating Revenues | | Actual Monthly Year 1 | | Year 2 | Projected Year 3 | Year 4 | Year 5 |
|---|---|---|---|---|---|---|---|
| Gross Scheduled Income | | 21,060 | 252,720 | 260,302 | 266,009 | 273,479 | 280,316 |
| Vacancy Rate | 7.0% | 1,474 | 17,690 | 18,221 | 18,677 | 19,144 | 19,622 |
| Net Rental Income | | 19,586 | 235,030 | 242,080 | 248,133 | 254,336 | 260,694 |
| Other Income | | 650 | 7,800 | 8,034 | 8,235 | 8,441 | 8,652 |
| Gross Income | 100.0% | 20,236 | 242,830 | 250,114 | 256,367 | 262,777 | 269,346 |
| **Operating Expenses** | | | | | | | |
| Repairs and Maintenance | 17.7% | 3,580 | 42,960 | 41,886 | 41,886 | 42,514 | 43,365 |
| Property Management Fees | 5.8% | 1,175 | 14,100 | 13,748 | 13,748 | 13,954 | 14,233 |
| Taxes | 10.5% | 2,115 | 25,380 | 24,746 | 24,746 | 25,117 | 25,619 |
| Insurance | 2.4% | 480 | 5,760 | 5,616 | 5,616 | 5,700 | 5,814 |
| Salaries and Wages | 4.9% | 1,000 | 12,000 | 11,700 | 11,700 | 11,876 | 12,113 |
| Utilities | 8.2% | 1,655 | 19,860 | 19,364 | 19,364 | 19,654 | 20,047 |
| Trash Removal | 0.6% | 115 | 1,380 | 1,346 | 1,346 | 1,366 | 1,393 |
| Professional Fees | 1.0% | 200 | 2,400 | 2,340 | 2,340 | 2,375 | 2,423 |
| Advertising | 1.2% | 250 | 3,000 | 2,925 | 2,925 | 2,969 | 3,028 |
| Other | 1.0% | 200 | 2,400 | 2,340 | 2,340 | 2,375 | 2,423 |
| Total Op. Exp. | 53.2% | 10,770 | 129,240 | 126,009 | 126,009 | 127,899 | 130,457 |
| Net Operating Income | 46.8% | 9,466 | 113,590 | 124,105 | 130,358 | 134,877 | 138,889 |
| Interest on Loan | 31.7% | 6,423 | 76,599 | 75,512 | 74,337 | 73,068 | 71,697 |
| Dep. Exp.—Building | | 2,500 | 30,000 | 30,000 | 30,000 | 30,000 | 30,000 |
| Dep. Exp.—Equip. | | 0 | 0 | 0 | 0 | 0 | 0 |
| Net Income Before Taxes | | 543 | 6,990 | 18,594 | 26,021 | 31,810 | 37,192 |
| Income Tax Rate | 0.0% | 0 | 0 | 0 | 0 | 0 | 0 |
| Net Income After Taxes | | 543 | 6,990 | 18,594 | 26,021 | 31,810 | 37,192 |

**Table 8.1**   *(Continued)*

| Cash Flow From Operations | | | | | | |
|---|---|---|---|---|---|---|
| Net Income After Taxes | 543 | 6,990 | 18,594 | 26,021 | 31,810 | 37,192 |
| Dep. Exp. | 2,500 | 30,000 | 30,000 | 30,000 | 30,000 | 30,000 |
| Total CF from Ops. | 3,043 | 36,990 | 48,594 | 56,021 | 61,810 | 67,192 |
| Interest on Loan | 6,423 | 76,599 | 75,512 | 74,337 | 73,068 | 71,697 |
| Total Cash Available for Loan Servicing | 9,466 | 113,590 | 124,105 | 130,358 | 134,877 | 138,889 |
| Debt Service | 7,512 | 90,141 | 90,141 | 90,141 | 90,141 | 90,141 |
| Remaining After Tax CF From Ops. | 1,954 | 23,449 | 33,965 | 40,217 | 44,736 | 48,748 |
| Plus Principal Reduction | 1,128 | 13,541 | 14,629 | 15,804 | 17,073 | 18,444 |
|    Total Return | 3,083 | 36,990 | 48,594 | 56,021 | 61,810 | 67,192 |
| CF/Debt Servicing Ratio | 126.01% | 126.01% | 137.68% | 144.62% | 149.63% | 154.08% |
| Net Income ROI | | 3.98% | 10.59% | 14.83% | 18.13% | 21.19% |
| Cash ROI | | 13.36% | 19.35% | 22.92% | 25.49% | 27.78% |
| Total ROI | | 21.08% | 27.69% | 31.92% | 35.22% | 38.29% |
| Net CFs From Investment—1 Yr Exit | (175,500) | 392,490 | | | | |
| Net CFs From Investment—3 Yr Exit | (175,500) | 23,449 | 33,965 | 599,692 | | |
| Net CFs From Investment—5 Yr Exit | (175,500) | 23,449 | 33,965 | 40,217 | 44,736 | 733,740 |

| | Exit Price | Gain on Sale | Cap Rate | | | IRR |
|---|---|---|---|---|---|---|
| Estimated Exit Price/Gain on Sale—1 Yr | 1,350,000 | 180,000 | 8.41% | Annualized IRR—1 Yr | | 123.64% |
| Estimated Exit Price/Gain on Sale—3 Yr | 1,510,000 | 340,000 | 8.63% | Annualized IRR—3 Yr | | 59.61% |
| Estimated Exit Price/Gain on Sale—5 Yr | 1,600,000 | 430,000 | 8.68% | Annualized IRR—5 Yr | | 43.91% |

assumptions. The Owner's Equity is a variable that is input by the user to determine the amount of money required to purchase the property. Since Improvements and Closing Costs are included in the Total Purchase Price, this must be taken into consideration when entering the amount of equity. Sometimes some of the closing costs can be rolled into the financing, and sometimes the seller will pay some of them. Inasmuch as every closing transaction is different, the model provides the user with the flexibility to estimate total cash outlay in this section. Whether some of the closing costs are rolled into the loan or paid for by the seller is irrelevant. The total amount of cash required by the investor, including closing costs or improvements, is input into this cell. The Interest Rate and Amortization Period are then entered to calculate both the annual and monthly payments. At the time I looked at this property, a competitive market rate of interest was considered 7.75 percent. Twenty-five years was offered by the lender I was working with for the Amortization Period. Based on the financing assumptions entered into the model, the monthly debt service is calculated to be $7,512 and the annual debt service is $90,141.

The next box in the model is labeled "Key Ratios." The only input for this section is the first value, Total Square Feet; all other data in this section are outputs automatically calculated by the model. In this example, the total square feet of the apartments was 47,220, which averages 908 square feet per unit. Following the Average Square Feet per Unit is the Average Rent per Square Foot, which in this example is calculated to be $0.45. The Average Cost per Square Foot is calculated at $24.78, giving the total cost per unit of $22,500. The Gross Rent Multiplier was calculated to be 4.63. Next is the Expenses per Unit, which divides the Total Operating Expenses by the number of units, resulting in $2,485. This number is then divided by the average square feet per unit to provide the average Expense per Unit, which in this example is $2.74. Both of these expense calculations were considered to be in line with the market.

The next section of the model is used to forecast changes that may affect both revenues and expenses. For example, if the rents for the property were below market, an adjustment to increase them could be made. Likewise, if expenses appeared to be out of line, they, too, could be increased or decreased as deemed appropriate. In this example, the rents were in line with current market conditions and there was little room to increase them in Year 1. The property's expenses also appeared to be in line with the market, so the value was set to zero.

The next section of the model is Operating Revenues. The model reads the Gross Monthly Revenues value from the Cost and Revenues section and inputs it automatically into Gross Scheduled Income, which in this example is $21,060. A vacancy factor, which is consistent with the local market, is then subtracted from Gross Scheduled Income to produce Net Rental Income. In this example, 7 percent was representative of vacancy rates in that area. The next value, Other Income, includes any type of income such as application fees, late fees, utility income, vending income, and interest income. This particular apartment building earned approximately $650 per month in Other Income, derived primarily from laundry and vending services. The sum of Net Rental Income and Other Income results in Gross Income. In this example, Gross Income is $20,236 per month and $242,830 per year.

After accounting for all of the Operating Revenues, we then move to Operating Expenses. Operating Expenses include all of the day-to-day costs incurred to operate the property with the exception of interest, which is accounted for later. Operating Expenses include such items as repairs and maintenance, management fees, taxes, insurance, utilities, landscaping, and any other day-to-day operating expenses. This section would not, however, include long-term capital improvements such as replacing an entire roof or expanding the parking lot. In this example, Total Operating Expenses amount to $10,770 per month and $129,240 per year. As indicated in the model, this figure represents approximately 53 percent of the property's Gross Income.

Total Operating Expenses for a multifamily property typically range anywhere from about 40 percent of Gross Income to as much as 60 percent of Gross Income. If expenses run any higher than that, the property will most likely have a difficult time cash-flowing properly. One primary factor that significantly affects operating expenses is whether the property is submetered. For example, in some older apartment buildings a master meter was installed at the time of construction. In this type of situation, the apartments are often rented out as "all-bills-paid" and the landlord or owner assumes the responsibility for paying all utilities. Conversely, in most newer apartment buildings, the units are individually metered so that the tenants become responsible for their own utilities. This significantly reduces the Total Operating Expenses for the owner.

The next section of the model is Net Operating Income. Recall that the value for NOI is crucial as it is the numerator in the cap rate calculation. The annual NOI in this example is $113,590, which gives us a cap rate of 9.71 percent calculated as follows:

$$\text{Cap Rate} = \frac{\text{net operating income}}{\text{price}} = \frac{\$113,590}{\$1,170,000} = 9.71\%$$

The model then calculates the first-year interest based on the loan amount, interest rate, and amortization period, which in this example is $76,599. Depreciation is then factored in for tax purposes; however, I prefer to evaluate income-producing properties on a before-tax basis since this is the way a lender will evaluate it. The tax rate was therefore set to zero, which means the value determined for depreciation is irrelevant in this example.

The next section of the model, Cash Flow from Operations, is especially important since it tells us how much cash is available to service any debt related to the property. The model begins by adding back in the Net Income After Taxes, Depreciation, and Interest to give us the total cash available to service the debt, which in this example is $113,590, the same value as NOI since the tax rate is set to zero. The annual Debt Service is $90,141, which means the property will generate a positive cash flow of $23,449 per year on a before-tax basis. Below that is Principal Reduction, which is the amount applied to pay down the loan in Year 1. When the Principal Reduction of $13,541 is factored in, the Total Return on this property is $36,990.

Below the Cash Flow from Operations section, the model provides the information necessary to make a decision on the viability of this opportunity. In this example, the Cash Flow to Debt Service Ratio, also known as the Debt Service Coverage Ratio, or DSCR, is 126 percent. Most lenders require a minimum DSCR of 1.00 to 1.20. I personally prefer to see the DSCR above 1.20 as a minimum standard so as to ensure that the property has adequate cash flow to cover any debt-related obligations. Notice also that although the Net Income and Cash ROIs indicate positive returns, they are somewhat marginal. The Total ROI, which factors in the returns attributed to the reduction in principal, provides a more favorable return of 21.08 percent. Below the returns is a section that shows the Net Cash Flows from Investment followed by my favorite section, Estimated Exit Price and Gain on Sale. This section of the model allows the user to evaluate what the potential resale value of a property is based on cap rates specific to its area. In this example, the value of $1,350,000 in Year 1 has a corresponding cap rate of 8.41 percent.

I made an offer for $1,100,000 with the standard 30-day feasibility period and ½ percent of the purchase price as earnest money matched with another ½ percent after the 30-day period when the earnest money goes hard, or becomes nonrefundable, and an additional 60 days to close. These terms are not at all out of the ordinary and in fact would be considered reasonable and customary in that market. The value-play opportunity for this property was to convert the units into condominiums and sell them individually. Conversion costs were estimated to be approximately $7,500 per unit, which would result in a total cost of $30,000 per unit. It was then estimated that the newly converted condominiums would resell for an average $50,000 each, resulting in a gross profit margin of $20,000, or $1,040,000 in aggregate.

As it turns out, the seller had an abrasive personality, was extremely arrogant, and had adopted a "my way or the highway" attitude. Since the seller demanded a 5 percent down payment up front as earnest money with no feasibility period and a closing in 30 days, I took the highway. No matter how promising a potential deal appears, I am not about to assume the risk for an investment in which I have not had the opportunity to perform due diligence. In this case, if the deal went south, I would have been out over $50,000 in earnest money.

Although this property would generate a rate of return that would be acceptable to some investors, let's take a moment to experiment with the model to see what it would take to improve an investor's returns in this project if it were purchased solely for the purpose of holding it rather than implementing a condo conversion. Take a moment to review Table 8.2.

Table 8.2 is identical to Table 8.1 with one exception—the purchase price has been reduced from $1,150,000 in Table 8.1 to an even $1,000,000 in Table 8.2. Now let us look at how the $150,000 reduction in price affects the output in the model. First of all, the Average Unit Cost in the Key Ratios section was reduced by approximately $2,885 in Table 8.2. Since the purchase price was reduced in Table 8.2, the cap rate increased from 9.71 percent to 11.14 percent. Revenues and operating expenses remain unchanged, so let us look at how the DSCR was affected. Recall that in Table 8.1, it was 1.26. That compares with 1.44 in Table 8.2. This improved ratio would certainly be considered more favorable to lenders. Now let us shift our focus to the section on returns. The Net Income ROI has improved from 3.98 percent in Table 8.1 to 13.96 percent in Table 8.2. Both the Cash ROI and the Total ROI also show significant improvements. Let's tweak the model one more time by adjusting the interest rate to a level more in line with today's market rates. Now take a moment to review Table 8.3.

Table 8.3 is identical to Table 8.2 with one exception—the interest rate in Table 8.3 has been adjusted downward from 7.75 percent to 6.00 percent. Let us start with the Financing Assumptions section this time. Note that the annual debt service has been reduced from $78,584 to $67,033—a differ-

**Table 8.2**  Property Analysis Worksheet—The Value-Play Income Analyzer

| Cost and Revenue Assumptions | | Financing Assumptions | | | Key Ratios | |
|---|---|---|---|---|---|---|
| Land | 300,000 | Total Purchase | 100.00% | 1,020,000 | Total Square Feet | 47,220.00 |
| Building | 700,000 | Owner's Equity | 15.00% | 153,000 | Avg Sq Ft/Unit | 908.08 |
| Improvements | 0 | Balance to Finc | 85.00% | 867,000 | Avg Rent/Sq Ft | 0.45 |
| Closing Costs | 20,000 | | | | Avg Cost/Sq Ft | 21.60 |
| Total | 1,020,000 | | | | Avg Unit Cost | 19,615.38 |
| | | | Annual | Monthly | Capitalization Rate | 11.14% |
| Number of Units | 52 | Interest Rate | 7.750% | 0.646% | Gross Rent Multiplier | 4.04 |
| Average Monthly Rent | 405 | Amort Period | 25 | 300 | Expense/Unit | 2,485.38 |
| Gross Monthly Revenues | 21,060 | Payment | 78,584 | 6,549 | Expense/Foot | 2.74 |
| Rental Increase Projections | | | 0.00% | 3.00% | 2.50% | 2.50% | 2.50% |
| Average Monthly Rent | | | 405 | 417 | 428 | 438 | 449 |
| Operating Expense Projections | | | 0.00% | −2.50% | 0.00% | 1.50% | 2.00% |

| Operating Revenues | | Actual Monthly | Year 1 | Year 2 | Projected Year 3 | Year 4 | Year 5 |
|---|---|---|---|---|---|---|---|
| Gross Scheduled Income | | 21,060 | 252,720 | 260,302 | 266,809 | 273,479 | 280,316 |
| Vacancy Rate | 7.0% | 1,474 | 17,690 | 18,221 | 18,677 | 19,144 | 19,622 |
| Net Rental Income | | 19,586 | 235,030 | 242,080 | 248,133 | 254,336 | 260,694 |
| Other Income | | 650 | 7,800 | 8,034 | 8,235 | 8,441 | 8,652 |
| Gross Income | 100.0% | 20,236 | 242,830 | 250,114 | 256,367 | 262,777 | 269,346 |

| Operating Expenses | | | | | | | |
|---|---|---|---|---|---|---|---|
| Repairs and Maintenance | 17.7% | 3,580 | 42,960 | 41,886 | 41,886 | 42,514 | 43,365 |
| Property Management Fees | 5.8% | 1,175 | 14,100 | 13,748 | 13,748 | 13,954 | 14,233 |
| Taxes | 10.5% | 2,115 | 25,380 | 24,746 | 24,746 | 25,117 | 25,619 |
| Insurance | 2.4% | 480 | 5,760 | 5,616 | 5,616 | 5,700 | 5,814 |
| Salaries and Wages | 4.9% | 1,000 | 12,000 | 11,700 | 11,700 | 11,876 | 12,113 |
| Utilities | 8.2% | 1,655 | 19,860 | 19,364 | 19,364 | 19,654 | 20,047 |
| Trash Removal | 0.6% | 115 | 1,380 | 1,346 | 1,346 | 1,366 | 1,393 |
| Professional Fees | 1.0% | 200 | 2,400 | 2,340 | 2,340 | 2,375 | 2,423 |
| Advertising | 1.2% | 250 | 3,000 | 2,925 | 2,925 | 2,969 | 3,028 |
| Other | 1.0% | 200 | 2,400 | 2,340 | 2,340 | 2,375 | 2,423 |
| Total Op. Exp. | 53.2% | 10,770 | 129,240 | 126,009 | 126,009 | 127,899 | 130,457 |

| Net Operating Income | 46.8% | 9,466 | 113,590 | 124,105 | 130,358 | 134,877 | 138,889 |
|---|---|---|---|---|---|---|---|
| Interest on Loan | 27.7% | 5,599 | 66,779 | 65,831 | 64,807 | 63,700 | 62,505 |
| Dep. Exp.—Building | | 2,121 | 25,455 | 25,455 | 25,455 | 25,455 | 25,455 |
| Dep. Exp.—Equip. | | 0 | 0 | 0 | 0 | 0 | 0 |
| Net Income Before Taxes | | 1,745 | 21,356 | 32,820 | 40,097 | 45,723 | 50,930 |
| Income Tax Rate | 0.0% | 0 | 0 | 0 | 0 | 0 | 0 |
| Net Income After Taxes | | 1,745 | 21,356 | 32,820 | 40,097 | 45,723 | 50,930 |

**Table 8.2** (Continued)

| Cash Flow From Operations | | | | | | |
|---|---|---|---|---|---|---|
| Net Income After Taxes | 1,745 | 21,356 | 32,820 | 40,097 | 45,723 | 50,930 |
| Dep. Exp. | 2,121 | 25,455 | 25,455 | 25,455 | 25,455 | 25,455 |
| Total CF From Ops. | 3,866 | 46,811 | 58,275 | 65,552 | 71,177 | 76,384 |
| Interest on Loan | 5,599 | 66,779 | 65,831 | 64,807 | 63,700 | 62,505 |
| Total Cash Available for Loan Servicing | 9,466 | 113,590 | 124,105 | 130,358 | 134,877 | 138,889 |
| Debt Service | 6,549 | 78,584 | 78,584 | 78,584 | 78,584 | 78,584 |
| Remaining After Tax CF From Ops. | 2,917 | 35,005 | 45,521 | 51,774 | 56,293 | 60,304 |
| Plus Principal Reduction | 984 | 11,805 | 12,754 | 13,778 | 14,884 | 16,080 |
| Total Return | 3,901 | 46,811 | 58,275 | 65,552 | 71,177 | 76,384 |
| CF/Debt Servicing Ratio | 144.54% | 144.54% | 157.93% | 165.88% | 171.63% | 176.74% |
| Net Income ROI | | 13.96% | 21.45% | 26.21% | 29.88% | 33.29% |
| Cash ROI | | 22.88% | 29.75% | 33.84% | 36.79% | 39.41% |
| Total ROI | | 30.60% | 38.09% | 42.84% | 46.52% | 49.92% |
| Net CFs from Investment—1 Yr Exit | (153,000) | 529,811 | | | | |
| Net CFs from Investment—3 Yr Exit | (153,000) | 35,005 | 45,521 | 733,111 | | |
| Net CFs from Investment—5 Yr Exit | (153,000) | 35,005 | 45,521 | 51,774 | 56,293 | 862,605 |

| | Exit Price | Gain on Sale | Cap Rate | | | IRR |
|---|---|---|---|---|---|---|
| Estimated Exit Price/Gain on Sale—1 Yr | 1,350,000 | 330,000 | 8.41% | Annualized IRR—1 Yr | | 246.28% |
| Estimated Exit Price/Gain on Sale—3 Yr | 1,510,000 | 490,000 | 8.63% | Annualized IRR—3 Yr | | 82.70% |
| Estimated Exit Price/Gain on Sale—5 Yr | 1,600,000 | 580,000 | 8.68% | Annualized IRR—5 Yr | | 57.22% |

ence of $11,551. Now take a look at the Key Ratios section. Not a single one of these values has changed, including the cap rate. Although it may initially seem that the cap rate should increase since we are adding more than $11,000 to the bottom line, the value remains unchanged because the interest expense falls below the NOI, which is the numerator in the cap rate equation. Let's move down now to the NOI section of the model. Notice that Net Income has improved by more than $15,000, which is the difference in the amount of interest paid annually. This favorable difference in interest expense has a significant impact on the amount of cash left over after satisfying all debt requirements, which in turn has a favorable impact

**Table 8.3**  Property Analysis Worksheet—The Value-Play Income Analyzer

| Cost and Revenue Assumptions | | Financing Assumptions | | | Key Ratios | |
|---|---|---|---|---|---|---|
| Land | 300,000 | Total Purchase | 100.00% | 1,020,000 | Total Square Feet | 47,220.00 |
| Building | 700,000 | Owner's Equity | 15.00% | 153,000 | Avg Sq Ft/Unit | 908.08 |
| Improvements | 0 | Balance to Finc | 85.00% | 867,000 | Avg Rent/Sq Ft | 0.45 |
| Closing Costs | 20,000 | | | | Avg Cost/Sq Ft | 21.60 |
| Total | 1,020,000 | | | | Avg Unit Cost | 19,615.38 |
| | | | Annual | Monthly | Capitalization Rate | 11.14% |
| Number of Units | 52 | Interest Rate | 6.000% | 0.500% | Gross Rent Multiplier | 4.04 |
| Average Monthly Rent | 405 | Amort. Period | 25 | 300 | Expense/Unit | 2,485.38 |
| Gross Monthly Revenues | 21,060 | Payment | 67,033 | 5,586 | Expense/Foot | 2.74 |

| | | | | | | | |
|---|---|---|---|---|---|---|---|
| Rental Increase Projections | | | 0.00% | 3.00% | 2.50% | 2.50% | 2.50% |
| Average Monthly Rent | | | 405 | 417 | 428 | 438 | 449 |
| Operating Expense Projections | | | 0.00% | −2.50% | 0.00% | 1.50% | 2.00% |

| Operating Revenues | | Actual Monthly | Year 1 | Year 2 | Projected Year 3 | Year 4 | Year 5 |
|---|---|---|---|---|---|---|---|
| Gross Scheduled Income | | 21,060 | 252,720 | 260,302 | 266,809 | 273,479 | 280,316 |
| Vacancy Rate | 7.0% | 1,474 | 17,690 | 18,221 | 18,677 | 19,144 | 19,622 |
| Net Rental Income | | 19,586 | 235,030 | 242,080 | 248,133 | 254,336 | 260,694 |
| Other Income | | 650 | 7,800 | 8,034 | 8,235 | 8,441 | 8,652 |
| Gross Income | 100.0% | 20,236 | 242,830 | 250,114 | 256,367 | 262,777 | 269,346 |
| **Operating Expenses** | | | | | | | |
| Repairs and Maintenance | 17.7% | 3,580 | 42,960 | 41,886 | 41,886 | 42,514 | 43,365 |
| Property Management Fees | 5.8% | 1,175 | 14,100 | 13,748 | 13,748 | 13,954 | 14,233 |
| Taxes | 10.5% | 2,115 | 25,380 | 24,746 | 24,746 | 25,117 | 25,619 |
| Insurance | 2.4% | 480 | 5,760 | 5,616 | 5,616 | 5,700 | 5,814 |
| Salaries and Wages | 4.9% | 1,000 | 12,000 | 11,700 | 11,700 | 11,876 | 12,113 |
| Utilities | 8.2% | 1,655 | 19,860 | 19,364 | 19,364 | 19,654 | 20,047 |
| Trash Removal | 0.6% | 115 | 1,380 | 1,346 | 1,346 | 1,366 | 1,393 |
| Professional Fees | 1.0% | 200 | 2,400 | 2,340 | 2,340 | 2,375 | 2,423 |
| Advertising | 1.2% | 250 | 3,000 | 2,925 | 2,925 | 2,969 | 3,028 |
| Other | 1.0% | 200 | 2,400 | 2,340 | 2,340 | 2,375 | 2,423 |
| Total Op. Exp. | 53.2% | 10,770 | 129,240 | 126,009 | 126,009 | 127,899 | 130,457 |
| Net Operating Income | 46.8% | 9,466 | 113,590 | 124,105 | 130,358 | 134,877 | 138,889 |
| Interest on Loan | 21.4% | 4,335 | 51,600 | 50,648 | 49,638 | 48,565 | 47,426 |
| Dep. Exp.—Building | | 2,121 | 25,455 | 25,455 | 25,455 | 25,455 | 25,455 |
| Dep. Exp.—Equip. | | 0 | 0 | 0 | 0 | 0 | 0 |
| Net Income Before Taxes | | 3,010 | 36,535 | 48,003 | 55,266 | 60,858 | 66,009 |
| Income Tax Rate | 0.0% | 0 | 0 | 0 | 0 | 0 | 0 |
| Net Income After Taxes | | 3,010 | 36,535 | 48,003 | 55,266 | 60,858 | 66,009 |

**Table 8.3** *(Continued)*

| Cash Flow From Operations | | | | | | |
|---|---|---|---|---|---|---|
| Net Income After Taxes | 3,010 | 36,535 | 48,003 | 55,266 | 60,858 | 66,009 |
| Dep. Exp. | 2,121 | 25,455 | 25,455 | 25,455 | 25,455 | 25,455 |
| Total CF From Ops. | 5,131 | 61,989 | 73,457 | 80,721 | 86,313 | 91,463 |
| Interest on Loan | 4,335 | 51,600 | 50,648 | 49,638 | 48,565 | 47,426 |
| Total Cash Available for Loan Servicing | 9,466 | 113,590 | 124,105 | 130,358 | 134,877 | 138,889 |
| Debt Service | 5,586 | 67,033 | 67,033 | 67,033 | 67,033 | 67,033 |
| Remaining After Tax CF From Ops. | 3,880 | 46,556 | 57,072 | 63,325 | 67,844 | 71,856 |
| Plus Principal Reduction | 1,286 | 15,433 | 16,385 | 17,395 | 18,468 | 19,607 |
| Total Return | 5,166 | 61,989 | 73,457 | 80,721 | 86,313 | 91,463 |
| CF/Debt Servicing Ratio | 169.45% | 169.45% | 185.14% | 194.47% | 201.21% | 207.19% |
| Net Income ROI | | 23.88% | 31.37% | 36.12% | 39.78% | 43.14% |
| Cash ROI | | 30.43% | 37.30% | 41.39% | 44.34% | 46.96% |
| Total ROI | 40.52% | 48.01% | 52.76% | 56.41% | 59.78% | |
| Net CFs from Investment—1 Yr Exit | (153,000) | 544,989 | | | | |
| Net CFs from Investment—3 Yr Exit | (153,000) | 46,556 | 57,072 | 755,538 | | |
| Net CFs from Investment—5 Yr Exit | (153,000) | 46,556 | 57,072 | 63,325 | 67,844 | 892,145 |

| | Exit Price | Gain on Sale | Cap Rate | IRR | | |
|---|---|---|---|---|---|---|
| Estimated Exit Price/Gain on Sale—1 Yr | 1,350,000 | 330,000 | 8.41% | Annualized IRR—1 Yr | 256.20% | |
| Estimated Exit Price/Gain on Sale—3 Yr | 1,510,000 | 490,000 | 8.63% | Annualized IRR—3 Yr | 88.77% | |
| Estimated Exit Price/Gain on Sale—5 Yr | 1,600,000 | 580,000 | 8.68% | Annualized IRR—5 Yr | 62.64% | |

on the DSCR, as well as the return ratios. For example, the DSCR has increased from about 1.44 in Table 8.2 to slightly over 1.69 in Table 8.3. The Cash ROI and Total ROI have also greatly improved and would certainly be considered an acceptable rate of return by most investors. So by simply reducing the interest rate, this investment has moved from a position of marginally acceptable to one that is definitely acceptable.

In this case study, we analyzed a 52-unit multifamily project to see if it met our investment criteria. The primary criteria used to evaluate this investment opportunity was based on its ability to generate an acceptable rate of return on a stand-alone basis. We concluded that although the property met an acceptable rate of return at the price it was being offered and that a potential value-play opportunity existed, the seller was unwilling to negotiate and therefore no deal was consummated. We also learned that reducing the price in the model improved the property's returns. Finally, by reducing the interest rate, the bottom line was favorably affected as Net Income improved dramatically and thereby had a positive effect on the property's Cash ROI and Total ROI. Using the Value Play Income Analyzer in this case study enabled us to quickly and easily make changes in the model and immediately see the effects on its output.

# Case Study 2: 12 Units in Saginaw— Below-Market Rents

While working as a mortgage broker, I had a client named Pam, for whom I had arranged financing on a smaller 12-unit property. After doing some market research to determine the average rental rate for comparable properties, Pam concluded that the apartments she was buying were being rented for considerably less than the market average. The price she was acquiring the apartments for reflected the existing income only, and not any upside potential. This should be true for any property you are considering, as well. Remember, you should be willing to pay only for what the property is worth as it is currently operating and not for any future upside potential the broker or seller may promise you exists. Pam knew going into the deal that she would be adjusting rents to market rates as soon as the tenants' respective leases expired. She also knew and accepted that there would probably be some tenant turnover as a result. Adjusting her rents to market rates would immediately add value to her apartments, as value is derived from a multiple of net operating income (NOI), as previously discussed.

In a discussion with Pam prior to closing her deal, she mentioned to me rather casually that she intended to buy the property and "just hold onto it" for a number of years. Pam's comments echoed what I had previously heard so many other investors say, that they just liked to buy a property, hold onto it, and eventually pay off the mortgage so they could live off the income. I knew Pam was creating value with the acquisition of the 12-unit apartment building; however, it was apparent to me that she did not fully realize the benefits of the value she would be adding. In an effort to educate Pam regarding the advantages of the value play, I faxed the following memo to her:

Pam,

I have been thinking about your deal . . . and decided to do some analysis of my own. Before I start, let me get the disclaimer out of the way. The following is NOT a recommendation by or on behalf of . . . Mortgage Company; rather, it is my own personal insight based on past experience intended to help you make the best decision regarding this transaction. Having said that, the attached pro forma income statements are from a proprietary model that I developed in Lotus and use to analyze my own real estate investments.

The first schedule shows an estimate, based on certain assumptions, of what your existing cash flows would look like if you made absolutely no changes to the property (i.e., income and expenses). The key lines that I like to focus on are:

1. Remaining After-Tax CF from Ops.
2. Cash ROI and Total ROI.
3. Annualized IRR—1 YR and 3 YR.
4. Estimated Exit Price/Gain on Sale—1 YR and 3 YR.

Remember that these are after-tax numbers and as such, more accurately reflect the true cash return on your investment (I have assumed a tax rate of 28%). You will note that your Cash ROI is okay, but certainly could be better.

The second schedule shows what I believe are realistic projections for the property with respect to increases in the rental income stream. These are only projections, as I am not specifically familiar with rental rates in the Saginaw market; however, some very basic market research could confirm market rates in that area. The Cash ROI is much more attractive under this scenario. What I believe to be even more impressive are the 1 YR and 3 YR IRRs. Look at the 1 YR IRR line—using the Estimated Exit Price of $465,000 gives you a Gain on Sale of $80,000. This is not a pie in the sky number. An Exit Price of $465,000 gives your buyer a Cap Rate of 9.5%, which is about what you are paying for the property. Now look at the 3 YR IRR line—using the Estimated Exit Price of $540,000 gives you a Gain on Sale of $155,000. Again, this provides your buyer with a Cap Rate of 9.5%. Cap Rates, remember, are a simple ratio measured by dividing NOI/Purchase Price. The higher the Cap Rate, the greater the value there is. Cap Rates generally range between 8.0% and 12.0%. They do of course deviate from that range depending on circumstances.

I will offer my thoughts for your consideration as a suggestion only (please forgive my frankness). To heck with the buy-and-hold strategy. Develop a well-defined plan going in, execute, and get out. Yes, you can make money by buying and holding, but the real money is made by buying and selling. Assume you sell in YR 1 and realize a gain of $80,000. You can then take the proceeds from the sale, which include your original investment, and reinvest them in a larger property (or two of the same size). For example, leveraging the proceeds from this deal of approximately $155,000 would allow you to purchase a property worth $775,000 using an LTV of 80%. If you sold in YR 3, you would realize a gain of $155,000, which would allow you to leverage approximately $230,000 and thereby purchase a property valued at $1,150,000.

Also, it really should not take a full three years to bring your rents up to market. Again, I don't know what the market is like in Saginaw, but it should be very easy for you to determine.

I will share one final thought with you that I mentioned in our telephone conversation earlier today. I used, and am using, this same strategy on properties of my own. As I mentioned, I had a 22-unit complex that was being rented for $425 each. I knew that similar properties in the area were renting for $575. When my first tenant moved out, I tested the waters at $540 and rented the property in no time. I tested the 2nd one at $575 and again rented it easily. I tested the 3rd one at $595 and still had no problem renting it. Finally, I went to $625, which is where I met some resistance, and subsequently lowered the rate back down to $595, which turned out to be market for my property. I had a firm contract on the property within six months of acquiring it and had the deal closed several months later. I then took the gain from the sale and leveraged it into a larger property. This property is another value play for me and should be ready to be placed on the market in the near future. And so the process goes, each deal a little larger than the last. I just wanted to share my perspective with you. Hope this helps.

Sincerely yours,
Steve

Look at Exhibit 8.1, Scenario 1. Note the cost and revenue assumptions, as well as the financing assumptions, that were used at the time of this analysis. These variables were keyed in to reflect as closely as possible the conditions under which the property would be operating. Now take a few minutes and examine the rest of the table closely.

The property had historically operated with very little turnover due in large part to the fact that the units were being leased out at rents well below market. Since the apartments had been well maintained over the years, it was assumed going forward, at least for the immediate future, that 10 percent would be adequate for repairs and maintenance. Pam would be managing the property herself, along with a partner, so the property management expense was assumed to be 0 percent. Although NOI was on the high end of our range of 40 to 60 percent, Pam felt comfortable with the assumptions, as she and I had previously discussed the total operating expenses for the

**Exhibit 8.1**  Scenario 1: Five-Year Pro Forma Income Statement. (from Berges Investment Group, Copyright © 1998)

### Cost and Revenue Assumptions

| | |
|---|---|
| Land | 75,000 |
| Building | 300,000 |
| Improvements | 0 |
| Closing Costs | 10,000 |
| Total | 385,000 |

| | | |
|---|---|---|
| Number of Units | 12 | |
| Average Monthly Rent | 445 | |
| Gross Monthly Revenues | 5,340 | |

### Financing Assumptions

| | | |
|---|---|---|
| Total Purchase | 100.00% | 385,000 |
| Owner's Equity | 20.00% | 77,000 |
| Balance to Finc | 80.00% | 308,000 |

| | | Annual | | Monthly | |
|---|---|---|---|---|---|
| Interest Rate | 8.125% | | | 0.677% | |
| Term | 25 | | | 300 | |
| Payment | 28,833 | | | 2,403 | |

### Key Ratios

| | |
|---|---|
| Total Square Feet | 12,000.00 |
| Avg Sq Ft/Unit | 1,000.00 |
| Avg Rent/Sq Ft | 0.45 |
| Avg Cost/Sq Ft | 32.08 |
| Avg Unit Cost | 32,083.33 |
| Capitalization Rate | 9.89% |
| Gross Rent Multiplier | 6.01 |
| Expense/Unit | 1,951.15 |
| Expense/Foot | 1.95 |

### Estimated Growth Rate Projections

| | | Year 2 | Year 3 | Year 4 | Year 5 |
|---|---|---|---|---|---|
| Average Monthly Rent | 0.00% | 445 | 445 | 445 | 445 |
| | | | Projected | | |
| | 0.00% | 445 | 445 | 445 | 445 |

| | | Actual Monthly | Actual Year 1 | Year 2 | Year 3 | Year 4 | Year 5 |
|---|---|---|---|---|---|---|---|
| **Operating Revenues** | | | | | | | |
| Gross Scheduled Income | | 5,340 | 64,080 | 64,080 | 64,080 | 64,080 | 64,080 |
| Vacancy Rate | 5.0% | 267 | 3,204 | 3,204 | 3,204 | 3,204 | 3,204 |
| Net Rental Income | | 5,073 | 60,876 | 60,876 | 60,876 | 60,876 | 60,876 |
| Other Income | | 50 | 600 | 600 | 600 | 600 | 600 |
| Gross Income | 100.0% | 5,123 | 61,476 | 61,476 | 61,476 | 61,476 | 61,476 |
| **Operating Expenses** | | | | | | | |
| Repairs and Maintenance | 10.0% | 512 | 6,148 | 6,148 | 6,148 | 6,148 | 6,148 |
| Taxes | 13.7% | 703 | 8,436 | 8,436 | 8,436 | 8,436 | 8,436 |
| Insurance | 3.0% | 152 | 1,824 | 1,824 | 1,824 | 1,824 | 1,824 |
| Property Mgmt. | 0.0% | 0 | 0 | 0 | 0 | 0 | 0 |
| Utilities | 9.9% | 507 | 6,084 | 6,084 | 6,084 | 6,084 | 6,084 |
| Trash Removal | 0.5% | 26 | 307 | 307 | 307 | 307 | 307 |
| Advt/Misc | 1.0% | 51 | 615 | 615 | 615 | 615 | 615 |
| Total Op. Exp. | 38.1% | 1,951 | 23,414 | 23,414 | 23,414 | 23,414 | 23,414 |

| | % | Mo. | Yr 1 | Yr 2 | Yr 3 | Yr 4 | Yr 5 | Yr 6 |
|---|---|---|---|---|---|---|---|---|
| Net Operating Income | 61.9% | 3,172 | 38,062 | 38,062 | 38,062 | 38,062 | 38,062 | 38,052 |
| Interest on Loan | 40.7% | 2,085 | 24,880 | 24,547 | 24,185 | 23,793 | 23,368 | 23,358 |
| Dep. Exp.—Building | | 909 | 10,909 | 10,909 | 10,909 | 10,909 | 10,909 | 10,909 |
| Dep. Exp.—Equip. | | 0 | 0 | 0 | 0 | 0 | 0 | 0 |
| Net Income Before Taxes | | 177 | 2,273 | 2,607 | 2,968 | 3,360 | 3,785 | 3,785 |
| Income Tax Rate | 28.0% | 50 | 637 | 637 | 637 | 637 | 637 | 637 |
| Net Income After Taxes | | 128 | 1,637 | 1,970 | 2,332 | 2,724 | 3,149 | 3,149 |
| **Cash Flow from Operations** | | | | | | | | |
| Net Income After Taxes | | 128 | 1,637 | 1,970 | 2,332 | 2,724 | 3,149 | 3,149 |
| Dep. Exp. | | 909 | 10,909 | 10,909 | 10,909 | 10,909 | 10,909 | 10,909 |
| Total CF from Ops. | | 1,037 | 12,546 | 12,879 | 13,241 | 13,633 | 14,058 | 14,058 |
| Interest on Loan | | 2,085 | 24,880 | 24,547 | 24,185 | 23,793 | 23,368 | 23,368 |
| Total Cash Available for Loan Servicing | | 3,122 | 37,426 | 37,426 | 37,426 | 37,426 | 37,426 | 37,426 |
| Debt Service | | 2,403 | 28,833 | 28,833 | 28,833 | 28,833 | 28,833 | 28,833 |
| Remaining After Tax CF from Ops. | | 719 | 8,593 | 8,593 | 8,593 | 8,593 | 8,593 | 8,593 |
| Plus Principal Reduction | | 329 | 3,953 | 4,287 | 4,648 | 5,040 | 5,465 | 5,465 |
| Total Return | | 1,049 | 12,546 | 12,879 | 13,241 | 13,633 | 14,058 | 14,058 |
| CF/Debt Servicing Ratio | 129.94% | 129.80% | 129.80% | 129.80% | 129.80% | 129.80% | 129.80% |
| Net Income ROI | | | 2.13% | 2.56% | 3.03% | 3.54% | 4.09% | 4.09% |
| Cash ROI | | | 11.16% | 11.16% | 11.16% | 11.16% | 11.16% | 11.16% |
| Total ROI | | | 16.29% | 16.73% | 17.20% | 17.70% | 18.26% | 18.26% |
| Net CFs from Investment—1 Yr Exit | | (77,000) | 169,546 | | | | | |
| Net CFs from Investment—3 Yr Exit | | (77,000) | 8,593 | 8,593 | 253,480 | | | |
| Net CFs from Investment—5 Yr Exit | | (77,000) | 8,593 | 8,593 | 8,593 | 8,593 | 308,986 | |

| | Exit Price | Gain on Sale | Cap Rate | | IRR |
|---|---|---|---|---|---|
| Estimated Exit Price/Gain on Sale—1 Yr | 465,000 | 80,000 | 8.19% | Annualized IRR—1 Yr | 120.19% |
| Estimated Exit Price/Gain on Sale—3 Yr | 540,000 | 155,000 | 7.05% | Annualized IRR—3 Yr | 55.14% |
| Estimated Exit Price/Gain on Sale—5 Yr | 585,000 | 200,000 | 6.51% | Annualized IRR—5 Yr | 38.45% |

**Exhibit 8.2** Scenario 2: Five-Year Pro Forma Income Statement. (from Berges Investment Group, Copyright © 1998)

| Cost and Revenue Assumptions | | Financing Assumptions | | | Key Ratios | |
|---|---|---|---|---|---|---|
| Land | 75,000 | Total Purchase | 100.00% | 385,000 | Total Square Feet | 12,000.00 |
| Building | 300,000 | Owner's Equity | 20.00% | 77,000 | Avg Sq Ft/Unit | 1,000.00 |
| Improvements | 0 | Balance to Finc | 80.00% | 308,000 | Avg Rent/Sq Ft | 0.45 |
| Closing Costs | 10,000 | | | | Avg Cost/Sq Ft | 32.08 |
| Total | 385,000 | | | | Avg Unit Cost | 32,083.33 |
| | | | Annual | Monthly | Capitalization Rate | 11.47% |
| Number of Units | 12 | Interest Rate | 8.125% | 0.677% | Gross Rent Multiplier | 5.46 |
| Average Monthly Rent | 445 | Term | 25 | 300 | Expense/Unit | 1,951.15 |
| Gross Monthly Revenues | 5,340 | Payment | 28,833 | 2,403 | Expense/Foot | 1.95 |

| | | Actual Monthly | Actual Year 1 | Year 2 | Year 3 | Year 4 | Year 5 |
|---|---|---|---|---|---|---|---|
| Estimated Growth Rate Projections | | | 10.00% | 10.00% | 7.00% | 5.00% | 3.00% |
| Average Monthly Rent Projected | | | 490 | 538 | 536 | 605 | 623 |
| **Operating Revenues** | | | | | | | |
| Gross Scheduled Income | | 5,340 | 70,488 | 77,537 | 82,964 | 87,113 | 89,726 |
| Vacancy Rate | 5.0% | 267 | 3,524 | 3,877 | 4,148 | 4,356 | 4,486 |
| Net Rental Income | | 5,073 | 66,964 | 73,660 | 78,816 | 82,757 | 85,240 |
| Other Income | | 50 | 600 | 660 | 706 | 742 | 764 |
| Gross Income | 100.0% | 5,123 | 67,564 | 74,320 | 79,522 | 83,498 | 86,003 |
| **Operating Expenses** | | | | | | | |
| Repairs and Maintenance | 10.0% | 512 | 6,148 | 7,432 | 7,952 | 8,350 | 8,600 |
| Taxes | 13.7% | 703 | 8,436 | 9,280 | 9,929 | 10,426 | 10,738 |
| Insurance | 3.0% | 152 | 1,824 | 2,006 | 2,147 | 2,254 | 2,322 |
| Property Mgmt. | 0.0% | 0 | 0 | 0 | 0 | 0 | 0 |
| Utilities | 9.9% | 507 | 6,084 | 6,692 | 7,161 | 7,519 | 7,744 |
| Trash Removal | 0.5% | 26 | 307 | 338 | 362 | 380 | 391 |
| Advt/Misc | 1.0% | 51 | 615 | 676 | 724 | 760 | 783 |
| Total Op. Exp. | 38.1% | 1,951 | 23,414 | 26,425 | 28,274 | 29,688 | 30,579 |

| | | | | | | |
|---|---|---|---|---|---|---|
| **Net Operating Income** 61.9% | 3,172 | 44,150 | 47,895 | 51,248 | 53,810 | 55,425 |
| Interest on Loan 40.7% | 2,085 | 24,880 | 24,547 | 24,185 | 23,793 | 23,368 |
| Dep. Exp.—Building | 909 | 10,909 | 10,909 | 10,909 | 10,909 | 10,909 |
| Dep. Exp.—Equip. | 0 | 0 | 0 | 0 | 0 | 0 |
| Net Income Before Taxes | 177 | 8 361 | 12,440 | 16,154 | 19,108 | 21,148 |
| Income Tax Rate 28.0% | 50 | 2,341 | 2,575 | 2,755 | 2,893 | 2,980 |
| Net Income After Taxes | 128 | 6 020 | 9,864 | 13,398 | 16,215 | 18,168 |
| **Cash Flow from Operations** | | | | | | |
| Net Income After Taxes | 128 | 6,020 | 9,864 | 13,398 | 16,215 | 18,168 |
| Dep. Exp. | 909 | 10,909 | 10,909 | 10,909 | 10,909 | 10,909 |
| Total CF from Ops. | 1,037 | 16,929 | 20,774 | 24,308 | 27,124 | 29,077 |
| Interest on Loan | 2,085 | 24,880 | 24,547 | 24,185 | 23,793 | 23,368 |
| Total Cash Available for Loan Servicing | 3,122 | 41,809 | 45,320 | 48,492 | 50,917 | 52,445 |
| Debt Service | 2,403 | 28,833 | 28,833 | 28,833 | 28,833 | 28,833 |
| Remaining After Tax CF from Ops. | 719 | 12,976 | 16,487 | 19,659 | 22,084 | 23,612 |
| Plus Principal Reduction | 329 | 3,953 | 4,287 | 4,648 | 5,040 | 5,465 |
| Total Return | 1,049 | 16,929 | 20,774 | 24,308 | 27,124 | 29,077 |
| CF/Debt Servicing Ratio | 129.94% | 145.00% | 157.18% | 168.18% | 176.59% | 181.89% |
| Net Income ROI | | 7.82% | 12.81% | 17.40% | 21.06% | 23.59% |
| Cash ROI | | 16.85% | 21.41% | 25.53% | 28.68% | 30.66% |
| Total ROI | | 21.99% | 26.98% | 31.57% | 35.23% | 37.76% |
| Net CFs from Investment—1 Yr Exit | (77,000) | 173,929 | | | | |
| Net CFs from Investment—3 Yr Exit | (77,000) | 12,976 | 15,487 | 264,547 | | |
| Net CFs from Investment—5 Yr Exit | (77,000) | 12,976 | 16,487 | 19,659 | 22,084 | 324,005 |

| | Exit Price | Gain on Sale | Cap Rate | | IRR |
|---|---|---|---|---|---|
| Estimated Exit Price/Gain on Sale—1 Yr | 455,000 | 80,000 | 9.49% | Annualized IRR—1 Yr | 125.88% |
| Estimated Exit Price/Gain on Sale—3 Yr | 540,000 | 155,000 | 9.49% | Annualized IRR—3 Yr | 61.62% |
| Estimated Exit Price/Gain on Sale—5 Yr | 585,000 | 200,000 | 9.47% | Annualized IRR—5 Yr | 45.83% |

apartments. In this particular example, 28 percent was assumed for income taxes.

Scenario 1 was designed to reflect the cash flows of the property as it was operating at the time of purchase; therefore, the estimated growth rate projections were assumed to be 0 percent. Toward the bottom of the income statement, you will see the debt service coverage ratio (DSCR), the cash ROI, and the total ROI as discussed in Chapter 7. The calculations are fairly straightforward, as previously described.

The last section in Exhibit 8.1 illustrates what effect a given exit price would have on the seller's gain on sale and its respective cap rate. In this example, the cap rate of 8.19 percent at an exit price of $465,000 would be hard to justify to an astute investor. There would have to be some other compelling reason to acquire the property at that price point. Quite frankly, I can't think of any.

Now take a look at Exhibit 8.2, Scenario 2. Note that the cost and revenue assumptions, as well as the financing assumptions, remain exactly the same as in the analysis in Exhibit 8.1. The only assumptions that have changed are the variables used for the estimated growth rate projections. Take a few minutes to study the table.

Once again, all assumptions remain exactly the same as in the analysis in Exhibit 8.1. Only the variables used for the estimated growth rate projections have changed. Recall that Pam, the buyer, believed the apartments were being rented for considerably less than market value, so an aggressive growth rate of 10 percent was used in the first two years to bring the rents in line with what the market would bear. Since this was a small 12-unit complex, it is entirely reasonable to assume that rents could be increased at this rate over a two-year period. A temporary increase in turnover would likely result, but once the new tenants were in, the property would become stabilized.

Note how all of the ratios have improved by changing only one set of variables. I should point out that you cannot, of course, arbitrarily adjust the variables to force the model to achieve a desired output. You must have some basis of fact for your assumptions, and in this case we clearly did. The DSCR has improved and is well within an acceptable range for a lender. The ratio would be even higher if the income tax rate were set to zero, so we are really looking at a conservative estimate here. The cash ROI and total ROI have also improved and are more in line with an acceptable degree at this level. Finally, if Pam were to sell the apartments at the end of Year 1, the exit price of $465,000 would be justifiable to the market. Holding the property for another two years could potentially yield an additional $75,000 in capital gains over and above the Year-1 exit price.

Pam and her partner did eventually acquire this 12-unit apartment building. I have not heard from her since they closed the deal, so I have no idea whether she took my value-play advice. Nevertheless, it provides an excellent case study, one that I hope you have learned something from. I am sure you will agree that there is great value in having a dynamic model such as the one I developed in Lotus. By keying in our basic assumptions, we can very easily change a few variables, which can help us to readily identify any upside potential. Additional information regarding the availability of the model used in the case studies is available on the Web at www.thevalueplay.com.

## Case Study 3: 16 Units in Beaumont— A Banker's REO

My brother, Tim, who is also a real estate investor, will from time to time ask my opinion when he is considering a particular deal. While my expertise lies in financial analysis, Tim's forte is more along the lines of property improvement, so while we have different talents, we are fortunate that they complement each other. This case study involves a 16-unit apartment building in Beaumont, Texas, that Tim was interested in, which happened to be about two hours from where he lived. While the property was being offered by a real estate broker, it was held by a bank in its real estate owned (REO) portfolio. The bank had foreclosed on the previous owner for defaulting on the loan and had subsequently turned it over to a property management firm to operate. The offering price was $364,000. Take a moment to review Exhibit 8.3, the investment summary information as provided by the broker.

We will analyze the financial information provided in Exhibit 8.3 in greater detail, but first, please examine the following excerpts from a series of e-mails Tim sent me.

Steve,

I went to look at the apartments in Beaumont yesterday. The apartments look to be acceptable. Roof and parking good. A few minor things need repairs . . . probably can do it myself. The area is mixed commercial and residential. Across the street are two nice looking homes, next to it is one that has been mostly remodeled (looks like by an investor). The one next to that is in really bad shape. Several homes in the neighborhood area are really nice looking. About 95% of lawns are cut and neat. A couple of attorneys have offices at the end of the block. About three blocks away is a very nice restaurant (4 yrs. there) that is reservation only. The restaurant list had several Drs. names on it . . . and looked pretty fancy inside. . . . The clientele looked like college age and older all dressed casually elegant. There are also a lot of for sale signs in the area. A neighbor told me that there is a nice house nearby on the market for $500K, but didn't think it was worth it. Some homes very nicely done. Victorian with the big columns and large porches. Area was peaceful and quiet with a sense of serenity. . . . Had to drive about 1 mile to find anything that looked like what I would call rough. About five blocks over were a few streets with lower income housing, but most were still in reasonably good shape. Not trashed and weeds in the yard like you see in some areas. . . . Also no cars being fixed in the drives or dead cars sitting around. Could be an area on the way up or on the way down. There are several other complexes in the area, some a little nicer and some not as nice. Only one about 5 blocks away was on the ratty side, looked a little trashy but not terribly. A neighbor said the complex has gotten better in the last year. She lives about three houses down and husband owns the restaurant one block away. I am waiting for the rent rolls that we talked about before proceeding. That will tell a story about the tenants. I don't feel at this point that I would be willing to pay more than $300K. If the area comes up it could be a great investment. If it stays the same it could be hard to sell unless the occupancy rate is very high and rents are solid.

Tim

The reply to my brother was short and direct.

Tim,

Sounds like you did a fairly thorough analysis of the area surrounding the apts. Rent rolls and a conversation with the management company should be telling.

Steve

Note the detail in Tim's e-mail regarding his observations of the area. It is apparent that he took the necessary time to examine every aspect of the sur-

**Exhibit 8.3**   Investment Summary.

| Property Information | | | |
|---|---|---|---|
| Price | $364,000 | Appraisal data | |
| Down payment | $72,800 | Income approach | $364,000 |
| Number of units | 16 | Cost approach | $408,000 |
| Price per unit | $22,750 | Sales comp approach | $375,000 |
| Lot size | 23,884 | | |
| Net rentable sq ft | 14,125 | Assessed tax values | |
| Zoning | RM-H | Total improvements | $177,800 |
| Price per sq ft | $25.77 | Total land | $14,000 |
| Cap rate | 14.00% | Total value | $191,800 |
| Land value | $14,000 | | |

| Income and Expenses as Reported by Owner/Seller | |
|---|---|
| **Income** | |
| 15 units × 460 | $6,900 |
| 1 unit × 325 | 325 |
| Less 10% vacancy | 723 |
| Gross income | $6,503 |
| **Expenses** | |
| Taxes | $ 455 |
| Insurance | 325 |
| Electric | 75 |
| Water and sewage | 400 |
| Management | 500 |
| Maintenance | 500 |
| Reserves | 333 |
| Refuse | 80 |
| Lawn | 195 |
| Extermination | 85 |
| Total expenses | $2,948 |
| Net operating income | $3,555 |

rounding community. As previously discussed, it is much easier to bring a Class C property up to the standards of a Class B neighborhood than it is to elevate the property's class or condition above that of the community. In some cases, it does not matter how much money you spend on improvements, prospective tenants will elect to reside elsewhere because they do not like the neighborhood. Although evaluating a community is a very subjective process, common sense usually dictates what action you should take—either to accept the deal and continue the due diligence process, or to reject it and move on to the next opportunity.

Tim raises some interesting issues in his e-mail. He states, "If the area comes up it could be a great investment. If it stays the same it could be hard to sell unless the occupancy rate is very high and rents are solid." Tim's observation here is that there have been some notable improvements to the area in recent years, but it is difficult to determine whether the improvements will continue and, if so, at what pace. He also mentions that, overall, the area appeared to be in relatively good condition; however, he also saw several For Sale signs. Is the area coming up, or is it going down? An interview with both the brokerage firm and the property management company overseeing the apartments could fill him in on the historical perspective. Remember, Tim lived a couple of hours away from the subject property and was therefore not that familiar with the area.

Now take a look at Exhibit 8.4, Scenario 1 for the Beaumont apartments. I used the information as provided in the investment summary in Exhibit 8.3 and entered it into our model.

Based on the assumptions used in Exhibit 8.4, the property appears to be operating reasonably well. The returns are modest; the DSCR and the cap rate are both acceptable. So what do you think—should Tim buy the property? Just to refresh your memory, Chapter 3 discusses the three basic components that must be considered when defining your objectives of acquiring an apartment building. They are your entry, postentry, and exit strategies. Chapter 4 discusses the merits of the value play at length. Keep these principles in mind as we continue our discussion with Tim's follow-up e-mail to me.

**Exhibit 8.4** Scenario 1: Five-Year Pro Forma Income Statement. (from Berges Investment Group, Copyright © 1998)

| Cost and Revenue Assumptions | | Financing Assumptions | | | Key Ratios | |
|---|---|---|---|---|---|---|
| Land | 14,000 | Total Purchase | 100.00% | 369,000 | Total Square Feet | 14,125.00 |
| Building | 350,000 | Owner's Equity | 20.00% | 73,800 | Avg Sq Ft/Unit | 882.81 |
| Improvements | 0 | Balance to Finc | 80.00% | 295,200 | Avg Rent/Sq Ft | 0.51 |
| Closing Costs | 5,000 | | | | Avg Cost/Sq Ft | 26.12 |
| Total | 369,000 | | Annual | Monthly | Avg Unit Cost | 23,062.50 |
| | | Interest Rate | 8.000% | 0.667% | Capitalization Rate | 11.57% |
| Number of Units | 16 | Term | 20 | 240 | Gross Rent Multiplier | 4.26 |
| Average Monthly Rent | 452 | Payment | 29,630 | 2,469 | Expense/Unit | 2,209.20 |
| Gross Monthly Revenues | 7,225 | | | | Expense/Foot | 2.50 |

| Estimated Growth Rate Projections | | | | | | |
|---|---|---|---|---|---|---|
| | | | 0.00% | 2.50% | 2.50% | 2.50% | 2.50% |
| Average Monthly Rent | | | 452 | 463 | 474 | 486 | 498 |

| | | Actual Monthly | Actual Year 1 | Year 2 | Year 3 | Year 4 | Year 5 |
|---|---|---|---|---|---|---|---|
| | | | | | Projected | | |
| Operating Revenues | | | | | | | |
| Gross Scheduled Income | | 7,225 | 86,698 | 88,865 | 91,087 | 93,364 | 95,698 |
| Vacancy Rate | 10.0% | 722 | 8,670 | 8,887 | 9,109 | 9,336 | 9,570 |
| Net Rental Income | | 6,502 | 78,028 | 79,979 | 81,978 | 84,027 | 86,128 |
| Other Income | | 0 | 0 | 0 | 0 | 0 | 0 |
| Gross Income | 100.0% | 6,502 | 78,028 | 79,979 | 81,978 | 84,027 | 86,128 |
| Operating Expenses | | | | | | | |
| Repairs and Maintenance | 12.8% | 832 | 9,988 | 10,237 | 10,493 | 10,756 | 11,024 |
| Taxes | 7.0% | 455 | 5,460 | 5,597 | 5,736 | 5,880 | 6,027 |
| Insurance | 5.0% | 325 | 3,900 | 3,998 | 4,097 | 4,200 | 4,305 |
| Property Mgmt. | 7.7% | 501 | 6,008 | 6,158 | 6,312 | 6,470 | 6,632 |
| Utilities | 7.3% | 475 | 5,700 | 5,843 | 5,989 | 6,138 | 6,292 |
| Trash Removal | 1.2% | 78 | 936 | 960 | 984 | 1,008 | 1,034 |
| Advt/Misc | 4.3% | 280 | 3,355 | 3,439 | 3,525 | 3,613 | 3,704 |
| Total Op. Exp. | 45.3% | 2,946 | 35,347 | 36,231 | 37,137 | 38,065 | 39,017 |

| | | | | | | |
|---|---|---|---|---|---|---|
| **Net Operating Income** | 54.7% | 3,557 | 42,631 | 43,748 | 44,841 | 45,962 | 47,111 |
| Interest on Loan | 30.3% | 1,968 | 23,391 | 22,873 | 22,312 | 21,704 | 21,047 |
| Dep. Exp.—Building | | 1,061 | 12,727 | 12,727 | 12,727 | 12,727 | 12,727 |
| Dep. Exp.—Equip. | | 0 | 0 | 0 | 0 | 0 | 0 |
| Net Income Before Taxes | | 528 | 6,553 | 8,148 | 9,802 | 11,531 | 13,338 |
| Income Tax Rate | 0.0% | 0 | 0 | 0 | 0 | 0 | 0 |
| Net Income After Taxes | | 528 | 6,553 | 8,148 | 9,802 | 11,531 | 13,338 |
| **Cash Flow from Operations** | | | | | | | |
| Net Income After Taxes | | 528 | 6,563 | 8,148 | 9,802 | 11,531 | 13,338 |
| Dep. Exp. | | 1,061 | 12,727 | 12,727 | 12,727 | 12,727 | 12,727 |
| Total CF from Ops. | | 1,589 | 19,290 | 20,875 | 22,530 | 24,258 | 26,065 |
| Interest on Loan | | 1,968 | 23,391 | 22,873 | 22,312 | 21,704 | 21,047 |
| Total Cash Available for Loan Servicing | | 3,557 | 42,681 | 43,748 | 44,841 | 45,962 | 47,111 |
| Debt Service | | 2,469 | 29,630 | 29,630 | 29,630 | 29,630 | 29,630 |
| Remaining After Tax CF from Ops. | | 1,088 | 13,051 | 14,118 | 15,211 | 16,332 | 17,481 |
| Plus Principal Reduction | | 520 | 6,240 | 6,757 | 7,318 | 7,926 | 8,584 |
| Total Return | | 1,608 | 19,290 | 20,875 | 22,530 | 24,258 | 26,065 |
| CF/Debt Servicing Ratio | 144.04% | 144.04% | 147.65% | 151.34% | 155.12% | 159.00% |
| Net Income ROI | | 8.89% | 11.04% | 13.28% | 15.62% | 18.07% |
| Cash ROI | | 17.68% | 19.13% | 20.61% | 22.13% | 23.69% |
| Total ROI | | 26.14% | 28.29% | 30.53% | 32.87% | 35.32% |
| Net CFs from Investment—1 Yr Exit | | (73,800) | 119,090 | | | | |
| Net CFs from Investment—3 Yr Exit | | (73,800) | 13,051 | 14,118 | 160,327 | | |
| Net CFs from Investment—5 Yr Exit | | (73,800) | 13,051 | 14,118 | 15,211 | 16,332 | 204,106 |
| | | Exit Price | Gain on Sale | Cap Rate | | | IRR |
| Estimated Exit Price/Gain on Sale—1 Yr | | 395,000 | 26,000 | 10.81% | Annualized IRR—1 Yr | | 61.37% |
| Estimated Exit Price/Gain on Sale—3 Yr | | 420,000 | 51,000 | 10.68% | Annualized IRR—3 Yr | | 40.82% |
| Estimated Exit Price/Gain on Sale—5 Yr | | 445,000 | 76,000 | 10.59% | Annualized IRR—5 Yr | | 35.11% |

Steve,

The Beaumont deal is moving slowly. Having a full-time job really makes try-ing to put a deal together difficult. I spoke with the management company's director this evening who will fax me the last six months' rent rolls and expense records. She says there are a lot of calls for that property, more than some others they manage. Over half of them don't qualify but because there is traffic they are able to rent them. Since they took the property to manage they have been upgrading the units so expenses will probably be high. Also, there are a lot of plumbing calls to unclog the main line, at least one or two a month and no suggestions from the plumber as to why. Evicted one tenant for nonpayment last month and are renovating the unit now. Feels the rent is at the top of the market for the area. Nearby 3 bedroom houses rent for $600 mo. She suggested gating the property. Was unsure about being able to attract a higher class of tenant, like employees who work at the hospital nearby.

   I guess you never feel completely comfortable with an investment, but the big question in my mind is how do I create value here to get the investment to profit at sale as we discussed?

Tim

Based on what Tim has told me so far, it sounds as if there is limited upside potential in this deal. Now take a look at Exhibit 8.5, Scenario 2.

Following is a memo I prepared for Tim based on my analysis of the 16-unit property in Beaumont.

Tim,

Attached are two scenarios from the output of my model pertaining to the 16 units in Beaumont. Following are the assumptions used in each.

### Scenario 1

- Purchase price of $364,000
- 20% down payment at 8% interest rate
- 0% growth in Year 1
- Revenues and expenses are as stated per the broker/seller
- Exit price of $395,000 in Year 1

### Scenario 2

- Purchase price of $300,000
- $20,000 for capital improvements
- Total of 15% down (which includes money for capitals)
- Rent increases of 3% in Year 1 following improvements
- Some adjustments to expenses
- Exit price of $395,000 in Year 1

I suggest a close examination of the sales comps to help you determine your upside potential for that market. A purchase price of $300,000 allows you to take advantage of what appears to be limited upside, while the $364,000 price leaves very little. If you're looking for a buy-and-hold property as opposed to a value-play opportunity, you may want to consider staying a little closer to home.

Hope this helps. Good luck!

Steve

The memo to Tim summarizes my thoughts on the 16-unit. Based on the information we have so far, if he were to pay the full asking price of $364,000, by the time transactions costs are factored in, there is not enough upside potential to qualify this as a value play. If Tim could pick the deal up

**Exhibit 8.5** Scenario 2: Five-Year Pro Forma Income Statement. (from Berges Investment Group, Copyright © 1998)

### Cost and Revenue Assumptions

| | |
|---|---|
| Land | 14,000 |
| Building | 286,000 |
| Improvements | 20,000 |
| Closing Costs | 5,000 |
| Total | 325,000 |

| | |
|---|---|
| Number of Units | 16 |
| Average Monthly Rent | 452 |
| Gross Monthly Revenues | 7,225 |

| | |
|---|---|
| Estimated Growth Rate Projections | 3.00% |
| Average Monthly Rent | 465 |

### Financing Assumptions

| | | |
|---|---|---|
| Total Purchase | 325,000 | 100.00% |
| Owner's Equity | 48,750 | 15.00% |
| Balance to Finc | 276,250 | 85.00% |

| | Annual | Monthly |
|---|---|---|
| Interest Rate | 8.000% | 0.667% |
| Term | 20 | 240 |
| Payment | 27,728 | 2,311 |

### Key Ratios

| | |
|---|---|
| Total Square Feet | 14,125.00 |
| Avg Sq Ft/Unit | 882.81 |
| Avg Rent/Sq Ft | 0.51 |
| Avg Cost/Sq Ft | 23.01 |
| Avg Unit Cost | 20,312.50 |
| Capitalization Rate | 14.92% |
| Gross Rent Multiplier | 3.64 |
| Expense/Unit | 2,271.94 |
| Expense/Foot | 2.57 |

| | | | Projected | | |
|---|---|---|---|---|---|
| | | | 2.50% | 2.50% | 2.50% |
| Estimated Growth Rate Projections | 3.00% | 2.50% | | | |
| Average Monthly Rent | 465 | 477 | 489 | 501 | 513 |

| | | Actual Monthly | Actual Year 1 | Year 2 | Year 3 | Year 4 | Year 5 |
|---|---|---|---|---|---|---|---|
| **Operating Revenues** | | | | | | | |
| Gross Scheduled Income | | 7,225 | 89,299 | 91,531 | 93,819 | 96,165 | 98,569 |
| Vacancy Rate | 5.0% | 361 | 4,465 | 4,577 | 4,691 | 4,808 | 4,928 |
| Net Rental Income | | 6,864 | 84,834 | 86,954 | 89,128 | 91,357 | 93,640 |
| Other Income | | 0 | 0 | 0 | 0 | 0 | 0 |
| Gross Income | 100.0% | 6,864 | 84,834 | 86,954 | 89,128 | 91,357 | 93,640 |
| **Operating Expenses** | | | | | | | |
| Repairs and Maintenance | 15.0% | 1,030 | 12,354 | 13,043 | 13,369 | 13,703 | 14,046 |
| Taxes | 6.6% | 455 | 5,460 | 5,597 | 5,736 | 5,880 | 6,027 |
| Insurance | 2.2% | 150 | 1,800 | 1,845 | 1,891 | 1,938 | 1,987 |
| Property Mgmt. | 7.7% | 528 | 6,342 | 6,500 | 6,663 | 6,830 | 7,000 |
| Utilities | 6.9% | 475 | 5,700 | 5,843 | 5,989 | 6,138 | 6,292 |
| Trash Removal | 1.2% | 82 | 988 | 1,013 | 1,038 | 1,064 | 1,091 |
| Advt/Misc | 4.5% | 309 | 3,706 | 3,799 | 3,894 | 3,991 | 4,091 |
| Total Op. Exp. | 44.1% | 3,029 | 36,351 | 37,640 | 38,581 | 39,545 | 40,534 |

| | % | | | | | | |
|---|---|---|---|---|---|---|---|
| Net Operating Income | 55.9% | 3,834 | 48,483 | 49,315 | 50,548 | 51,811 | 53,107 |
| Interest on Loan | 26.8% | 1,842 | 21,889 | 21,404 | 20,879 | 20,311 | 19,695 |
| Dep. Exp.—Building | | 867 | 10,400 | 10,400 | 10,400 | 10,400 | 10,400 |
| Dep. Exp.—Equip. | | 0 | 0 | 0 | 0 | 0 | 0 |
| Net Income Before Taxes | | 1,125 | 16,194 | 7,510 | 19,268 | 21,100 | 23,011 |
| Income Tax Rate | 0.0% | 0 | 0 | 0 | 0 | 0 | 0 |
| Net Income After Taxes | | 1,125 | 16,194 | 17,510 | 19,268 | 21,100 | 23,011 |
| **Cash Flow from Operations** | | | | | | | |
| Net Income After Taxes | | 1,126 | 16,194 | 17,510 | 19,268 | 21,100 | 23,011 |
| Dep. Exp. | | 867 | 10,400 | 10,400 | 10,400 | 10,400 | 10,400 |
| Total CF from Ops. | | 1,993 | 26,594 | 27,910 | 29,668 | 31,500 | 33,411 |
| Interest on Loan | | 1,842 | 21,889 | 21,404 | 20,879 | 20,311 | 19,695 |
| Total Cash Available for Loan Servicing | | 3,834 | 48,483 | 49,315 | 50,548 | 51,811 | 53,107 |
| Debt Service | | 2,311 | 27,728 | 27,728 | 27,728 | 27,728 | 27,728 |
| Remaining After Tax CF from Ops. | | 1,524 | 20,755 | 21,587 | 22,820 | 24,083 | 25,379 |
| Plus Principal Reduction | | 487 | 5,839 | 6,324 | 6,848 | 7,417 | 8,033 |
| Total Return | | 2,010 | 26,594 | 27,910 | 29,668 | 31,500 | 33,411 |
| CF/Debt Servicing Ratio | | 165.94% | 174.85% | 177.85% | 182.30% | 186.86% | 191.53% |
| Net Income ROI | | | 33.22% | 35.92% | 39.52% | 43.28% | 47.20% |
| Cash ROI | | | 42.57% | 44.28% | 46.81% | 49.40% | 52.06% |
| Total ROI | | | 54.55% | 57.25% | 60.86% | 64.62% | 68.54% |
| Net CFs from Investment—1 Yr Exit | | (48,750) | 145,344 | | | | |
| Net CFs from Investment—3 Yr Exit | | (48,750) | 20,755 | 21,587 | 185,581 | | |
| Net CFs from Investment—5 Yr Exit | | (48,750) | 20,755 | 21,587 | 22,820 | 24,083 | 228,589 |

| | Exit Price | Gain on Sale | Cap Rate | | IRR |
|---|---|---|---|---|---|
| Estimated Exit Price/Gain on Sale—1 Yr | 395,000 | 70,000 | 12.27% | Annualized IRR—1 Yr | 198.14% |
| Estimated Exit Price/Gain on Sale—3 Yr | 420,000 | 95,000 | 12.04% | Annualized IRR—3 Yr | 81.93% |
| Estimated Exit Price/Gain on Sale—5 Yr | 445,000 | 120,000 | 11.93% | Annualized IRR—5 Yr | 63.68% |

for $300,000 as assumed in Scenario 2, spruce it up with about $20,000 in capital improvements, and turn around and sell it for $395,000, then I believe it would be worth pursuing. Conversely, as I mentioned in my memo to him, if he is looking for a buy-and-hold property, he will likely be better off acquiring something a little closer to home.

As it turned out, the management company faxed over the actual expenses, along with a recent history of rent collections. The actuals turned out to be much worse than the financial statements had originally reported. Expenses across the board were high, while collections were slow—all indicating underlying problems that likely had contributed to the property's ending up in the bank's REO portfolio. With this new information, the purchase of the 16-unit apartment complex became marginal even at the $300,000 price point. Tim wisely decided to pass on the deal.

Remember, you must define your objectives from the outset. Entry, postentry, and exit strategies must all be clearly established. If you are a value-play buyer, your investment philosophy will by definition be to assume a short-term approach. Every potential acquisition candidate you analyze should meet your established criteria for a value-play opportunity. You cannot afford to implement the buy-and-hold technique if you truly intend to maximize the return on your investment capital.

## Case Study 4: 98 Units in Houston—Creating Synergism through Consolidation

This case study involves the consolidation of a 73-unit apartment complex and a 25-unit apartment complex located in close proximity to each other in Houston, Texas. A few years ago, these properties were brought to my attention simultaneously by two different brokers. They happened to be located about one-half mile from each other. The 73-unit had a full-time manager who had been there for eight years, while the 25-unit was being operated by the owners, a husband and wife, who also happened to be residents. The couple had owned the property for 25 years and had just made their last payment on the mortgage. Selling the apartments would allow them to cash out and retire comfortably.

My idea was to combine the two properties by operating them as a single entity because they were located just a couple of minutes from each other. Because the 73-unit property's full-time manager had already proven herself to be quite capable, I believed she could assume the responsibility for an additional 25 units without becoming overloaded. I would, of course, be willing to compensate her for taking on the additional workload. The difference in her salary would certainly be less than that of hiring another manager for the 25-unit building.

Both properties were operating at over 95 percent capacity and both appeared to have been fairly well maintained, although they were in need of some minor cosmetic repairs. The 73-unit complex had a full-time maintenance person, while repairs on the 25-unit complex were being made by the owners. The 73-unit property had originally been constructed with a master meter for the electric service, but had since been submetered, with collections from the tenants being made on-site. The 25-unit had also been constructed with a master meter, but had not yet been retrofitted with submeters. Both were solid Class C properties in a Class B– to C+ community. After personally calling 14 competing apartment complexes within a 1- to 3-mile radius, I discovered that most of the comps in the surrounding area enjoyed high occupancy. A limited supply with strong demand—just the way I like it. My survey of the other 14 apartment buildings indicated that rents at the 73-unit complex were fully 10 percent below market, while rents at the 25-unit were only slightly below market.

**Exhibit 8.6** Scenario 1: Five-Year Pro Forma Income Statement. (from Berges Investment Group, Copyright © 1998)

**Cost and Revenue Assumptions**

| | |
|---|---|
| Land | 125,000 |
| Building | 1,290,000 |
| Improvements | 0 |
| Closing Costs | 20,000 |
| Total | 1,435,000 |
| | |
| Number of Units | 98 |
| Average Monthly Rent | 368 |
| Gross Monthly Revenues | 36,064 |
| | |
| Estimated Growth Rate Projections | 0.00% |
| Average Monthly Rent | 368 |

**Financing Assumptions**

| | | |
|---|---|---|
| Total Purchase | 100.00% | 1,435,000 |
| Owner's Equity | 20.00% | 287,000 |
| Balance to Finc | 80.00% | 1,148,000 |
| | Annual | Monthly |
| Interest Rate | 7.375% | 0.615% |
| Term | 25 | 300 |
| Payment | 100,686 | 8,390 |
| | 0.00% | 0.00% |
| | 368 | 368 |

**Key Ratios**

| | |
|---|---|
| Total Square Feet | 70,486.00 |
| Avg Sq Ft/Unit | 719.24 |
| Avg Rent/Sq Ft | 0.51 |
| Avg Cost/Sq Ft | 20.36 |
| Avg Unit Cost | 14,642.86 |
| Capitalization Rate | 11.90% |
| Gross Rent Multiplier | 3.32 |
| Expense/Unit | 3,080.27 |
| Expense/Foot | 4.28 |
| | 0.00% |
| | 368 |

| | | | | Projected | | |
|---|---|---|---|---|---|---|
| **Operating Revenues** | | Actual Monthly | Actual Year 1 | Year 2 | Year 3 | Year 4 | Year 5 |
| Gross Scheduled Income | | 36,064 | 432,768 | 432,768 | 432,768 | 432,768 | 432,768 |
| Vacancy Rate | 4.2% | 1,515 | 18,176 | 18,176 | 18,176 | 18,176 | 18,176 |
| Net Rental Income | | 34,549 | 414,592 | 414,592 | 414,592 | 414,592 | 414,592 |
| Other Income | | 4,840 | 58,080 | 58,080 | 58,080 | 58,080 | 58,080 |
| Gross Income | 100.0% | 39,389 | 472,672 | 472,672 | 472,672 | 472,672 | 472,672 |
| **Operating Expenses** | | | | | | | |
| Repairs and Maintenance | 15.6% | 6,145 | 73,737 | 73,737 | 73,737 | 73,737 | 73,737 |
| Taxes | 5.1% | 2,015 | 24,180 | 24,180 | 24,180 | 24,180 | 24,180 |
| Insurance | 2.1% | 821 | 9,850 | 9,850 | 9,850 | 9,850 | 9,850 |
| Mgmt. and Payroll | 8.5% | 3,348 | 40,177 | 40,177 | 40,177 | 40,177 | 40,177 |
| Utilities | 29.3% | 11,527 | 138,324 | 138,324 | 138,324 | 138,324 | 138,324 |
| Trash Removal | 1.0% | 394 | 4,727 | 4,727 | 4,727 | 4,727 | 4,727 |
| Advr/Misc | 2.3% | 906 | 10,871 | 10,871 | 10,871 | 10,871 | 10,871 |
| Total Op. Exp. | 63.9% | 25,156 | 301,866 | 301,866 | 301,866 | 301,866 | 301,866 |

164

| | | | | | | | |
|---|---|---|---|---|---|---|---|
| Net Operating Income | 36.1% | 14,234 | 170,806 | 170,806 | 170,806 | 170,806 | 170,806 |
| Interest on Loan | 17.9% | 7,055 | 84,112 | 82,848 | 81,487 | 80,022 | 78,445 |
| Dep. Exp.—Building | | 3,909 | 46,909 | 46,909 | 46,909 | 46,909 | 46,909 |
| Dep. Exp.—Equip. | | 0 | 0 | 0 | 0 | 0 | 0 |
| Net Income Before Taxes | | 3,269 | 39,784 | 41,049 | 42,410 | 43,875 | 45,451 |
| Income Tax Rate | 0.0% | 0 | 0 | 0 | 0 | 0 | 0 |
| Net Income After Taxes | | 3,259 | 39,784 | 41,049 | 42,410 | 43,875 | 45,451 |
| **Cash Flow from Operations** | | | | | | | |
| Net Income After Taxes | | 3,269 | 39,784 | 41,049 | 42,410 | 43,875 | 45,451 |
| Dep. Exp. | | 3,909 | 46,909 | 46,909 | 46,909 | 46,909 | 46,909 |
| Total CF from Ops. | | 7,178 | 86,693 | 87,958 | 89,319 | 90,784 | 92,360 |
| Interest on Loan | | 7,055 | 84,112 | 82,848 | 81,487 | 80,022 | 78,445 |
| Total Cash Available for Loan Servicing | | 14,234 | 170,806 | 170,806 | 170,806 | 170,806 | 170,806 |
| Debt Service | | 8,390 | 100,686 | 100,686 | 100,686 | 100,686 | 100,686 |
| Remaining After Tax CF from Ops. | | 5,843 | 70,120 | 70,120 | 70,120 | 70,120 | 70,120 |
| Plus Principal Reduction | | 1,381 | 16,574 | 17,838 | 19,199 | 20,664 | 22,241 |
| Total Return | | 7,224 | 86,693 | 87,958 | 89,319 | 90,784 | 92,360 |
| CF/Debt Servicing Ratio | 169.64% | 169.64% | 169.64% | 169.64% | 169.64% | 169.64% | 169.64% |
| Net Income ROI | | 13.86% | 14.30% | 14.78% | 15.29% | 15.84% |
| Cash ROI | | 24.43% | 24.43% | 24.43% | 24.43% | 24.43% |
| Total ROI | | 30.21% | 30.65% | 31.12% | 31.63% | 32.18% |
| Net CFs from Investment—1 Yr Exit | (287,000) | 488,693 | | | | | |
| Net CFs from Investment—3 Yr Exit | (287,000) | 70,120 | 70,120 | 550,731 | | | |
| Net CFs from Investment—5 Yr Exit | (287,000) | 70,120 | 70,120 | 70,120 | 70,120 | 618,636 | |

| | Exit Price | Gain on Sale | Cap Rate | | IRR |
|---|---|---|---|---|---|
| Estimated Exit Price/Gain on Sale—1 Yr | 1,550,000 | 115,000 | 11.02% | Annualized IRR—1 Yr | 70.28% |
| Estimated Exit Price/Gain on Sale—3 Yr | 1,575,000 | 140,000 | 10.84% | Annualized IRR—3 Yr | 39.92% |
| Estimated Exit Price/Gain on Sale—5 Yr | 1,600,000 | 165,000 | 10.68% | Annualized IRR—5 Yr | 33.80% |

I decided to make an offer on both properties, referred to here as the Franklin I and II Apartments, with Franklin I being the 73-unit and Franklin II being the 25-unit. Before we proceed with the details of the offer, take a few minutes to study Exhibit 8.6, Scenario 1, which is a consolidated income statement for the two properties operating together.

Assuming a total purchase price of $1,435,000, including closing costs, the two properties operating together "as is" with no changes provided a fairly generous cap rate of about 11.9 percent, which is at the upper end of our range of 8 to 12 percent, which is good. Remember, the higher the cap rate, the better. Multifamily properties you are considering should almost always be able to sustain themselves and be capable of generating a profit, as this example shows. I know this has been stated before, but it is worth repeating: *You should be willing to pay a price based only on how the property is operating today, not based on how the broker or seller tells you it can potentially operate.* If you do not remember anything else in this book, please remember at least this one principle. By doing so, you will prevent yourself from paying more than a property is really worth. Examine the actual operating statements and use them to negotiate to your advantage.

My analysis of the two properties revealed a number of revenue-enhancing and cost-savings measures that I felt certain would allow me to create value. The first of these items has already been mentioned—the opportunity to consolidate the two properties and operate them as a single entity, thereby achieving synergies through management and maintenance personnel. Also, my market research of the 14 neighboring apartment buildings indicated that Franklin I's rents were well below market. By sprucing it up a bit, I could justify raising the rents and thereby increase the revenue. While Franklin II's rents were at market, the owner's financial statements reflected income for only 24 units rather than 25, because he and his wife were occupying one of them. It just so happened that their unit was really the size of three units combined, so the rent from their apartment would be at least twice that of a normal apartment. In effect, it was like getting 26 units for the price of 24. Franklin II was also being operated as a master-metered property, so the installation of submeters would shave 20 to 30 percent off the electric utility expense; however, this would be offset somewhat by a slight reduction in the rent to compensate the tenants for assuming responsibility for their electric bills. Finally, an on-site inspection of the premises at Franklin II revealed that although the owner had maintained the property fairly well overall, he was not much of a plumber. Probably 20 of the 25 units had leaky faucets and commodes. I estimated that repairing all of the leaks would save at least another 10 percent on the water bill.

Now take a look at Exhibit 8.7, Scenario 2. It includes both the revenue enhancements and the cost-savings measures per my analysis. Note also the $75,000 allocated for capital improvements, which brought the total project value to $1,510,000. The $75,000, by the way, is not included in the owner's equity of 14.25 percent and $215,175 because I was able to finance it with a bank line of credit. I was able to negotiate with the owners of both properties to have them carry back a second mortgage for 10 percent of the purchase price. The lender offered what is known as *75/10/15 financing,* meaning they loaned 75 percent, the seller carried a note for 10 percent, and my required down payment was 15 percent of the purchase price, which did not include capital improvements.

The assumption of 8 percent for the estimated growth rate projections is not an arbitrarily selected number, but is based on the market data gathered from my survey of surrounding apartment buildings. Table 8.4 provides a detailed analysis of the rental income, but I used the more conservative estimate of 8 percent—realizing, of course, that it would take time to achieve this level.

**Exhibit 8.7** Scenario 2: Five-Year Pro Forma Income Statement. (from Berges Investment Group, Copyright © 1998)

| Cost and Revenue Assumptions | | Financing Assumptions | | | Key Ratios | |
|---|---|---|---|---|---|---|
| Land | 125,000 | Total Purchase | 100.00% | 1,510,000 | Total Square Feet | 70,486.00 |
| Building | 1,290,000 | Owner's Equity | 14.25% | 215,175 | Avg Sq Ft/Unit | 719.24 |
| Improvements | 75,000 | Balance to Finc | 85.75% | 1,294,825 | Avg Rent/Sq Ft | 0.51 |
| Closing Costs | 20,000 | | | | Avg Cost/Sq Ft | 21.42 |
| Total | 1,510,000 | | | | Avg Unit Cost | 15,408.16 |
| | | | Annual | Monthly | Capitalization Rate | 14.24% |
| Number of Units | 98 | Interest Rate | 7.375% | 0.615% | Gross Rent Multiplier | 3.23 |
| Average Monthly Rent | 368 | Term | 25 | 300 | Expense/Unit | 3,047.57 |
| Gross Monthly Revenues | 36,064 | Payment | 113,563 | 9,464 | Expense/Foot | 4.24 |

| | Estimated Growth Rate Projections | 8.00% | 6.00% | 3.50% | 2.50% | 2.50% |
|---|---|---|---|---|---|---|
| | Average Monthly Rent | 397 | 421 | 436 | 447 | 458 |

| | | | Actual Year 1 | Projected | | | |
|---|---|---|---|---|---|---|---|
| Operating Revenues | | Actual Monthly | | Year 2 | Year 3 | Year 4 | Year 5 |
| Gross Scheduled Income | | 36,064 | 467,389 | 495,433 | 512,773 | 525,592 | 538,732 |
| Vacancy Rate | 5.0% | 1,803 | 23,369 | 24,772 | 25,639 | 26,280 | 26,937 |
| Net Rental Income | | 34,261 | 444,020 | 470,661 | 487,134 | 499,313 | 511,795 |
| Other Income | | 5,800 | 69,600 | 73,776 | 76,358 | 78,267 | 80,224 |
| Gross Income | 100.0% | 40,061 | 513,620 | 544,437 | 563,492 | 577,580 | 592,019 |
| Operating Expenses | | | | | | | |
| Repairs and Maintenance | 16.0% | 6,410 | 76,917 | 87,110 | 90,159 | 92,413 | 94,723 |
| Taxes | 5.6% | 2,250 | 27,000 | 28,620 | 29,622 | 30,362 | 31,121 |
| Insurance | 2.0% | 821 | 9,850 | 10,441 | 10,806 | 11,077 | 11,354 |
| Mgmt. and Payroll | 9.5% | 3,806 | 45,669 | 48,409 | 50,104 | 51,356 | 52,640 |
| Utilities | 25.5% | 10,200 | 122,400 | 129,744 | 134,285 | 137,642 | 141,083 |
| Trash Removal | 1.0% | 401 | 4,807 | 5,096 | 5,274 | 5,406 | 5,541 |
| Advr/Misc | 2.5% | 1,002 | 12,018 | 12,739 | 13,185 | 13,515 | 13,853 |
| Total Op. Exp. | 62.1% | 24,888 | 298,662 | 322,159 | 333,435 | 341,771 | 350,315 |

| | | | | | | | |
|---|---|---|---|---|---|---|---|
| Net Operating Income | 37.9% | 15,172 | 214,958 | 222,278 | 230,057 | 235,809 | 241,704 |
| Interest on Loan | 19.9% | 7,958 | 94,870 | 93,444 | 91,909 | 90,256 | 88,478 |
| Dep. Exp.—Building | | 3,909 | 46,909 | 46,909 | 46,909 | 46,909 | 46,909 |
| Dep. Exp.—Equip. | | 0 | 0 | 0 | 0 | 0 | 0 |
| Net Income Before Taxes | | 3,305 | 73,179 | 81,925 | 91,240 | 98,643 | 106,317 |
| Income Tax Rate | 0.0% | 0 | 0 | 0 | 0 | 0 | 0 |
| Net Income After Taxes | | 3,305 | 73,179 | 81,925 | 91,240 | 98,643 | 106,317 |

**Cash Flow from Operations**

| | | | | | | |
|---|---|---|---|---|---|---|
| Net Income After Taxes | 3,305 | 73,179 | 81,925 | 91,240 | 98,643 | 106,317 |
| Dep. Exp. | 3,909 | 46,909 | 46,909 | 46,909 | 46,909 | 46,909 |
| Total CF from Ops. | 7,215 | 120,089 | 128,834 | 138,149 | 145,552 | 153,226 |
| Interest on Loan | 7,958 | 94,370 | 93,444 | 91,909 | 90,256 | 88,478 |
| Total Cash Available for Loan Servicing | 15,172 | 214,958 | 222,278 | 230,057 | 235,809 | 241,704 |
| Debt Service | 9,464 | 113,563 | 113,563 | 113,563 | 113,563 | 113,563 |
| Remaining After Tax CF from Ops. | 5,709 | 101,395 | 108,714 | 116,494 | 122,245 | 128,141 |
| Plus Principal Reduction | 1,558 | 18,693 | 20,120 | 21,655 | 23,307 | 25,085 |
| Total Return | 7,267 | 120,089 | 128,834 | 138,149 | 145,552 | 153,226 |

| | | | | | | |
|---|---|---|---|---|---|---|
| CF/Debt Servicing Ratio | 160.52% | 189.28% | 195.73% | 202.58% | 207.65% | 212.84% |
| Net Income ROI | | 34.01% | 38.07% | 42.40% | 45.84% | 49.41% |
| Cash ROI | | 47.12% | 50.52% | 54.14% | 56.81% | 59.55% |
| Total ROI | | 55.81% | 59.87% | 64.20% | 67.64% | 71.21% |

| | | | | | | |
|---|---|---|---|---|---|---|
| Net CFs from Investment—1 Yr Exit | (215,175) | 775,264 | | | | |
| Net CFs from Investment—3 Yr Exit | (215,175) | 101,395 | 108,714 | 882,137 | | |
| Net CFs from Investment—5 Yr Exit | (215,175) | 101,395 | 108,714 | 116,494 | 122,245 | 992,176 |

| | Exit Price | Gain on Sale | Cap Rate | | IRR |
|---|---|---|---|---|---|
| Estimated Exit Price/Gain on Sale—1 Yr | 1,950,000 | 440,000 | 11.02% | Annualized IRR—1 Yr | 260.29% |
| Estimated Exit Price/Gain on Sale—3 Yr | 2,000,000 | 490,000 | 11.50% | Annualized IRR—3 Yr | 88.84% |
| Estimated Exit Price/Gain on Sale—5 Yr | 2,050,000 | 540,000 | 11.79% | Annualized IRR—5 Yr | 67.42 |

**Table 8.4**  Franklin Apartments Projected Rents

Franklin I

| Apt Type | Number of Units | Per-Unit Data | | | Total Unit Data | | |
|---|---|---|---|---|---|---|---|
| | | Sq Ft | Rent | Rent per Sq Ft | Sq Ft | Rent | Annualized Rent |
| 1-1 | 1 | 336 | $295 | $0.878 | 336 | $  295 | $  3,540 |
| 1-1 | 2 | 368 | 300 | 0.815 | 736 | 600 | 7,200 |
| 1-1 | 1 | 418 | 320 | 0.766 | 418 | 320 | 3,840 |
| 1-1 | 1 | 423 | 325 | 0.768 | 423 | 325 | 3,900 |
| 1-1 | 13 | 447 | 330 | 0.738 | 5,811 | 4,290 | 51,480 |
| 1-1 | 9 | 637 | 365 | 0.573 | 5,733 | 3,285 | 39,420 |
| 1-1 | 1 | 649 | 375 | 0.578 | 649 | 375 | 4,500 |
| 1-1 | 22 | 656 | 375 | 0.572 | 14,432 | 8,250 | 99,000 |
| 2-1 | 4 | 812 | 465 | 0.573 | 3,248 | 1,860 | 22,320 |
| 2-1 | 13 | 894 | 480 | 0.537 | 11,622 | 6,240 | 74,880 |
| 2-1 | 4 | 918 | 490 | 0.534 | 3,672 | 1,960 | 23,520 |
| 2-1 | 1 | 925 | 495 | 0.535 | 925 | 495 | 5,940 |
| 2-1 | 1 | 947 | 495 | 0.523 | 947 | 495 | 5,940 |
| Totals | 73 | | | | 48,952 | $28,790 | $345,480 |
| Averages | | | $394 | $0.588 | 671 | | |

Franklin II

| Apt Type | Number of Units | Per-Unit Data | | | Total Unit Data | | |
|---|---|---|---|---|---|---|---|
| | | Sq Ft | Rent | Rent per Sq Ft | Sq Ft | Rent | Annualized Rent |
| 2-1 | 20 | 750 | $470 | $0.627 | 15,000 | $9,400 | $112,800 |
| 2-1 | 4 | 871 | 495 | 0.568 | 3,484 | 1,980 | 23,760 |
| 5-2.5 | 1 | 3,050 | 895 | 0.293 | 3,050 | 895 | 10,740 |
| Totals | 25 | | | | 21,534 | $12,275 | $147,300 |
| Averages | | | $491 | $0.570 | 861 | | |

Franklin I and II Combined

| | | | | | | | |
|---|---|---|---|---|---|---|---|
| Totals | 98 | | | | 70,486 | $41,065 | $492,780 |
| Averages | | | $419 | $0.583 | 719 | | |

SOURCE: Berges Investment Group, copyright © 1998.

As you will recall, the three basic components that must be considered when defining your objectives are your entry, postentry, and exit strategies. My entry strategy on this property was to identify as many opportunities as possible to create value, adjust the variables in my model, and then determine whether the project would provide a reasonable return on my invested capital. According to the model's output, I could expect a potential gain of $440,000 on my initial investment of $215,000 at an exit price of $1,950,000 while still providing a generous cap rate to the buyer of about 11 percent. The market research I conducted on the 14 surrounding apartment complexes gave me the confidence to move forward with the purchase of this property. The two primary factors that contributed to my decision were the high occupancy rates in the area and the fact that Franklin I was being rented at approximately 10 percent below market rates. I also liked the idea of combining the two properties and operating them as a single entity. The next step was to secure financing in a manner that would require a minimal capital outlay, which in this case turned out to be the 75/10/15 loan previously described.

Immediately after I acquired the property, I began implementing my postentry strategy by making the required capital improvements identified during the analysis phase, enhancing the revenue stream according to the projections outlined in Table 8.4, and finally by applying the cost-savings measures necessary to operate the property more efficiently. The capital improvements shown in Table 8.5 were all accomplished within the first six months. I did experience higher than expected turnover at Franklin II as a result of the submetering process. All but 5 of the original 25 tenants moved within six months. Franklin I, however, continued to remain very stable during this period and was profitable enough to offset losses incurred from the higher turnover. The new tenants moving into Franklin II understood that they would be responsible for their own utilities, so by the eighth to ninth month, both Franklin I and II were stabilized. It was time to begin preparing my exit strategy.

With all capital improvements, revenue enhancements, and cost-savings measures now fully completed, it was time to implement my exit strategy. I knew that by the time I made the property available for sale and put it on the market, I would be well beyond my desired 12-month holding period, the

**Table 8.5** Franklin Apartments Schedule of
Capital Improvements

| Description | Cost |
|---|---|
| A/C & heating | $2,485 |
| Appliances | 1,750 |
| Building repairs | 3,412 |
| Carpet and tile | 3,430 |
| Contract labor | 16,485 |
| Driveways and parking lots (asphalt and striping) | 18,747 |
| Drapes and blinds | 1,036 |
| Electrical (submetering) | 5,250 |
| Painting | 17,330 |
| Roof | 1,500 |
| Signage | 4,954 |
| Miscellaneous | 2,574 |
| Total capital improvements | $78,953 |

minimum required for taking advantage of the lower long-term capital gains tax rate of 20 percent. Franklin I and II, by the way, is the same apartment complex discussed in the previous chapter—the one the broker recommended selling at a price of $1.8 million, claiming I would be lucky to get $1.65 million for it. As you may recall, my own analysis—which suggested an exit price of $2 million to $2.1 million—was ultimately corroborated by two other brokerage firms and an appraiser, and the property eventually sold for a price of $1,995,000.

Take a minute to refer back to the Estimated Exit Price YR 1 line in Exhibit 8.7. My original estimate of $1,950,000 proved to be quite accurate and slightly on the conservative side. You can see firsthand from this example the value of having a powerful and dynamic model, such as the one I developed, to help you with your analysis. By simply adjusting the variables to reflect realistic projections based on your research and analysis, within minutes you can determine the latent potential of any multifamily property *before* you buy it.

In summary, the case studies presented in this chapter illustrate the fundamental precepts of this book. As an investor with capital to employ, you should strike with surgical precision when an opportunity presents itself. I also want to emphasize how important it is to do your homework. Familiarize yourself with every aspect of the area where your acquisition target is located by taking the time to conduct the research necessary to make a sound and prudent business decision.

## CHAPTER 9

*All the strength and force of man comes from his faith in things unseen.*
*He who believes is strong; he who doubts is weak.*
*Strong convictions precede great actions.*
**—JAMES FREEMAN CLARKE**

# Negotiation Strategies and the Due Diligence Process

Chapter 7 describes the financial analysis principles used to value income-producing assets in considerable detail, and Chapter 8 discusses the practical application of those principles, so by now you should have a fairly good understanding of the valuation process used to analyze multifamily properties. Once you have identified a value-play opportunity and have determined through your research and analysis the maximum amount you are willing to pay for a property, the next logical step is to negotiate for the best possible price and terms. Upon reaching an agreement that is acceptable to both parties, you are then ready to implement your due diligence process. This chapter explores the five cardinal rules of artfully and skillfully negotiating the best deal possible, and then examines a step-by-step approach to performing the required due diligence.

# Five Cardinal Rules of Successful Negotiation

Negotiating the purchase price and terms of your acquisition requires a combination of art and skill. As in playing a game of poker, you must be careful not to reveal your own hand, while simultaneously attempting to force the hand of your opponent. The master negotiator will implement every one of the cardinal rules of successful negotiation.

### Five Cardinal Rules of Successful Negotiation

1. Engage a competent broker to act as your intermediary.
2. Justify your offering price armed with the seller's operating statements.
3. Know why the seller is selling.
4. Safeguard yourself with a 30-day "free look."
5. Know when to walk away from a deal.

## Rule 1: Engage a Competent Broker

Hiring a qualified and capable real estate broker to represent you as your fiduciary agent can easily be the difference between making or breaking a deal. Here is why. Sellers tend to have a deep level of emotional attachment to or involvement with their properties. They have likely owned their properties for a number of years and have personally devoted a great deal of time and energy to them. They have worked hard to maintain their apartment buildings and likely have considerable resources invested in them. While the level of emotional attachment diminishes among more sophisticated investors who own large portfolios of multifamily properties, you should still consider using a competent broker to act as your intermediary. As a prospective buyer, you can say things to the broker that you would never say to the seller, and the seller can say things to the broker that the seller should never say to the buyer. The broker's role is to diffuse the emotional aspects of negotiating by acting as an intermediary, or a go-between, for the buyer and the seller. A seller who is offering a 200-unit apartment complex for sale at $5 million, for example, may take offense to a buyer offering a lowball offer of only $3.5 million. The seller may in fact choose to not even respond to the offer because of the insult, "feeling" that the property is worth much more than the $3.5 million offered. If the seller had been represented by a broker, however, the broker would either encourage the buyer to offer more, knowing that the seller's price point was higher, or encourage the seller to counter with an offer closer to the original asking price. Without the broker in place, the lowball offer would likely have no chance at all of going anywhere with the seller. The broker has a strong incentive to keep the deal going—the commission. No deal, no commission.

On several occasions, I have seen buyers and sellers attempt to circumvent a broker who did not have an exclusive listing on an apartment complex, thinking they could save the commission. More often than not, the negotiations fell apart because the two parties were unable to reach an agreement. Consider the seller who, for example, stands to gain $500,000 from a sale, less a $50,000 commission if a broker is involved. Trying to save the $50,000 by dealing directly with the buyer may very well end up costing the seller the entire $500,000 gain. Yes, eventually the seller will be able to sell, but this opportunity to do so is lost, and it may be another three months, or six months, or even a year before he or she is able to sell. Meanwhile, a seller using a broker could have taken a net gain of $450,000 and been on to the next value-play opportunity. So you see, while the possibility is there to save the broker's commission, it is a potentially risky strategy and could ultimately derail the transaction.

I do not want to imply that you should never talk directly to the seller, because there are times when it is appropriate to do so. The negotiation phase just is not one of them. If, for example, you are gathering general information about the property that is not readily available in the documentation already provided, sometimes it is better to take the broker out of the communication loop and ask the seller directly. Preliminary discussions with the seller can also provide you with greater insight into his or her motive for selling. Subtle comments made by the seller that would probably not be picked up by the broker can be used to your advantage when it does become time to enter the negotiation phase. These comments can offer clues as to the seller's underlying motive for selling, regardless of the reason stated by the broker. The seller will have in essence revealed his or her hand, and it will be time for you to call the bluff.

## Rule 2: Justify Your Offering Price

By the time you are ready to make an offer, you should have reviewed the seller's financial statements in great detail. At a minimum, you should have reviewed a recent income statement for the trailing 12 months and the last 3 months' worth of rent rolls. If you have not yet examined these crucial operating statements, you are not ready to make an offer. You are setting yourself up for failure if you do. On the other hand, assuming you have studied the requisite financial statements, you will have a very good idea of the true value of the property under consideration. The value you have derived is the basis for your offering price.

If a seller is asking, for example, $1 million for the apartments, and your analysis indicates a value of only $800,000, you should use that information to your advantage by explaining to the broker exactly why the subject property is worth that amount and no more. Walk the broker through your analysis, and help the broker understand why you believe the value is only $800,000, so the broker, in turn, can use your rationale to explain it to the seller. Because cap rates vary within a range and are somewhat subjective, I recommend starting below your target price of $800,000. If in this example, the net operating income (NOI) is $80,000 and the market comps suggest a cap rate of 10.00 percent, then

$$\text{Cap rate} = \frac{\text{NOI}}{\text{price}}$$

$$\text{Price} = \frac{\text{NOI}}{\text{cap rate}} = \frac{\$80,000}{0.10} = \$800,000$$

If your target price is $800,000 and that is the first offer you make, guess what? You are not going to get the deal for $800,000. You must be prepared to start lower so that you end up achieving your true objective. As you walk the broker through your analysis, simply state that you believe the property falls into the 10 to 11 cap-rate range, and that at a cap rate of 10.5, the property is worth only $761,905; therefore, you want to start the bidding at $760,000.

$$\text{Price} = \frac{\text{NOI}}{\text{cap rate}} = \frac{\$80,000}{0.1050} = \$761,905$$

Okay, I am going to repeat it one more time: *You should be willing to pay a price based only on how the property is operating today, not based on how the broker or seller tells you it can potentially operate.* Repetition is the key here. I hope that by repeating this one point, you will not get caught in the trap of overpaying for an apartment complex. If the broker is the seller's agent, the broker is going to tell you every reason he or she can think of as to why the apartments are worth the $1 million the seller is asking. You politely but firmly explain to the broker that if the property were truly worth the full asking price, then it should be generating a minimum of $100,000 of net operating income today—not tomorrow, not a year from now, but *today*. If all of the potential the broker claims to be in the property truly exists, then why has the current owner not achieved that level of performance yet? Why is the property generating only $80,000 of NOI instead of $100,000? These are the types of arguments to make to support your position. The more knowledgeable brokers who correctly comprehend value will better understand your position and tend to agree with you, while those brokers with limited experience may not. In the case of the latter, it will be up to you to educate them.

### Rule 3: Know Why the Seller Is Selling

As a prospective buyer, it is important for you to know why the seller is disposing of the property. Knowing the underlying reasons for the sale can potentially give you the upper hand at the negotiating table. Is the seller burned out and just trying to get rid of the apartments (and the headaches of operating them), or is the seller just testing the waters to determine what price the market will bear? In other words, you want to know whether your seller is *motivated,* and if so, to what degree. The more motivated the seller, the more likely the seller is to be flexible on both price and terms. Reasons for selling typically fall into one or more of the following six categories:

**Six Reasons Sellers Sell Their Property**

1. Need proceeds from sale for another investment opportunity.
2. Burned out due to poor management.
3. Changes in economic conditions.
4. Tax considerations.
5. Life-changing event.
6. Retirement.

One of the most compelling reasons for a seller to divest property is that the seller is a value player like yourself and is ready to take the gain on sale and move on to the next deal. The degree of motivation will vary depending on factors such as how much value was created and the timing for entry into the next investment. If, for example, the seller created $600,000 in value on a $3-million apartment complex over a 12-month period, the seller may in fact be willing to accept $2.85 million for the deal, thinking that a bird in the hand is worth two in the bush. In other words, instead of holding out for the full $600,000 in profits—which could take as long as another six months to a year—the seller can go ahead and accept the lower price, lock in a gain of $450,000, and be ready to move on to the next deal. You may be inclined to think that $150,000 is a lot to leave on the table, and, granted, it is, but a value player has a different mindset. The value player is thinking about the next deal and the $500,000 he or she will make on it.

Poor management is another primary reason sellers look to dispose of their apartments. The degree of motivation will correlate directly with the seller's degree of distress. This is where subtle clues can be detected by direct communication with the seller. A meeting with both the broker and the seller at the property site for a general tour can be very revealing to the astute investor who is attuned to the seller's needs. Does the seller seem anxious, frazzled, or short with the staff? Indications of poor management will also show up in the financial statements. For example, the vacancy rate may be high relative to the area as a whole; the unit turnover ratio may be high; and make-ready costs may be higher than normal. If the seller is suffering from burnout related to managing the property, the seller will most likely be highly motivated, and a highly motivated seller is a flexible seller.

Changes in macroeconomic conditions are changes that occur outside of and unrelated to a specific property, but which may affect the property either positively or negatively. A shift in demographics, crime, or employment trends, for example, are all changes over which the owner has no direct control, but may affect the operations of the property anyway. The apartment owner may have been doing an excellent job over the years of keeping up the property and managing it, but something like an increase in crime or job layoffs will have a direct adverse impact on the property's level of profitability. As a buyer, you will want to tune in to and absorb as much information as possible about these conditions, because as the new owner, you, too, will have very little control over them.

Another primary reason for selling an apartment building is the seller's tax considerations. If the seller is involved in an exchange, then the seller is limited by law to a fixed number of days to identify another property and subsequently close on it. These strict time constraints can impact the seller on both ends of this transaction—the divestment of the current property and the acquisition of the new one. If the seller has not identified a new property to purchase yet, the seller may not be that motivated, and may, in fact, stall the sale.

Life-changing events can radically and immediately alter a seller's position. These events include such things as divorce, illness in the family, or the death of a loved one. If something were to happen to one spouse—being seriously injured in a car wreck, for example—the other spouse may be forced to sell if he or she has had little involvement in operating the property.

In *Rich Dad Secrets to Money, Business, and Investing* (Niles, IL: Nightingale-Conant, 1998), Robert Kiyosaki tells the story of an 18-unit apartment building he was negotiating for. A group of six partners, who were all elderly, put their building up for sale at a price of $1.2 million. Kiyosaki made an offer of $1.1 million, which was rejected by the partners.

Three months later, the apartments were still available for sale, and Kiyosaki again made an offer of $1.1 million, which was again rejected.

Another three months passed and the property was still available, so Kiyosaki decided to call a meeting with the partners and their broker. As they all sat down at the negotiating table, he noticed one of the partners was missing. Instead of six partners, there were only five.

Kiyosaki asked about the missing partner's whereabouts. The reaction from the partners who were present was one of nervousness, clearing of throats, and evasive eye contact. Because they refused to discuss the missing partner, Kiyosaki got up from the table and promptly excused himself. He said that as he did so, he could almost feel a sense of despair and disappointment from those partners who were present.

A phone call to the broker confirmed his suspicions—something had happened to the missing partner. He had had a stroke and was hospitalized.

Kiyosaki now knew the remaining five partners no longer had the luxury of holding out for their full asking price of $1.2 million. If they did so, they ran the risk of the sixth partner dying and the property ending up in probate court. He immediately made an offer of $500,000, and ultimately settled at a price of $695,000. In retrospect, it appears the sellers should have taken Kiyosaki's initial offer of $1.1 million, but a life-changing event forced them to settle for much less than that.

Finally, another reason for selling is retirement. At some time in everyone's life, they reach a point at which they are ready to retire. I shared an example earlier of a 25-unit building I bought. The couple had owned the apartment complex for 25 years and had just made their last mortgage payment. They were both of retirement age, and selling the apartments would give them a sizable lump sum of cash on which to retire.

## Rule 4: Safeguard Yourself with a 30-Day "Free Look"

One key point you should include in your negotiating technique is to protect yourself by providing an open-ended out for any reason whatsoever within the first 30 days of signing the contract. This initial period, also known as a "free look" or feasibility period, gives you the right to walk away from the deal for any reason at all, or for no reason at all. Once you are under contract, the 30-day period is the time for you to complete all phases of your due diligence. Any number of factors could arise that might cause you to change your mind. You might find excessive deferred mainte- nance, or discover after looking through the records that the turnover ratio is higher than you initially thought, or you might just simply not like the flowers planted outside the building. Whatever the reason, be sure to safe- guard yourself with a free-look period. The seller may not always give you a full 30 days, but you should have a minimum of 15 days to perform your due diligence.

## Rule 5: Know When to Walk

If you cannot convince the seller and broker of the validity of your offering price (see Rule 2), then it is time for you to move on to the next opportunity. An exception you may consider, however, is when the seller is willing to offer you some compensating incentive, such as more favorable terms. For example, if the seller offers to carry back a second mortgage for 10 percent of the purchase price, enabling you to get in with less money down, then you will want to reconsider the deal. Simply change the variables in the model you use for your analysis from 20 percent down to 10 percent down, adjust the offering price to what the seller is requiring, and examine the effect on your return on investment (ROI). On a $1-million apartment complex, your cash investment is reduced from $200,000 to only $100,000. This one change in your model is likely to have a significant effect on your returns. As a value player, to create enough value to double your money in this example, you need to create only an additional $100,000 of value, or 10 percent of the deal value. Assuming a cap rate of 10 percent, we know that NOI is $100,000. To create an additional $100,000 of value, NOI must be increased to $110,000. This could be done with a 5 percent increase in rents and a 5 percent decrease in expenses, or any combination thereof.

$$Price \times cap\ rate = NOI$$
$$\$1,000,000 \times 0.10 = \$100,000$$
$$\$1,100,000 \times 0.10 = \$110,000$$
$$\$1,100,000 - \$1,000,000 = \$100,000\ of\ value\ created$$

Now, back to Rule 5. The bottom line is, do not be afraid to walk away from a deal if it does not make sound financial sense for your investment capital. Earlier, in Chapter 8, I used the example of a nice 52-unit value-play opportunity that presented some unique twists in the way the financing for the acquisition could be structured. The asking price, at $1.15 million, was very reasonable. I made an offer of $1.1 million with the standard 30-day feasibility period and 0.5 percent of the purchase price as earnest money, matched with another 0.5 percent after the 30-day period when the earnest money *goes hard,* or becomes nonrefundable, and an additional 60 days to close. These terms are not at all out of the ordinary, and in fact would be considered reasonable and customary. As it turns out, the seller in this case had an abrasive personality, was extremely arrogant, and had adopted a "my way or the highway" attitude. Because the seller demanded 5 percent down up front as earnest money with no feasibility period and a closing in 30 days, I took the highway. No matter how promising a potential deal appears, I am not about to assume the risk for an investment on which I have not had the opportunity to perform due diligence. In this case, if the deal went south, I would have been out over $50,000 in earnest money.

# The Due Diligence Process

Your preliminary analysis brought you to the negotiation phase and you have successfully reached an agreement. Now it is time to thoroughly research and analyze virtually every aspect of the property in question through the process known as *due diligence.* The due diligence process should include an exhaustive review of the apartment's physical condition and a review of the seller's records and documentation. It should also take into consideration various zoning and environmental ordinances, as well as any outstanding legal issues. Finally, preliminary market studies should now be supported with solid documentation.

## Physical Inspection

As a value player, your inspection of the physical condition of the property should include an examination of every unit, in addition to the general premises. You want to note items that could materially impact your decision to move forward with the purchase. There will always be minor repairs, messy apartments that need painting, and the like. These types of conditions are largely cosmetic and have no material impact. Your focus should be on the larger issues that will require a major injection of capital, such as the replacement of a roof, or foundation problems, or a parking lot that needs resurfacing. Air-conditioning and heating equipment should also be closely inspected. Note as a percentage how many of the air-conditioning units look like the original equipment, and how many of them have been replaced within the last five years or so. Take a look at Exhibit 9.1, a physical inspection checklist for the exterior. This will provide a good guideline as you conduct your own inspections.

Now take a look at Exhibit 9.2, a physical inspection checklist for the interior. You should use a checklist similar to this one in inspecting every unit. One final note on the physical inspection—you may want to hire a professional who will do an independent exhaustive inspection. If an engineering report is required by your lender, however, this report should be more than sufficient to tell you everything you need to know regarding the condition of the property, so hiring a professional inspector would only be redundant. I highly recommend you do your own inspection even if you decide to pay a

**Exhibit 9.1**    Exterior Physical Inspection Checklist.

| Physical Inspection Checklist—Exterior | |
| --- | --- |
| General Information | |
| Property name | |
| Number of units | |
| Number of buildings | |
| Total square footage | |
| Date of inspection | |

| Description | Comments |
| --- | --- |
| Drives | |
| Boiler equipment | |
| Central cooling and heating | |
| Common area flooring | |
| Common area grounds | |
| General neighborhood area | |
| Hallways | |
| Individual air-conditioners | |
| Individual furnaces | |
| Landscaping | |
| Laundry facility | |
| Lawns | |
| Lighting | |
| Mailboxes | |
| Office | |
| Parking lots | |
| Pool equipment | |
| Roofs | |
| Sidewalks | |
| Signage | |
| Swimming pools | |
| Trees | |
| Washers and dryers | |

**Exhibit 9.2**    Interior Physical Inspection Checklist.

| Physical Inspection Checklist—Interior |
| --- |
| General Information |
| Property name |
| Number of units |
| Number of buildings |
| Total square footage |
| Date of inspection |

*(continued)*

**Exhibit 9.2**  *(Continued)*

| Description | Comments |
|---|---|
| Living room | |
|    Paint | |
|    Flooring | |
|    Fixtures | |
|    Other | |
| Dining room | |
|    Paint | |
|    Flooring | |
|    Fixtures | |
|    Other | |
| Kitchen | |
|    Oven/stove | |
|    Microwave | |
|    Refrigerator | |
|    Cabinets | |
|    Flooring | |
|    Fixtures | |
|    Other | |
| Bedroom 1 | |
|    Paint | |
|    Flooring | |
|    Fixtures | |
|    Other | |
| Bedroom 2 | |
|    Paint | |
|    Flooring | |
|    Fixtures | |
|    Other | |
| Bedroom 3 | |
|    Paint | |
|    Flooring | |
|    Fixtures | |
|    Other | |
| Bathroom 1 | |
|    Tubs/sinks/commodes | |
|    Paint | |
|    Flooring | |
|    Fixtures | |
|    Other | |
| Bathroom 2 | |
|    Tubs/sinks/commodes | |
|    Paint | |
|    Flooring | |
|    Fixtures | |
|    Other | |

professional. Your own eyes and ears act as receptors and can tell you things about a property no inspector could ever tell you.

## Records and Documentation

Your due diligence should also include a thorough review of financial statements and their supporting documentation, lease agreements, maintenance contracts, zoning ordinances, environmental issues, and any pending litigation. The preliminary market research you conducted prior to entering into an agreement should now be supported with solid documentation. Most apartment owners will have much of this information available to you on-site. You should be able to meet with the apartment manager and owner and have ready access to all of the lease agreements, tax statements, utility records, tenant deposits, collection information, and the like. Now take a few minutes to review the due diligence checklist presented in Exhibit 9.3.

**Exhibit 9.3**   Due Diligence Checklist.

| Due Diligence Checklist | |
| --- | --- |
| General Information | |
| Property name | |
| Number of units | |
| Number of buildings | |
| Total square footage | |
| Date of inspection | |

| Description | Comments |
| --- | --- |
| Financial statements | |
|   Income statement | |
|   Balance statement | |
|   Rent roll | |
| Income statement—revenues | |
|   Scheduled income | |
|   Utility income | |
|   Other income | |

*(continued)*

**Exhibit 9.3**  *(Continued)*

| Description | Comments |
| --- | --- |
| Income statement—expenses | |
| General & Administrative | |
| Repairs & Maintenance | |
| Salaries & Payroll | |
| Utilities | |
| Taxes | |
| Insurance | |
| Rent roll | |
| Number of months | |
| Vacancy rate | |
| Turnover ratio | |
| Lease agreements | |
| Balance statement—assets | |
| Supplies | |
| Prepaid items | |
| Utility deposits | |
| Assessed land value | |
| Personal property list | |
| Balance statement—liabilities | |
| Accounts payable | |
| Notes payable | |
| Mortgages payable | |
| Taxes payable | |
| Security deposits | |
| Other | |
| Market analysis | |
| Competitor analysis | |
| Demographics study | |
| Environmental compliance | |
| Pending litigation | |
| Zoning ordinances | |
| Compliance with local codes | |

In summary, obtaining the best possible price and terms when acquiring an apartment building requires a combination of art and skill. As a master negotiator, you will take care to exercise each one of the five cardinal rules to successful negotiations. Upon reaching an agreement with the seller, you will then be ready to implement the requisite due diligence steps.

## CHAPTER 10

*The credit belongs to those people who are actually in the arena . . . who know the great enthusiasms, the great devotions to a worthy cause; who at best, know the triumph of high achievement; and who, at worst, fail while daring greatly . . . so that their place shall never be with those cold and timid souls who know neither victory nor defeat.*
**—THEODORE ROOSEVELT**

# Financing Your Acquisition

Obtaining the proper financing for your acquisition is a crucial step that must be implemented with exactness in order to ensure your success as a multifamily real estate investor. As a value player strategist, your needs are very different from those of the investor who buys and holds; nevertheless, you must take care to educate yourself with respect to the long-term investor's needs, because that is precisely whom you will be selling your property to. This chapter examines the many alternatives available and carefully analyzes each one of them. Some of the terminology may be new and unfamiliar to less experienced investors. Take time to fully acquaint yourself with the various characteristics of each of these financing mechanisms. The better you understand the array of options available, the greater will be your success.

# Traditional Financing Alternatives

Apartment financing is a very specialized and multifaceted discipline that requires intimate familiarity with the process. You need to know and understand the advantages and disadvantages of each type of financing arrangement so that you can make a sound investment decision that will best meet your objectives. I hope I have convinced you by now that the value-play methodology is where the most money is to be made. As a value player, your focus is short term. This means you have to be very careful about the type of financing you put in place. You cannot afford to make the mistake of procuring a long-term loan, which may tie up the property for 10 years and potentially lock out prospective buyers for as many years. You must take care to examine all aspects of the loan arrangements you are considering. This includes knowing the effect each component of the financing instrument has on your entry, postentry, and exit strategy. For example, you should know the implications of the type of financing, the term, the interest rate, points paid at closing, requisite third-party reports, assumability of the loan, recourse provisions, lockout periods, and, finally, prepayment penalties that may be imposed. To become a master of the value-play strategy, you must also become a master of the financing alternatives.

## Conventional Bank, Wall Street Conduit, and Specialty Programs

While a number of borrowing alternatives are available to investors for financing apartment deals, they can generally be classified as conventional bank loans, conduit loans, or specialty loans. Each type of loan has its advantages and disadvantages, and each specific loan will vary among lenders. The type of financing you select will be determined by your specific needs for the property under contract.

*Conventional bank financing* is typically available through smaller local banks. Such banks may operate with just a single branch and $25 million in total assets, or they may be slightly larger, with as many as 5 to 10 branches and $250 million in total assets. One advantage of utilizing local banks is that they can often offer a greater degree of flexibility. For example, they may provide money for capital improvements, or tailor your loan to best fit your needs, such as by providing a release clause for a condominium conversion project. Smaller banks are also likely to be much more familiar with the local area and would therefore have a greater degree of confidence in the specific market than a larger regional or national lender would. Personal relationships with your local banker are more easily established, as well. You can go into the bank, introduce yourself, and sit down and talk directly with the lender. This gives you the opportunity to sell yourself and your project. Once a relationship has been established and the banker gets to know you and is comfortable with you, future loan requests will be much easier and likely require less documentation, possibly as little as updating your personal financial statement.

However, one disadvantage of using smaller banks is their limitations on the size of loans to any one borrower. If you need to borrow $2.5 million from a bank with only $25 million in total assets, your chances of getting the loan are not good. In this case, a loan of $2.5 million represents 10 percent of the bank's assets. If the loan went into default, the bank would be in serious trouble. Larger lenders with billions of dollars in assets can much more easily facilitate this type of loan.

The biggest disadvantage to using your local lender is pricing. You may find a bank that will charge only the prime lending rate, but in my experience, most banks charge a minimum of prime plus 1 and may charge as much as prime plus 3. This means, for example, that if the lender is charging you prime plus 2.75 and the prime rate is 8.00 percent, your interest rate will be 10.75 percent. Depending on the size of your loan, the higher rate will adversely impact your cash flow by hundreds or even thousands of dollars. If you have used a lower rate of 8.00 percent in your initial analysis and found the related returns to be acceptable, you might very well discover that at the higher rate, the deal no longer makes sense. Good thing you have remembered the five cardinal rules of negotiating and have a 30-day feasibility period built into your contract. If the numbers do not make sense at the higher rate, you may need to exercise your option to terminate the contract.

*Conduit loans* are typically originated by huge Wall Street firms, which usually have billions of dollars in total assets. I should mention that having an office on Wall Street is certainly not a requirement, but many of these firms do. Conduit lenders represent pools of institutional investors such as insurance companies with large amounts of capital to invest, and they are often well connected with some of the largest companies in the world.

Conduit financing differs from conventional bank loans in several ways. First, conduit loans are pooled together when a certain dollar amount is reached, say $500 million. They are then *securitized* or packaged together and sold to investors who seek to maintain a specific yield or return on their capital. Because the loans are pooled together, it is very difficult to pay off a single loan out of the pool prior to the end of the term, and, in many cases, the borrower is *locked out* or prohibited from prepaying the loan. Conventional bank loans, on the other hand, are not securitized but are instead treated as individual loans and maintained and serviced directly by the issuing bank.

Another key difference is that unlike conventional bank loans, which are priced off of the prime lending rate, conduit loans are generally priced off of an index, such as Treasury notes, which corresponds to the term of the loan. A loan with a 10-year term, for example, may use the 10-year Treasury bill as its benchmark. A spread is then factored into the rate by adding the spread to the 10-year Treasury bill. Spreads are stated in *basis points,* so a spread of 215 basis points is equivalent to 2.15 percent. If the 10-year treasury is currently priced at 5.30 and the spread is 215 basis points (or *bips,* as lenders like to call them), the interest rate applied to the loan would be 7.45 percent.

Conduit loans also differ from conventional bank loans in the degree of personal liability associated with each type. With conduit loans, there is usually no personal liability, while there is almost always full personal liability with conventional bank financing.

*Specialty apartment lending programs* are designed specifically with the small multifamily property investor in mind. They are the result of listening to feedback from investors such as yourself, and they have been streamlined and tailored especially for borrowers in the apartment business. In addition, because many lenders focus on the larger-sized loans, these programs were devised to serve a once overlooked segment of the apartment lending business. Interest rates for this type of loan are usually very competitive, typically below prime. Loan amounts vary according to the underwriting guidelines established by each lender, but generally range from approximately $100,000 to $2 million. A variety of terms are offered, including 1, 3, 5, 7, and 10 years. Amortization periods are commonly 20 or 25 years, with some lenders offering 30-year periods. Other advantages of this type of loan include minimal lender fees and often less stringent third-party report requirements. A primary disadvantage of the specialty apartment lending programs is that the maximum loan amount is usually around $2 million. Because this type of loan was designed with the smaller investor in mind, the maximum loan amounts are capped at lower levels.

## Recourse versus Nonrecourse Loans

*Recourse* and *nonrecourse* are terms used by investors and lenders to refer to the degree of personal liability attached to a given loan. For example, if you apply for a recourse loan, this means you are willing to accept personal liability for repayment in the event of default. The bank has full recourse against you and can attempt to force you to repay any loss incurred as a result of the default. The bank's redress is not limited to the collateral used to secure the loan; in addition, it can look to your own personal assets to offset any deficiencies. Do not let this frighten you. Think about any personal loan you already have—including your mortgage, car loan, or other notes—and you will have a good idea of what a recourse loan is. You have agreed to accept personal liability for all these types of loans. For many first-time multifamily property owners, especially on smaller loans, the bank or lender will expect to have full recourse against the borrower.

A nonrecourse loan is just the opposite of a recourse loan. There is no personal liability attached to the loan. In other words, if you default on the note, the lender's only redress is to take the property back. You, as the borrower, can essentially walk away from the deal, and your loss will be limited to the equity you have in it. So if you put down 20 percent on a $1-million apartment building, your loss is limited to your $200,000 down payment plus any additional funds you may have invested for capital improvements. As the borrower, you are personally indemnified from any additional liability, while the lender is precluded from seeking restitution through your personal assets. Most conventional bank loans are full-recourse loans, while most conduit loans are nonrecourse loans. Specialty programs designed for smaller-sized loans are typically full recourse, but there are some lenders who offer varying degrees of nonrecourse loans under this type of program.

## Loan Term

The *term* of a loan refers to its duration, or life. A loan with a five-year term, for example, must be renewed or paid in full at the end of the five-year period. As a value-play investor, your focus is on the short term; therefore, you must take the necessary precautions to ensure that the type of financing you secure coincides with your exit strategy. Longer-term loans, such as 5, 7, or 10 years, may not be appropriate for a value-play opportunity for reasons related to prepayment and transferability of the loan. The shorter-term loans offered, such as 1 and 3 years, work to your advantage by providing you with the flexibility needed to facilitate your exit strategy. Don't lock yourself into a loan that will create problems for you if you intend to sell the property in one to two years. Let the individual you sell to, who will most likely be someone who has adapted a buy-and-hold methodology, obtain the long-term loan.

## Amortization Period

While the term of a loan refers to its duration, the *amortization period* refers to the length of time used to calculate loan payments. The shorter the amortization period, the higher the payment; conversely, the longer the amortization period, the lower the payment. Take a look at this simple example:

Loan amount = present value = PV = $500,000
Interest rate – $i$ – 8 percent
Amortization period = $n$ = 240 months;
    payment = pmt = $4,182
Amortization period = $n$ = 360 months;
    payment = pmt = $3,669

In this example, the difference between a 20-year loan period and a 30-year loan period is $513 per month. Cash flow is the name of the game in this business. You should do everything possible to minimize your monthly cash outflows. Who really cares if it takes an extra 10 years to pay off the loan? As a value player, you are not concerned with what happens in 20 or 30 years anyway. All you care about is the immediate future. I have worked with a number of clients whose intentions were to buy an apartment building and hold it for the long term, however, who preferred the shorter amortization periods. Even then, I recommend building flexibility into the loan by using the longer amortization period. If you want to pay the loan off over a shorter period of time, you have the *option* of paying a little extra each month, but you are not required to do so.

## Interest Rates

Interest rates vary widely among lenders. For conventional financing, local banks tend to be the highest, usually charging anywhere from prime plus 1 to prime plus 3. Depending on the nature of your transaction, this may end up being the most appropriate financing alternative even though the loan costs more. Conduit loans are normally priced off an index such as Treasury bills and are usually more competitive than conventional bank loans. Specialty apartment lending programs also offer competitive rates and are usually priced below prime.

## Loan Fees

Among the biggest expenses related to funding your project are the loan fees assessed. These include origination fees and mortgage broker fees. Lenders' origination fees are usually equivalent to 1 point, or 1 percent, of the total amount of the loan. On a $1-million loan, the fee would be $10,000. Mortgage brokers typically charge between 1 and 2 percent of the loan amount, depending on the size of the loan. On a smaller loan, say $500,000, mortgage brokers may charge as much as 2 percent, while on larger loans, fees of 1 percent are common. When combined, these fees can add up. For example, on a $1-million loan, a 1 percent origination fee plus a 1 percent mortgage brokerage fee totals $20,000. While these fees are sometimes negotiable, you still need to be prepared for these added expenses when undertaking your acquisition.

## Third-Party Reports

Lenders often require third-party reports, which may include an appraisal, an environmental report, an engineering inspection, and a survey. While local banks, conduit lenders, and specialty lenders all require an appraisal and a survey of the property, they may or may not require environmental and engineering reports.

Conduit lenders are usually the most stringent with their requirements. Individual loans must conform to uniform standards before they can be pooled together, securitized, and sold to investors.

Conventional financing can often be obtained with just an appraisal and a survey. An environmental inspection is sometimes required, while an engineering report usually is not.

Specialty lenders fall somewhere in between conventional banks and conduit lenders. They typically require an appraisal, survey, and environmental report, but not a full engineering report. They do, however, require a limited physical inspection, which is not nearly as exhaustive as an engineering report.

You should be aware that environmental inspections may encompass far more than you might expect. Believe it or not, while the actual property being inspected may be completely free from any underground contaminants or physical problems such as asbestos, a convenience store with a gas station across the street may derail your deal. Some lenders, especially conduit lenders, are very particular about anything that may pose some unforeseen threat or create a potential liability, such as seepage from an underground fuel storage tank located at a neighboring property.

Finally, third-party report fee expenses can range anywhere from $2,500 to $25,000, depending on the size of the apartment building you are buying and the particular lender requirements.

## Assumption of Loan

The assumability of loans varies widely among lenders. As a value player, you may or may not be concerned with this feature of your loan. If your intentions are to turn the property within 12 to 18 months, you will most likely seek financing with a shorter term that meets your needs, not your prospective buyer's needs. When you prepare to implement your exit strategy, the new buyer can obtain his or her own financing, which will be in the new buyer's best interest anyway, because the required down payment will be less. For instance, assume you purchase a property for $1 million and subsequently create $200,000 in value. Twelve months later you decide to resell the apartments at the new price of $1.2 million. Now take a look at the following example:

| | |
|---|---|
| Your original purchase price | $1,000,000 |
| Down payment at 20% | 200,000 |
| Amount financed | $ 800,000 |

*Scenario 1*

| | |
|---|---|
| Value created by you | $ 200,000 |
| New sales price to buyer | 1,200,000 |
| Buyer assumes original loan | 800,000 |
| Required down payment | $ 400,000 |

*Scenario 2*

| | |
|---|---|
| Value created by you | $ 200,000 |
| New sales price to buyer | 1,200,000 |
| Obtains new loan at 80% LTV | 960,000 |
| Required down payment at 20% | $ 240,000 |

Under Scenario 1, if the new buyer decides to assume your original loan, he or she will assume the existing loan balance of approximately $800,000 (actually less, because the principal will have been paid down somewhat) and then be required to make up the difference of $400,000 out of pocket. Under Scenario 2, the borrower only has to come up with $240,000, which is $160,000 less than Scenario 1. We know that investors are seeking to maximize their ROI, so in most cases, they will choose Scenario 2.

## Lockout Periods

The *lockout period* does exactly as its name suggests: it locks you out of prepaying a loan for a given period of time. Lockout periods primarily apply to conduit type financing. Because individual loans are pooled together and sold to investors as a package, it would be extremely difficult to break up the securitized instrument by prepaying one loan out of the pool. The investors who purchase these types of securities are guaranteed a specific return or yield for a minimum period of time; therefore, borrowers of conduit loans are precluded, or locked out, from prepaying their loans. On a loan with a 10-year term, the lockout period could be as short as 1 year, or as long as 9.5 years. Before obtaining a loan, I strongly recommend that you be aware of any lockout provisions in your loan agreement. Using the previous example, if you bought a property for $1 million and placed a conduit loan with a lockout provision on it, you would have no choice but to sell to a new buyer as described under Scenario 1. This would limit your ability to divest the property and take your gain, because even though the loan had an assumption feature, the new buyer would be forced to come up with an additional $160,000. A prudent investor will use $400,000 to buy a $2-million apartment building, not a $1.2-million apartment building. In summary, my advice is to simply be very careful about lockout provisions and how they affect the marketability of your property.

## Prepayment Penalties

Most lenders impose penalties for prepaying a loan before the expiration of its term. For instance, if you obtained a loan with a three-year term, but decided to sell your property after just 12 months, the lender would most likely assess a fee, or penalty, for prepaying the loan. Prepayment penalty fees are structured in numerous ways and can sometimes be substantial. A loan with a five-year term, for example, may have a declining prepayment penalty fee structure, as follows:

| Payoff in Year | Prepayment Penalty |
| --- | --- |
| 1 | 5% |
| 2 | 4% |
| 3 | 3% |
| 4 | 2% |
| 5 | 1% |

If your intentions are to acquire an apartment building, create value, and turn around and sell it within 12 to 18 months, you will need to take the prepayment penalty structure of the loan into consideration. It is best to minimize your exposure by procuring a loan with a shorter term, such as a one-year or three-year term.

# Secondary Financing Alternatives

While traditional financing sources primarily rely on debt in the form of loans, secondary financing alternatives include both debt and equity financing. In fact, apartment owners often use a combination of traditional sources with secondary alternatives to achieve a blended financing package. Secondary alternatives include either debt or equity financing from sellers through an owner-financing arrangement, equity financing from institutional investors, and debt or equity funding from partners.

## Owner Financing

Sellers of multifamily properties will often consider debt and equity arrangements with prospective buyers. A common form of debt financing is for the seller to carry back a second lien for 5 to 10 percent of the total sales price. Here is how it works: in a 75/10/15 program, which is allowed by many lenders, 75 percent of the purchase price comes in the form of debt from the lender, who holds a first-lien position secured by the property; 10 percent of the purchase price comes in the form of debt from the seller, who holds a second-lien position that may be secured by the property or any other collateral; and the remaining 15 percent of the purchase price is provided by the buyer, in the form of equity. Sellers are often amenable to carrying back small portions of the total sales price because they do not always need 100 percent of the cash provided by an outright sale. Moreover, if the seller believes that the buyer has a solid interest and is willing to accept the offering price, the seller becomes motivated to work with the buyer to facilitate the transaction. Under the 75/10/15 program on a transaction valued at $2.5 million, a lender would furnish debt financing of $1,875,000, the seller would take a second lien for $250,000, and the buyer would be required to provide the remaining balance of $375,000. This is truly a win-win-win situation for all three parties. The lender has a fairly secure loan with only a 75 percent loan-to-value ratio, rather than the more common 80 percent; the seller has divested the property but retains a small interest in it; and the buyer is able to achieve a greater degree of leverage and therefore earn a higher rate of return on the invested capital.

Although second-lien positions are the most common form of owner-financing arrangements, owners or sellers are not limited to just debt financing. They may be open to an equity agreement wherein they retain a small portion of ownership interest. Instead of being required to make monthly payments to the seller, the buyer and seller would now share in the profits of the newly formed entity. Depending on the specifics of the agreement, the original seller may also be entitled to a share of any capital gains when the property is sold again.

Another form of owner financing is known as a *wraparound mortgage*. Under this arrangement, the seller retains title and continues to make mortgage payments to the lender, while the new owner makes mortgage payments directly to the seller. Wraparound mortgages are more common on smaller multifamily properties such as duplexes and fourplexes than on their larger counterparts. Be careful of any due-on-sale clauses in the deed of trust, which may expressly prohibit this type of financing arrangement. Lenders typically are not too fond of the transfer of ownership interests without their knowledge.

## Equity Financing

Although not as common as lenders who provide financing in the form of loans, or debt, a number of institutional investors exist who are willing to part with their capital in the form of equity. In other words, instead of loaning money to buyers, equity investors form a partnership agreement with them. This allows smaller multifamily property buyers to leverage themselves into larger properties. The investors funding the equity portion of the financing usually require a minimum return on their investment and will expect to share in any gain on sale, as well. It should be noted, however, that most of these types of investors are looking to employ large pools of capital, so the minimum purchase price of an apartment building is often $5 million or more.

## Partnerships

Using the resources of a partner can be an excellent form of secondary financing. The type of partner referred to in this subsection is a friend, family member, or business acquaintance, not the large institutional investor described in the Equity Financing subsection.

Partnerships can be structured in any number of ways. For instance, capital injections by partners can take the form of debt or equity; partners can play an active or passive role; and terms for the repayment provisions can be defined in various creative ways. If your partner agrees to invest in your project using equity, then your partner will share the risk with you. If you lose, your partner loses, but if you win, your partner also wins and shares in the profits. Conversely, if you do not want to give up any of your profits, you would have your partner participate on the debt side by making a loan to you. In this case, the loan can be secured by the property or any other collateral you may have, or it may be an unsecured loan.

You may decide to have your partner actively participate by exploiting whatever skill sets the partner may have. If your partner is mechanically inclined, for example, you may consider having the partner perform some of the maintenance. Conversely, you may choose to have your partner play a passive role, wherein the partner's only function is to provide capital.

Repayment provisions should take into consideration the cash flow generated from the apartments. Periodic debt payments can be made monthly, quarterly, or annually, or you might agree to repay the debt with all interest due when the property is sold.

In summary, the participation of a partner can benefit you by providing additional capital for a project that might otherwise have been out of reach, and by contributing services in the form of specific skills you may be lacking.

# Additional Financing Considerations

Besides primary and secondary funding for the acquisition of your multifamily property, there are additional financing issues you should consider. They include using the services of a mortgage broker, familiarizing yourself with your credit score and how it affects your ability to secure financing, and having a working knowledge of lender underwriting guidelines.

## Mortgage Brokers

As a former mortgage broker specializing in apartment loans, I had the honor of working with numerous investors such as yourself. I know firsthand that sorting out the myriad of financing options can be thoroughly confusing, especially if you are just getting started. Unless you have been through the financing process for apartments at least a couple of times, I recommend working with a mortgage broker.

Just as real estate brokers play an important role in matching up buyers and sellers, mortgage brokers play an important role in matching up buyers and lenders. Mortgage brokers usually have many contacts in the industry. They know which lender is best suited for the type of financing you are seeking, and they know who is offering the best deal. Experienced brokers have well-established direct relationships with the lenders and usually do a high volume of business with two or three of them. Because the brokers already have professional or personal relationships with their contacts, they can often persuade a lender that your deal is worth the risk of taking on a loan that might otherwise be considered borderline.

While you can generally expect to pay 1 point to the broker for his or her services, the fee can be well worth it if you are working with a professional broker who has solid relationships with several lenders. The broker's service can sometimes make the difference as to whether the financing for your deal goes through. Furthermore, brokers know how to qualify your particular property before ever sending it to a lender, because they know what each lender will and will not accept. For example, if the apartment complex you are buying has aluminum wiring, you absolutely will not be able to get financing from some lenders, as they consider this type of wiring to be a fire hazard. While aluminum wiring may sound like a trivial and even insignificant factor, it represents an unacceptable level of risk for some lenders, and your loan will be flatly rejected.

A good mortgage broker can usually tell you if he or she can place your loan after spending just ten to fifteen minutes with you on the phone. The broker knows what questions to ask to qualify your property and which lender is likely to be the most interested in financing it.

## Credit Scores: The Good, the Bad, and the Ugly

The majority of lenders today use what are known as *FICO scores* to determine your ability to repay a loan. *FICO* is an acronym for Fair, Isaac, and Company, a firm that uses a complex model to calculate a credit score from data collected over a period of time. The scoring system uses factors such as payment history, number of creditors, outstanding balances relative to credit limits, length of credit history, types of credit, and reported income. Before the final score is calculated, previously established weights are assigned to each variable according to the criteria set forth in the model. When lenders order your credit history, they typically get it from all three of the major reporting services—Equifax, Experian, and Trans Union. All three services may not have exactly the same information, so credit scores will vary among them. Lenders will often use either an average or the median of the three scores.

The credit score range is from 300 to 850, with 300 being extremely poor and 850 being a perfect score. I strongly recommend that you do everything within your power to maintain as high a score as possible. If your score is 700 or better, you are considered to be an A borrower and will have no problem qualifying for a loan, provided you meet whatever other criteria the lender has set forth.

Credit scores are used much like Scholastic Aptitude Test (SAT) or Graduate Management Admissions Test (GMAT) scores. The first thing university administrators want to know when students apply for admission is how well they did on standardized tests. The tests are used to measure students' knowledge and aptitude in various subjects, and the results are summarized in the form of a numeric score. Just as administrators use these scores to set minimum standards for matriculation into their schools, lenders use credit scores to set minimum standards for loaning money to prospective borrowers.

Credit scores serve as a valuable tool to lenders because they are purely objective in measuring the ability of a borrower to repay and the probability that the borrower will default. They remove all elements of subjective judgments that could be considered discriminatory, such as race or religious preference.

While conventional banks and specialty lenders tend to place greater emphasis on credit scores, conduit lenders are not as concerned about your personal credit history. This is because conduit lenders look to the property itself for its ability to repay the loan in the event of a default. This is not to say that conduit lenders will not examine your credit history; rather, they do not place as much importance on it as do more traditional lenders. One primary reason conventional banks and specialty lenders place more emphasis on personal credit is that, in most cases, they require personal guarantees. On the other hand, conduit lenders, as you recall, typically issue nonrecourse loans, which require no personal guarantee from the borrower.

Some lenders will make loans to just about anyone. They do not care what your score is as long as the property is generating adequate income to service the debt. These lenders will, however, charge accordingly by applying a matrix grid that plots your ability to repay against the condition of the property. As you can see in Table 10.1, borrowers who fail to maintain good credit are usually penalized. The logic is simple. Lenders must charge a higher rate of interest to offset the higher risk that borrowers with poor credit represent. The bottom line for you as an investor is to work hard to maintain the best credit rating possible. It will make life so much easier in the pursuit of your goal of creating lasting and permanent wealth.

## Underwriting Guidelines

All lenders have established criteria for making loan decisions, referred to as *underwriting guidelines*. These guidelines form the basis for all decisions made to either approve or decline a loan applicant's request. They are, in essence, the lender's bible; loans under review must conform to them before being approved. Underwriting guidelines include items such as the loan-to-value (LTV) ratio, the debt service coverage ratio (DSCR), the size and term of the loan, and information about the subject property.

**Table 10.1**   Interest Rate Matrix

| Property Rating | Borrower Rating | | | |
|---|---|---|---|---|
| | A | B | C | D |
| A | 7.00% | 7.50% | 8.00% | 8.50% |
| B | 7.50% | 8.00% | 8.50% | 9.00% |
| C | 8.00% | 8.50% | 9.00% | 9.50% |
| D | 8.50% | 9.00% | 9.50% | 10.00% |

While most of these guidelines are clearly and objectively stated, more often than not, a property under review will not completely fit into the lender's box—meaning that many properties will meet most of the established criteria, but it is rare when they meet 100 percent of the lender's guidelines. Lenders therefore have to take into consideration what are known as *additional compensating factors*. For example, suppose a lender has set 680 as the minimum FICO score, and the borrower's score is only 640. A valid compensating factor would be that the net operating income generated by the apartments exceeds the lender's requirements enough to increase the amount of cash available to service the loan. In other words, if the DSCR minimum requirement is 1.20, but the income from the property is high enough to yield a ratio of 1.35, this fact would be favorably considered and might be sufficient to offset the borrower's lower credit score.

Take a look at the underwriting guidelines in Table 10.2 for an example of typical lender requirements. Once you have located a lender who provides the best fit to meet your needs, all required terms, conditions, and documentation will be provided to you.

## Required Loan Documentation

Lenders and mortgage brokers often require certain information about the property and the borrower in order to do a preliminary analysis of a loan

**Table 10.2**  Underwriting Guidelines

| Eligible Property Types | Minimum DSCR | Maximum LTV | Ineligible Property Types |
|---|---|---|---|
| Office | 1.35 | 75% | Auto dealerships |
| Multifamily | 1.20 | 80 | Bowling alleys |
| Industrial | 1.25 | 75 | Car washes |
| Retail | 1.30 | 75 | Churches |
| Mixed use | 1.30 | 75 | Gas stations |
| Mobile home parks | 1.25 | 75 | Marinas |
| Hotels and motels | 1.45 | 80 | Nightclubs |
| Health care facilities | 1.40 | 70 | RV parks |
| Self-storage | 1.30 | 75 | Schools |

| General Loan Terms and Conditions | |
|---|---|
| Loan size | $150,000–$2.5 million |
| Index | Treasury bill |
| Term | 7, 10, 15, 20, or 25 years |
| Amortization period | 20, 25, or 30 years |
| Lien position | First lien only |
| Property age | May not be older than 40 years |
| Vacancy | 10% or less |
| Management fees | 10% or less |
| Operating history | Minimum of 2 years full financials |
| Recourse | Nonrecourse |
| Replacement reserves | $250 per unit |
| Escrows | No escrow required |
| Assumability | Assumable with 1% transfer fee |
| Deferred maintenance | Escrowed at closing as required |
| Bankruptcy | Not allowed where borrower has filed in last 5 years |
| Phase I environmental survey | Required |
| Engineering report | May be required on properties older than 10 years |
| Appraisal report | Required |
| Estimated third-party costs | $4,500–$9,500 |
| Loan origination fees | 2% under $500,000; 1% over $500,000 |

request before submitting the package to a loan review committee. The required preliminary information includes a summary memorandum, an underwriting sheet, operating history, rent rolls, and maps and photos. The summary memorandum section should include a summary of all the pertinent information for the prospective loan, such as the borrower's credit and personal financial statement, the requested loan amount, the underwriting overviews and sponsor information, a review of the general market conditions, and property management information. In addition, any major issues should be addressed in this section. The underwriting sheet section provides an evaluation of the stability of the property by comparing prior period cash flows with the current cash flows. The net operating income of the property is examined to determine whether minimum DSCRs and LTV ratios are met. Two to three years' worth of operating history data are also required if available, along with a current year-to-date income statement. All financial statements provided should be signed and certified as true and correct by the seller. Copies of the last three months' rent rolls, along with a current rent roll, are also needed. Furthermore, a sample of a current lease should be made available to the lender. Finally, the maps and photos section should include maps of the general vicinity, a site plan showing the layout and building configuration, and floor plans of the units to be rented. Photos of the property exterior and interior, as well as the neighboring properties, are also essential. Furnishing a complete and thorough preliminary information package will enable the lender to expedite the processing of your loan in a timely and efficient manner.

Once a lender or mortgage broker has completed a preliminary review of the loan documents and approved them, it is time to prepare a full loan application package. While pulling all of the necessary documentation together can be a rather tedious and laborious process, keep in mind what it is you are attempting to achieve and recognize that once you have submitted your application, you are well on your way to becoming an apartment owner. Following is a list of some of the items your lender will likely require at some point in the application process:

- Formal loan application form
- Copies of executed agreements between the buyer and seller, such as the purchase agreement
- Personal financial statement showing all assets, including other real estate owned

- Income tax returns for a minimum of the previous two years
- Credit references, along with full FICO reports
- Statement of the borrower's real estate experience
- Historical and current operating statements for the subject property
- Historical and current rent rolls for the subject property
- Sample leases used for the subject property
- Profile of the management company operating the property (if applicable)
- Verification of property tax amounts
- Property insurance verification
- Copies of any maintenance or vendor agreements
- Third-party reports including a survey, appraisal report, environmental report, and engineering inspections
- An attorney opinion letter stating that your attorney has reviewed the loan documents with you and that you understand them

By now you should have a good understanding of the various issues that must be considered when preparing to secure financing for your apartment project. As you can see, there is much more to the process than simply filling out a loan application at your local bank. You must be able to weigh the advantages and disadvantages of each type of financing mechanism, whether it be through traditional or secondary sources, or a combination of the two, and evaluate them to determine how they fit with your stated objectives. Following is a summary of the many issues to consider when preparing to finance your investment.

### Summary of Financing Considerations

1. Conventional bank, conduit, or specialty loan.
2. Recourse versus nonrecourse loan provisions.

3. Loan term.
4. Amortization period.
5. Interest rate.
6. Loan fees.
7. Third-party reports.
8. Assumability of loan.
9. Lockout period.
10. Prepayment penalties.
11. Owner financing.
12. Equity financing.
13. Partnerships.
14. Mortgage broker.
15. Credit scores.
16. Underwriting guidelines.
17. Loan documentation.

## CHAPTER 11

*To put the world right in order, we must first put the nation in order; to put the nation in order, we must first put the family in order; to put the family in order, we must first cultivate our personal life; we must first set our hearts right.*
**—CONFUCIUS**

# Closing the Deal

After securing financing for your property, the next step is to prepare to finalize and close the transaction. Depending on the size of your acquisition, the closing process can be fairly simple and straightforward, or it can be quite involved, with extensive documentation required. It is also time to begin planning and defining what your role as a strategic manager will be. This, too, will depend on the size of the transaction, as well as your level of experience.

# Closing Fundamentals

The closing process is the time when everything comes together to finalize your transaction. You have studied the market and analyzed numerous apartment buildings, you have successfully negotiated terms and conditions acceptable to both you and the seller, and you have sought out the best financing alternative for your property. It is now time to bring all the parties together to close the sale. Before you do so, however, there are several factors to consider that may affect the closing. They include a thorough review of all related closing documents, a final inspection of the property, and the timing of the close.

## Closing Documents

While numerous ancillary closing forms and letters will need your attention, the primary closing documents that will require a careful review are the title report, closing statement, deed of trust, and promissory note.

The *title report,* also known as the *abstract of title,* provides information about the property's chain of title. In other words, it gives a history of ownership, judgments, liens, and anything else that may have been recorded against the property over time. The title insurance company issues an insurance policy to the buyer and a separate policy to the lender that ensures the title is clean and there are no encumbrances that may adversely affect the new owner.

*Closing statements,* also known as *settlement statements,* are commonly prepared by the title company handling the closing. They detail by line item all of the associated debits and credits assessed to both buyer and seller, such as:

- Contract sales price
- Earnest money deposit

- Principal amount of new loan(s)
- Existing loan(s)
- Seller financing
- Prorated tax adjustments
- Prorated rent adjustments
- Tenants' deposits
- Lender fees
- Title fees
- Attorney fees

You should take the necessary time to review each charge on the settlement statement and verify its accuracy. I cannot think of a deal that I have been involved in where all settlement charges on the closing statement were completely accurate. Errors are inadvertently made for one reason or another. For example, the title company may have an incorrect payoff amount for the seller's loan, or it may prorate the rents or taxes incorrectly, or it may not be aware of a credit you are entitled to because of a specific clause in your purchase agreement negotiated by you and the seller.

Do not assume that because the closing officer works at the title company and acts as the facilitator in numerous closings, the officer must be right because the closer should know. Precisely the opposite is true. The fact that the closer does act as the facilitator in numerous closings is all the more reason that he or she must rely on you to provide accurate information for the settlement statement. The inherent risk to you by neglecting to review the closing statement can be substantial and potentially cost you hundreds or even thousands of dollars.

The lender is responsible for preparing the *deed of trust* and the promissory note. These documents outline the terms and conditions under which the lender has agreed to loan you money. Repayment terms are specified, including the amount of the loan, the interest rate and amortization period, and any prepayment penalties that may be imposed. Other lender requirements that may also be included are escrow conditions for taxes and insurance, minimum insurance amounts, standard of care for property condition, and default provisions.

Many years ago, when I was first getting started in real estate, I bought my first two single-family rental houses. The seller owned 10 or 12 rental properties and was beginning to sell some of them. He offered each of the two houses that I bought for a sales price of $23,000, with only $1,000 down. In addition, the seller wanted to defer the gain on sale for tax purposes, so he was also willing to provide owner financing. Because I was buying both properties from the same seller at the same time, it was only natural to close on both houses at the same time with the same closing officer. The closing went smoothly, and, as far as I knew, everything appeared to be in order. However, when I decided to sell the properties years later, I discovered that the legal descriptions were mixed up and had accidentally been switched in several of the closing documents. This was an easy mistake for anyone to make, but one that should have been caught by either the closing officer, the seller, myself, or all three of us. Rectifying the mistake ended up costing me several hundred dollars in attorney fees.

To help avoid some of the problems that can occur in closings, some lenders may require you to sign what is commonly known as an *attorney opinion letter.* It is often prepared by the lender's attorney and subsequently forwarded to your attorney. The letter serves two primary functions. First, it forces you, as the borrower, to review all of the pertinent and relative language affecting the transaction with your attorney. Your attorney will advise you regarding the legal content and may recommend changes to help protect you. By signing the attorney opinion letter, you are stating that you understand all of the legal documents and that you are in agreement with them. By taking time to have a competent attorney review these documents, you will minimize your exposure to risk from any inadvertent errors, such as the ones previously discussed. Second, an attorney opinion letter serves to indemnify and hold harmless the lender. By outlining all of the terms and conditions and by requiring you to review them with an attorney, the lender is effectively adding an extra measure of self-protection.

## Final Inspection

Several days before the closing, you should take the necessary precaution of performing one final physical inspection of the apartment building. Doing so could potentially save you thousands of dollars. On one particular acquisition I was involved in, a cracked slab was discovered on one of the buildings about two weeks before the scheduled closing. The weather had been extremely hot and arid that summer, with no rain for several weeks. The soil below the foundation (which was a cement slab; there was no basement) had completely dried up due to the lack of moisture in the ground. This caused a portion of the building's foundation to settle downward and subsequently crack. Fortunately for me, this incident occurred before I took possession of the property. While this was an unfortunate incident for the seller, he knew he had an obligation to repair the foundation at his expense. A repair crew was called out to lift up the settled portion of the slab with hydraulic jacks and then pour several cement footings underneath to support the building. Although I did not see the final bill for the repair work, I am sure it was not cheap.

# Closing Credits Can Add Up

Closing credits most often consist of prorated credits for rental income, security deposits, and taxes. The time of month your closing is held can have a significant impact on the credits you are entitled to as a buyer. Suppose you close on the very first day of the month. Although you would technically be entitled to receive the full month's rent at the time of closing, assuming rents are due on the first of the month, chances are the seller will have collected very little of the rental income yet. Most landlords provide a two- to three-day grace period before rents are considered late. If the seller were to give credit for the full month, this would put the seller in the precarious position of having to collect the remainder of the rent after the date of closing when he or she is no longer the owner. It is better to wait until the fifth of the month or so. By then, over 95 percent of all rents should have been collected and as the buyer, you will be entitled to receive a prorated credit for 25 days' worth of rent without having to expend the time and effort to collect them. Depending on the monthly revenues generated by the apartment complex, the credit due from rents collected can be quite substantial. Take a look at the following example:

$$100 \text{ units} \times \$600/\text{unit average rent} = \$60,000/\text{month}$$

$$\frac{25}{30} \times \$60,000 = \$50,000 \text{ closing credit for rental income}$$

Conversely, closing at the end of the month, say on the twenty-eighth, would have the following effect:

$$100 \text{ units} \times \$600/\text{unit average rent} = \$60,000/\text{month}$$

$$\frac{2}{30} \times \$60,000 = \$4,000 \text{ closing credit for rental income}$$

By studying this simple example, you can see the potential impact of closing at the beginning of the month versus closing at the end of the month. In this case, you would have had to come to the closing table with $46,000 less by closing on the fifth rather than the twenty-eighth. I should mention that a prepaid interest payment to the lender would be greater at the beginning of the month, which would partially offset the difference collected in rental income. In this example, the prepaid interest would be around $12,000 to $14,000, so you would still come out ahead by more than $32,000.

While timing does affect the amount of rental income received at closing, it has no effect on the credit you are entitled to for security deposits. As with the rental income credit, however, this can also be quite substantial. Using the same 100-unit apartment building example from before, assume an average security deposit of $300:

$$100 \text{ units} \times \$300 \text{ average security deposit} = \$30,000$$

Now assume the seller required a security deposit equal to the first and last months' rent:

$$100 \text{ units} \times \$600/\text{unit average rent} \times 2 = \$120,000$$

Keep in mind that although you will receive a credit at closing in the form of cash, there is an offsetting liability equal to the credit received. The money you receive at closing really belongs to the tenants; however, because they move in and out over a period of time, the cash flow from operations is not materially affected. As old tenants move out and are reimbursed for their security deposits, new tenants move in and replace the funds. The primary benefit to you as the buyer is received at the time of closing when the transfer of the asset (cash) is made.

Depending on the area where the property you purchase is located and also on the lender's specific requirements, you will either receive a credit, give the seller a credit, give the lender a credit, or some combination of these. I have purchased property both in areas where taxes are paid in arrears and in areas where taxes are paid in advance. In the case of the former, you will receive a prorated credit at closing, because the seller's liability for unpaid taxes is transferred to you. In other words, you will receive a credit in the form of cash, an asset, and an offsetting liability in the form of taxes payable. Receiving a cash credit at closing may significantly reduce the amount of cash you need for the down payment. Of course, eventually you will be responsible for paying the taxes, but for the time being, you effectively have an interest-free loan. Your lender may, however, require that funds be set aside in an escrow account. In that case, the cash credit is transferred to the lender, who, in turn, assumes responsibility for the offsetting liability.

If the area where your property is located requires that taxes be paid in advance, you, as the buyer, will be required to give the seller a prorated credit at closing, because the seller has already paid the taxes for the given time period. The seller has an asset, prepaid taxes, which is transferred to you as the buyer. In this case, there is no offsetting liability, but rather an offsetting owner's contribution, or contributed capital, which is applied in the form of cash. The transfer is made between the seller and the buyer only. No lender is involved under these circumstances; however, the lender may require that an additional two months' prepaid taxes or so be set up in an escrow account.

In summary, familiarity with all aspects of the closing process, including a thorough review of all related closing documents, a final inspection of the property, and the timing of the close can potentially save you thousands of dollars.

## CHAPTER 12

*The harder the conflict, the more glorious the triumph.*
*What we obtain too cheaply, we esteem too lightly.*
**—THOMAS PAINE**

# Managing Your Property

Now that you have successfully closed your apartment transaction, the real fun begins. It is time to implement your postentry strategy. This includes putting together a winning management team. Depending on the size of the apartment building, your management team may consist of just yourself, or it may include a professional management company to administer the day-to-day operations. You must also give serious consideration to the role you will play in this process, which should be a function of where you can contribute the most value. Finally, even after taking all the necessary precautions of careful planning and execution, you must take care to expect the unexpected. In the apartment business—or in any other business for that matter—unforeseen events have a way of challenging you. While almost impossible to anticipate, you can take steps to mitigate the effects of these incidents.

## Hiring a Professional Property Management Firm

If this is your first purchase and the property is smaller than 50 units, you will likely want to be as directly involved in managing the property as possible. There is no substitute for the kind of experience you will get while directing the daily affairs of your apartment complex. Conversely, if you are a seasoned real estate investor and are acquiring a larger property, you will likely want to employ a *competent* management company to assist you. Note the emphasis on "competent." A property management firm must be capable of operating your property effectively and efficiently. The firm's representatives may promise a great deal over the phone when you are conducting your search. I recommend that the initial telephone conversation be followed up by a face-to-face interview at the management company's office. This way you can sit down with them, look them directly in the eye, and discuss the issues that are most important to you in executing your pos-tentry strategy.

I remember conducting one such interview myself. It was with the vice president of a fairly well known and well respected management company. I expected him to be able to elaborate in considerable detail on the benefits his company could offer me. When I asked him what the company did to train the on-site managers and personnel for the apartments, his response astounded me.

The company's on-site property managers had to meet two basic criteria: (1) they were required to be 18 years of age or older, and (2) they were required to undergo a drug screening test. For whatever reason, the vice president seemed really proud of requirement number two.

I commended him on the fact that all of their managers were over 18 and had passed drug screening tests, but what about training? His answer led me to believe that the only training the on-site personnel received came from on-the-job experience and that most managers started out with little to no experience.

"That's terrific," I thought to myself. "I'm about to buy a $1.6-million apartment complex, and you expect me to turn it over to some 18-year-old kid with no experience who happened to pass a drug test. No thanks." I left the interview certain I would not be engaging this firm to represent my interests.

There are several things to be aware of when considering a property management firm. One of these is a proper understanding of your manager's most basic role. Most management agreements are structured such that the management firm acts as your legal agent. An agent has the right to conduct business on your behalf and therefore acts as an extension of you, the owner. While the agent is limited by the agreement in place between you, the agent is generally given broad powers to make a myriad of decisions that directly affect the operations and, consequently, the profitability of your business. By integrating your strategic plan with the role of the agent, you are taking steps to ensure a successful partnership for both parties. The goals of the management company must be the same as the goals of the property owner. Sharing common goals will facilitate a cooperative effort and provide an environment conducive to success.

The property management agreement is vital for the protection of both the owner and the management company. It sets forth in express language the duties and responsibilities of all parties entering into the contract and helps to minimize any misconceptions either party may have. A management agreement should at minimum provide the following stipulations:

- *It acts as a service agreement between the owner and the management company.* Ideally, the management company should act as an independent contractor, not an employee. You avoid a number of legal issues, such as federal, state, and social security taxes, with an independent contractor arrangement.

- *It establishes an agency relationship between you and the management company.* The relationship is expressly limited by the powers set forth in the agreement.

- *It provides for the management firm's compensation.* This is typically done as a percentage of collections as opposed to a stated monthly rate. It is similar to a real estate broker's compensation in that the broker earns a commission only when he or she sells a property. Because the management company's compensation is, in a sense, commission driven, the company is penalized if the manager does a poor job of collecting rent. Management fees are often applied to all moneys collected, including rents, application and late fees, and other income, such as that collected from vending machines and laundry rooms.

- *It provides for the termination of the relationship.* Be careful not to get locked into too long a minimum duration, such as one year. For example, if you are bringing in a new management company to help resolve problems at your complex, you should begin seeing signs of improvement within 90 days. If you have signed a one-year agreement and are not seeing any signs of a turnaround within three to four months, you may be in trouble. Protect yourself by limiting the duration of the agreement. Most professional management firms know that if they do not perform, they will soon be replaced by another company. If the management company requires anything more than 90 to 120 days— except in special circumstances, such as when complete rehabilitation of the property is required—it is a red flag that should prompt you to reconsider.

In addition to the terms of the agency agreement, you should also be aware of the specific obligations the management firm has to you, the apartment owner. While these obligations will certainly vary from project to project and company to company, they generally include the following:

- To act in a professional manner at all times when representing you
- To make every effort to collect rents and all revenue due on a timely basis
- To maximize apartment occupancy and minimize apartment vacancy
- To minimize individual apartment unit downtime by completing make-readies as quickly as possible
- To maintain the physical condition of the property at all times
- To disburse payments for moneys owed in a timely manner
- To keep accurate records for the property, including lease agreements and occupancy, collections, disbursements, maintenance, and personnel records

A careful interviewing and selection process will enable you to employ a firm that will help you maximize the value of your apartment building. A professional and competent management company will make every effort to discharge its duties and responsibilities in accordance with your stated objectives. The company's managers know it is in the best interests of all parties to do so.

## Your Role as a Strategic Manager

Depending on the size of the apartments you will be managing and your level of experience, you may or may not decide to get involved in the minutiae of operating a property. You must determine the best use of your time. Where can you make the most valuable contribution to the process? Is it in mowing the grass, cleaning out the pool, or collecting the rents? It may be initially, but by your second or third property, it should not be. Your primary function is to stay focused on your role as a strategic manager, whether you decide to take a hands-on approach by actively participating in the daily management or not. Long before you got to this point, you mapped out a plan that included your entry, postentry, and exit strategies. You must keep those concepts in the forefront of your mind at all times; otherwise, you will find yourself off course. Use your well-thought-out plan as a compass to guide you in accomplishing your objectives.

## Expect the Unexpected

Regardless of how much training or experience you and your staff have, there will always be those unexpected incidents that are difficult, if not impossible, to prepare for. What really counts is how you choose to act, or react, when they arise. Seemingly random events that affect the operation and profitability of your apartment building stem from both internal and external sources. Internal sources include the personnel working for you, your tenants, or your building and equipment, while external sources may include weather-related events, nontenants, and equipment that is not your property.

Here are a couple of examples. Recently, one of my apartment buildings sustained damage from both internal and external sources. The event from the external source occurred first. It happened late one Saturday night, or rather, early Sunday morning, shortly after the bars had closed. A drunk driver swerved off the road and crashed into one of my buildings. The car was apparently still operable, because the driver promptly left the scene of the accident. Fortunately, none of my tenants were injured. The building sustained about $2,200 in damage, which was slightly less than my deductible of $2,500, so no insurance claim was made and, of course, the $2,200 came right out of the operating profits of the apartment complex (and hence, right out of my pocket). As you can imagine, I was not too happy about this incident. In this case, there was not much I could do except to have the repairs made immediately.

The second event occurred from an internal source and happened exactly one week after the drunk driver hit my building. My property manager called me and said, "Steve, you remember how one of the buildings got hit last week? Well, you're not going to believe this, but another one of them got hit earlier today."

He was right. I didn't believe it. At least, I didn't want to believe it.

The internal source was one of the tenants. Actually, it was the tenant's daughter. As it turned out, the tenant was teaching his teenage daughter, who had just received her learner's permit, how to drive a car with a five-speed stick shift. The daughter had obviously not yet mastered the coordination required to operate the clutch, brake, and accelerator simultaneously. As she was pulling into a parking space, which happened to be against the side of one of the buildings, she stepped on the gas pedal instead of the brake and drove right up over the curb, through the wall of the building, and into another tenant's living room.

Well, that was certainly the kind of news that can cheer an apartment owner right up, especially after shelling out $2,200 the week before for some hit-and-run drunk. Once again, fortunately, no one was injured. The tenant whose daughter ran through the wall was at least honest enough to admit what had happened and, moreover, was honorable enough to accept responsibility for it. He agreed to pay for the damages a little at a time over the next several months.

In this example, I could have reacted by having the tenant evicted, but he had been a good paying tenant for several years and was decent enough to agree to pay for the damages. My manager worked out a repayment schedule with him, and after several months, the tenant fulfilled his obligation. I never did hear whether his daughter passed her driving exam.

Stay with me as I share one more car story. This one occurred at a different property and, once again, involved late-night drunks. The apartment units backed up to a public street that ran parallel across the back of the units. Intersecting this street was another street that ran perpendicular to the back of the apartments. The two streets together formed a T because the street that ran perpendicular stopped at the street that ran parallel. If a car traveling on the street running perpendicular ran the stop sign, it would crash into the back of the apartments. For whatever reason, young kids liked to use this particular strip for late-night drag racing. On many occasions, I saw black tire marks at the intersection of the two streets where cars had come to a screeching halt.

One night at about 2 A.M., the kids were at it again. Most likely inebriated, they pushed it a little too far. One of the drivers failed to hit the brakes in time, so instead of coming to a screeching halt at the stop sign, he skidded through the intersection and slammed into the chain-link fence behind the apartment building. Thank goodness the fence was there, because it acted as a barrier between the car and the apartment unit.

The tenants happened to be sleeping in a bedroom that backed up to the fence. Needless to say, they were immediately awakened by all of the commotion. The police were notified, and one of the kids was picked up. I attempted to press charges but had a difficult time doing so. The police seemed too busy with other things and did not even bother to return my phone calls. I finally just dropped the matter.

The fence that had caught the car was ruined and had to be replaced. That was another $1,100 pop to the pocketbook.

The tenants expressed concern for their safety, and rightly so. After all, who can sleep at night in a bedroom where there is a very real possibility that a car could come careening through the wall at any moment? As an added measure of protection, I had 15 steel posts, each 8 feet in length and 4 inches in diameter, set in the ground about 6 feet apart inside the fence. The posts were anchored 4½ feet in the ground and filled with concrete. This left 3½ feet protruding out of the ground to act as a solid reinforcement to the fence and prevent any cars from hitting the building.

To my knowledge, the kids laid low on the drag racing for awhile, and no other incidents occurred while I owned the property.

These are not intended to be horror stories, so please do not let them dissuade you from your pursuit of apartment ownership. They are meant to illustrate the point that you must expect the unexpected. In other words, any number of things can adversely affect the operation of your apartment building, and it is impossible to anticipate all of them. Lightning could strike a building, a tornado could tear a roof off, or a smoker could fall asleep in bed with a lit cigarette and cause a fire. Anything can happen, and many things *do* happen. There is risk in everything you do. You could get in an accident while driving, or trip and fall while walking, or bump your head on a low-lying tree branch. Life is full of challenges. Accept these challenges and risks as opportunities to grow, and do not allow yourself to be defeated by them. You have to taste the bitter before you can appreciate the sweet.

As a prudent apartment owner, you must take all of the precautions you can and be as well prepared as possible. Two of the most important things you can do are to have the proper insurance coverage and to have a small cash reserve on hand. Having the proper insurance coverage will protect you from what might otherwise prove to be catastrophic, while maintaining a small cash reserve will provide the measure of safety needed to endure some of the mishaps, such as the ones previously mentioned.

In summary, employing a capable and professional property management company can mean the difference between success and failure in your efforts to achieve your stated objectives for your postentry and exit strategies. Mastering the concepts outlined in this chapter will enable you to enjoy a smooth and successful transition into apartment ownership.

## CHAPTER 13

*Great spirits have always found violent opposition from mediocrity. The latter cannot understand it when a man does not thoughtlessly submit to hereditary prejudices, but honestly and courageously uses his intelligence.*
**—ALBERT EINSTEIN**

# Four Effective Exit Strategies

You have worked hard over the past 12 to 24 months implementing your entry and postentry strategies. You started by searching for and locating a property that met your specific needs. You then acquired the property using various closing and management techniques that enabled you to make the most efficient use of your available resources. You have since utilized the necessary tools to find ways to create value by enhancing revenues and reducing expenses. It is now time to capture as much of the newly created value from the property as possible in order to more fully employ the capital created by maximizing its leverage into a greater investment opportunity in another apartment building. Your exit strategy may include selling the property outright, refinancing it, bringing in an equity partner, exchanging the property for a similar one, or any combination of these.

**Four Effective Exit Strategies**

**1.** Outright sale.

**2.** Refinancing.

**3.** Equity partnership.

**4.** Exchange of properties.

# Outright Sale

Perhaps the most common method of exiting a property is by disposing of it through an outright sale to another buyer. Selling your apartment complex outright has both advantages and disadvantages over the other exit strategies.

One primary advantage of disposing of your property by selling it is that you are able to obtain full control of the gain at the time of sale. Remember, your objective is to unlock the newly created value and leverage it into another opportunity. Selling allows you to do exactly that. Another advantage of selling versus the other exit strategies is that you are free from all legal liabilities and encumbrances imposed by the lender when the sale is consummated. This depends, of course, on how the sale is structured and assumes you are not carrying a second note. While this may sound like a minor point, it is important, especially for less experienced investors, to note that by selling a property, you relinquish all responsibility for it. This allows you the mental and emotional freedom to focus on your next acquisition. Finally, depending on what your accountant recommends, you may be able to take advantage of long-term capital gains treatment for tax purposes, which has historically offered much more favorable tax rates than those applied to ordinary income.

One disadvantage of an outright sale is that you abdicate control of the property. This is just the opposite of the advantage stated previously. Some more experienced investors prefer to maintain control of an asset once it is acquired. A smaller portion of the gain can be captured through other methods, such as through refinancing, while still maintaining control of the asset. Several properties can be acquired over time to build up a sizable portfolio worth several million dollars. Retaining the property allows you to do this; however, you would still be responsible for any liabilities related to the transaction. Another disadvantage of selling the property outright is the tax payments associated with the gain on sale. Although you will likely be able to take advantage of the more favorable capital gains tax rate, you will still be giving some of your hard-earned equity to Uncle Sam.

# Refinancing

Another common method of unlocking the newly created value from your apartment building is through refinancing. While you may not have ever refinanced an apartment building, you have probably refinanced a single-family house, perhaps even your own residence, at one time or another. Refinancing an apartment building is not that much different, it is just done on a larger scale.

Many of the concepts discussed in Chapter 10 will apply to refinancing your property. An additional issue not covered in Chapter 10 is *seasoning,* a term lenders and investors generally apply to the length of time you have owned the property. Most lenders require a minimum of 12 months of seasoning before they will consider refinancing your property, while other lenders require anywhere from 18 to 36 months. Lenders require this seasoning period to ensure that you, as the investor, have committed adequate time, energy, and resources to the property. Many lenders do not understand the process of creating value, so you may have to educate them. They sometimes erroneously believe that the only way a property can increase in value is through a series of natural rental increases that occur over an extended period of time due to general price appreciation.

Lenders may grow suspicious if your property has had a significant increase in value over a short period of time. They will want to know when you bought the property and how much you paid for it. If the apartment building you bought 12 months ago for $2 million is now worth $2.6 million, they will want to know why, and rightfully so. You must be prepared to sell the lender on the process you used to create value. If the property was being poorly managed and rents were below market and expenses were unusually high, explain to the lender what you did to turn the property around. Be confident in your presentation, and describe in detail how you injected needed funds for various capital improvements, then initiated a series of rent increases while simultaneously reducing expenses. Remember that lenders want your patronage. They are in business to loan money. You just need to give them a good reason to do so. You can do this by telling your story convincingly and thereby earning the lender's trust and confidence in you as an investor.

To refinance your apartment building, you must also be prepared to objectively justify the higher value. In the example mentioned in the previous paragraph, you need to validate to the lender, as well as to the appraiser, why the apartments you paid $2 million for a year ago are now worth $2.6 million. This requires a sound understanding of both the valuation methodologies discussed earlier in this book and the financing principles covered in Chapter 10. You have to know what the appraiser will look for to justify the value, and you also have to know what the lender will look for.

Recall Chapter 7 for a minute. The three valuation methods most commonly used by appraisers are (1) the sales comparison approach, (2) the replacement cost approach, and (3) the income capitalization approach. Remember that while each method has its place in determining property values, appraisers place the most weight on the income approach for income-producing properties such as apartment buildings. We have already determined that value is a function of net operating income (NOI) and is directly driven by the property's ability to generate income. Assuming a capitalization rate of 10 percent, we know that the apartment building should have been producing $200,000 of net operating income:

$$\text{Cap rate} = \frac{\text{NOI}}{\text{price}}$$

$$\text{Price} = \frac{\text{NOI}}{\text{cap rate}} = \frac{\$200,000}{0.10} = \$2,000,000$$

To justify the new value of $2.6 million using the same assumptions, we know that we must have $260,000 of net operating income:

$$\text{Cap rate} = \frac{\text{NOI}}{\text{price}}$$

$$\text{NOI} = \text{price} \times \text{cap rate} - \$2,600,000 \times 0.10 = \$260,000$$

You will need to be prepared to demonstrate the higher value to both the lender and the appraiser by presenting each with current financial statements, including operating statements and rent rolls. The $260,000 net operating income will probably not represent the trailing 12 months, but is more likely to represent the most recent quarter annualized. Lenders and appraisers understand this process and will even use the most recent month to estimate gross revenues by annualizing the current rent roll. When you first acquired the property, NOI represented $200,000 on an annualized basis. Over time, as you improved the property's physical condition, as well as its financial condition, the NOI increased.

| Item | Quarter | | | |
| | 1 | 2 | 3 | 4 |
|---|---|---|---|---|
| Revenues | $125,000 | $127,500 | $130,000 | $132,500 |
| Expenses | 75,000 | 72,500 | 70,000 | 67,500 |
| NOI | $ 50,000 | $ 55,000 | $ 60,000 | $ 65,000 |
| Annualized NOI | $200,000 | $220,000 | $240,000 | $260,000 |

You can see from this example that getting from $200,000 to $260,000 in a 12-month period is entirely feasible. An increase in revenues of only $2,500 per quarter augmented by a decrease in expenses of $2,500 per quarter adds $5,000 to NOI, and by the end of the fourth quarter adds $15,000 to NOI, or $60,000 on an annualized basis. This is all that was needed to create the additional $600,000 in value for this property. To better put this in perspective, the increase in revenues represents a total increase of only 6 percent, while the decrease in expenses represents a total decrease of only 10 percent. Identify the right property with the right opportunities, and such results are easily achievable.

$$\frac{\$132,500 - \$125,000}{\$125,000} = 6.00\%$$

or a 6 percent increase in rents

$$\frac{\$67,500 - \$75,000}{\$75,000} = -10.00\%$$

or a 10 percent decrease in expenses.

As you can see, this is not rocket science. You just need a basic understanding of the mechanics of this analysis to apply these methods to the process of creating value. It should not be too difficult to identify an apartment building that is under market rents by a factor of only 6 percent, nor to identify one that is a little heavy on the expense side. Putting the right management team in place can make all the difference in the world. As the owner, an understanding of the valuation process is crucial to placing you on the fast track to wealth accumulation. Without it, you will be just like most other apartment owners, who buy properties for the long term, hold them forever, and hope they will somehow appreciate in value. Remember the lender and the seasoning process? The long-term holder is the type of investor lenders are accustomed to dealing with, and that is exactly why you must be prepared to educate the lenders.

Now that you know what the appraiser will be looking for, consider what the lender will be looking for. Although the criteria for refinancing apartment buildings among lenders vary widely, three factors most of them will focus on are (1) the seasoning period, (2) the loan-to-value (LTV) ratio, and (3) the debt service coverage ratio (DSCR).

As stated earlier, the minimum seasoning period is usually 12 months. While there may sometimes be flexibility in this requirement, the requisite seasoning period is usually written into the lender's underwriting guidelines, which means the proposed loan must meet the specified criteria. Because most loans take anywhere from 60 to 120 days to process, some lenders will allow you to start the process before fulfilling the seasoning requirement. For example, suppose the lender's required period is 12 months and you approach the lender in Month 10. The lender knows that by the time all of the third-party reports are completed, a minimum of 60 days will have passed, and you will have therefore met the seasoning requirement of 12 months.

The second factor lenders focus on is the LTV ratio. From my experience as a mortgage broker, I know that the majority of lenders will usually provide only 75 percent financing for the new loan. While these same lenders will offer 80 percent and even 85 percent financing for acquisitions, they are often reluctant to allow you to pull cash out of your property. The feeling among lenders is that if you pull your equity out in the form of cash, you will no longer have a vested interest in the property. While there may be some truth to this, I do not personally know many investors who would leave the remaining 25 percent on the table. On the $2.6-million project, walking away from the remaining equity would be the equivalent of leaving $650,000 on the table. While the possibility exists, it is not likely to happen. I should mention that although most lenders offer only 75 percent financing for a "cash-out refi," as it is called, there are lenders who will provide up to 80 percent LTV financing. Anything above 80 percent is rare.

Finally, lenders also focus on the DSCR when considering refinancing. They want to ensure that the income generated from your apartment building is sufficient to service the new debt you will be placing on it. You must be prepared to demonstrate to them that it will. The lenders will take the information from your operating statement to calculate this ratio. They may or may not make some adjustments to the revenues and expenses as reported on your operating statement. For example, it is standard practice for underwriters to use either the actual vacancy rate or 5 percent, whichever is greater. So, if the vacancy rate for your property is only 3.5 percent, the underwriter would use 5 percent instead, because it is greater than 3.5 percent. This would adversely affect your NOI, and, consequently, the DSCR. Calculating this ratio is fairly straightforward, as described in Chapter 7. The formula is included here again.

**Debt Service Coverage Ratio**
$$DSCR = \frac{\text{net operating income}}{\text{debt payment}}$$

When searching for a lender to refinance a property, I have found that it is best to spend 10 to 15 minutes on the phone with them to determine what their requirements are. This way, you know before ever submitting any of the requisite loan documentation whether your loan has a chance of being approved. Good loan officers are well aware of this interviewing process and want to maximize the value of their time by prequalifying your loan. If you have owned the property for one year and you know the lender's seasoning requirement is two years, you know you need to go on to the next lender. If you are looking for an 80 percent LTV and the lender only offers 75 percent LTV, you know you need to go on to the next lender. Finally, if under the terms and conditions the lender offers, your DSCR is 1.20 and the lender requires 1.30, you know you need not spend any more time with this lender. Mortgage brokers can play a valuable role in helping you to secure your desired loan financing. They often have relationships with several lenders and are familiar with the requirements of each. Mortgage brokers can save you a great deal of time because they are likely to know who will be interested in refinancing your property and who will not.

Since you know what the lenders will be looking for, I suggest you make some initial calculations before even contacting them. As you familiarize yourself with this process, you will be able to determine well in advance how much capital you can expect to pull out of your property through the refinancing process. With the proprietary model I have developed, I actually make these calculations before ever acquiring a multifamily property. The calculations are made automatically at the time of the initial analysis. Take a minute to examine the refinancing model in Table 13.1. By simply adjusting variables such as the interest rate, the term, or the DSCR, you can quickly make changes to better analyze your property.

Refinancing your property offers both advantages and disadvantages when compared to other exit strategies. One primary advantage for more experienced investors is that you retain control of a sizable asset—your apartment building. As you acquire more and more properties, the size of your real estate portfolio can grow quite large—initially into the millions of dollars, and eventually into the hundreds of millions of dollars. Maintaining control of such a sizable portfolio can, in itself, offer several advantages. Because

**Table 13.1**   Refinancing Model

| Maximum Refinance—Cash-Out | | | Key Factors | |
|---|---|---|---|---|
| Net operating income | | 276,597 | Required DSCR | 135.00% |
| | | | Total sq ft | 75,000.000 |
| Max refinance | (80%) | 2,165,497 | Avg sq ft/unit | 765.306 |
| Owner's equity at | 20% | 541,375 | Avg rent/sq ft | 0.542 |
| required appraisal | | 2,706,871 | Avg cost/sq ft | 36.092 |
| | | | Avg unit cost | 27,621.136 |
| | Annual | Monthly | Capitalization rate | 10.218% |
| Interest rate | 8.250% | 0.688% | Gross rent multiplier | 5.546 |
| Term | 25 | 300 | Expense/unit | 2,520.831 |
| Payment | 204,886 | 17,074 | Expense/sq ft | 3.294 |

you have already actualized all of the property's current potential value, the only remaining value is that which will accrue in the future through economic appreciation. Even a modest increase through appreciation, however, can increase your net worth substantially. Using our previous example, if you only held one property valued at $2.6 million and achieved a modest increase of 3 percent annually for five years, the value of your apartment building would grow to almost $3.0 million. In addition, the amount of the mortgage would also be reduced, thereby creating even more equity. Although the equity remains in the property in an illiquid form, it is not rendered useless. It can actually be employed as collateral, which can be used to acquire additional multifamily properties.

Another advantage refinancing offers over other methods is that there are no taxes imposed as a result of the refinancing cash-out. Because you are not selling your property, but are instead borrowing against it, taxes are not levied against the transaction as they would be in an outright sale. In a sale, you are taxed on the net gain. In refinancing, there is no net gain to tax because you are borrowing funds that must be repaid. Even though you have created new value, your gain represents an *unrealized* gain until such time as you dispose of the property through a sale. Furthermore, even though there will likely be a new mortgagor, no transfer of property rights has been made. It is like borrowing money to buy a car, or anything else, for that matter. You do not pay taxes for incurring liabilities. In fact, you may even be able to write off some of the expenses related to the refinancing process, such as origination fees.

Although refinancing your apartment building can be a very attractive alternative to pulling cash out, this method does have its disadvantages. One principal disadvantage is that you will receive only up to 80 percent of the value of the property rather than 100 percent as you would in a sale. The difference is, however, partially offset by the taxes that would be imposed on the net gain on sale (unless the transaction were handled as an exchange, in which case the tax liability would still exist, but would be deferred until a later date). Compare the two methods using the example of the $2.6 million apartment building. Take a minute to review Table 13.2.

This example is fairly simple and does not take into consideration factors such as transaction costs related to brokerage fees, third-party reports, and loan fees. Reduction in principal on the original loan is also not considered. In addition, the example assumes under Exit Strategy 1 that the seller is able to obtain the full asking price of $2.6 million. To procure that price, the property would most likely have to be offered at a slightly higher price initially, say $2.7 to $2.8 million. Using the assumptions illustrated in this example would provide the seller with an additional $400,000 of capital to employ. Assuming an 80 percent LTV, you could purchase a complex valued at $4.4 million under Exit Strategy 1, while under Exit Strategy 2, your capital would only be sufficient to acquire a complex valued at $2.4 million. This is, of course, a rather significant difference.

Another disadvantage of refinancing is that because you retain the apartment building in your real estate portfolio, you are increasing your risk

**Table 13.2** Cash Sale versus Refinancing

| Original Assumptions | | | |
|---|---|---|---|
| Original purchase price | 2,000,000 | | |
| Equity at 20% | 400,000 | | |
| Amount to finance | 1,600,000 | | |
| Exit Strategy 1: Cash Sale | | Exit Strategy 2: Refinancing | |
| Sales price | 2,600,000 | Appraised value | 2,600,000 |
| Purchase price | 2,000,000 | | |
| Gain on sale before taxes | 600,000 | New Loan at 80% | 2,080,000 |
| Tax at 20% LT capital gains rate | 120,000 | Payoff of existing loan | 1,600,000 |
| Gain on sale after taxes | 480,000 | Available cash proceeds | 480,000 |
| Original down payment | 400,000 | Tax liability | 0 |
| Cash available at closing | 880,000 | Cash available at closing | 480,000 |
| Difference between methods | **400,000** | Difference between methods | **(400,000)** |

exposure in the event of a downturn in the economy. As long as the economy remains healthy and unemployment remains at acceptable levels, you are likely to enjoy strong occupancy. Conversely, if the economy suffers a recession, vacancy rates and delinquencies may increase. There are ways, however, to insulate yourself from any personal liability. As you recall from Chapter 10, refinancing with a nonrecourse conduit loan will absolve you from personal liability. The financial institutions that make these loans have much deeper pockets than do individual investors, and if need be, they can draw on these additional resources to see the property through in tough times. It goes without saying that a careful investor should take every precaution to ensure that the lender is not forced to take the property back.

Another layer of protection investors have at their disposal is the use of corporations. If you did not originally form a separate legal entity such as a limited liability corporation, S corporation, or C corporation, you can do so when you refinance. The lender may place some constraints on the formation of the new entity, but in most cases, you can put the apartments in the name of the corporation. In addition to protecting you from economic downturns, the newly created entity can also protect you from incidents, such as accidents, which may occur on the property. Although your apartment building will be fully insured, if someone slips on a stairway and suffers an injury as a result, they will not be able to sue you personally for the mishap. The injured party will have every right to collect a settlement check from the insurance company, and can even sue the entity that owns the property. If you create a legal entity through which to own the apartments, you add an extra layer of protection to shield yourself and your personal assets from being seized in the event of some misfortune.

Finally, refinancing an apartment building for more than the previous loan amount with similar terms and conditions will reduce the cash flow from the property. If the newly procured debt is maximized with an 80 percent loan, the net cash you had become accustomed to receiving each month will be diminished due to the increase in the new mortgage payments. The lender will require a minimum positive DSCR to ensure that the debt can be adequately serviced each month, but nevertheless, you must be prepared for the reduction in net cash flow. Although in the first two to three years the remaining cash flow may be minimal, these net cash flows will gradually increase over time as rents are raised against mortgage payments, which are fixed.

## Equity Partnership

Another effective method of pulling capital from the newly created value of your property is by introducing an equity partner. Creating a partnership at this juncture is not that much different from bringing in a partner at the time of the original purchase. The principal difference here is that you have increased the value of your investment and are now looking to recoup your original investment capital, in addition to whatever other arrangements you agree to with the new partner. Referring to our previous example, in which an apartment was purchased for $2.0 million and is now worth $2.6 million, you would seek an investor willing to participate at an effective level of 20 percent equity of the new value. Take a minute to study Table 13.3.

In this example, assume you purchased the property for $2.0 million with 20 percent down, or $400,000, and financed it at 7.25 percent over 25 years. This would give you monthly debt service of $11,565 and annual debt service of $138,779. Now assume you brought in an equity partner willing to put down 20 percent of the new value, or $520,000. In exchange for the new investor's equity, you agree to forgo all income from the property, with the exception of the difference in debt service payments of $3,806 monthly or $45,673 annually. This arrangement is very similar to what is commonly known as a *wraparound mortgage,* with one notable exception—you are not transferring any property rights. Wraparounds are used to sell property

**Table 13.3** Purchase and Financing Assumptions

| Original Assumptions | | |
|---|---|---|
| Original purchase price | | 2,000,000 |
| Owner's equity at 20% | | 400,000 |
| Balance to finance (80%) | | 1,600,000 |
| | Annual | Monthly |
| Interest rate | 7.250% | 0.604% |
| Term | 25 | 300 |
| Payment | 138,779 | 11,565 |
| Equity Partner Assumptions | | |
| Appraised value | | 2,600,000 |
| Equity at 20% | | 520,000 |
| Remaining balance (80%) | | 2,080,000 |
| | Annual | Monthly |
| Interest rate | 7.500% | 0.625% |
| Term | 25 | 300 |
| Payment | 184,452 | 15,371 |
| **Difference in debt service** | **45,673** | **3,806** |

directly to a buyer, usually without the lender's knowledge. The new buyer agrees to make payments on the new amount financed, while the original buyer agrees to continue making the original payments to the lender. Most mortgages have due-on-sale clauses that preclude such agreements. Any transfer of rights that may occur under a wraparound mortgage can trigger the due-on-sale clause, enabling the lender to accelerate the note, causing it to be due in full immediately.

Introducing an equity partner is a way of circumventing the due-on-sale clause. Under this type of arrangement, no property rights are transferred. As the legal owner of the apartment building, you have the right to bring in a partner at any time under whatever conditions you agree to. No sale of the property takes place. Legal documents that outline the terms and conditions of the new partnership are drawn up. In this example, you have agreed to take $520,000 of cash in exchange for the income generated by the investment, minus the difference between what a new mortgage would be and the existing mortgage. Note also that you have increased the spread on the interest rate by 25 basis points by adjusting the new rate to 7.50 percent from the original rate of 7.25 percent.

Now that you understand the mechanics of this strategy, let us examine the advantages and disadvantages. One primary advantage is that just as with the refinancing strategy, you avoid any tax liability. Because no sale has occurred, no taxes are due. With an equity partner, you receive an injection of capital, and with a lender, you receive an injection of debt. Both of these injections are in the form of cash on which taxes cannot be imposed because there has been no sale, and therefore no gain on sale.

Another advantage to this method is that very few costs are incurred in forming the new partnership; conversely, under the refinancing strategy, third-party reports, lender fees, and legal and title fees can all be quite significant. The only real costs related to the equity partnership method are those fees assessed by the attorneys hired to draw up the partnership agreement.

Finally, the new equity partner also benefits, due to the ease with which he or she can assume control of the property. The partner does not have to secure new financing. The partner does not have to jump through the myriad of hoops required by most lenders. The partner does not have to worry about all of the third-party reports, nor the expenses associated with them. If the partner is comfortable with the terms and conditions, a partnership agreement can be drawn up in as little as a few days.

Perhaps the biggest drawback to this method is the problem of enforcing each party's responsibilities. This disadvantage can be addressed by putting controls in place to satisfy each party with respect to the fulfillment of the other's responsibilities. For example, the new equity partner may be concerned that the original owner will not make the requisite payments to the lender in a timely manner. The partnership agreement can mandate proof of payment through documentation each month, thus ensuring that no default occurs. If it is the new partner who will be responsible for making the payment to the lender, the same documentation would be required of him or her. Likewise, the original owner may be concerned that the new partner will not operate and maintain the property satisfactorily. Again, this can be addressed in the partnership agreement by requiring the new partner to maintain the property in as good or better condition as at the time of forming the agreement.

As you can see, the equity partnership method can be a very powerful exit strategy. Although you still retain a significant interest in the property, in this example you have effectively recouped your original investment of $400,000, plus an additional $120,000 of capital that can be employed elsewhere. In the process, you have also managed to create an annual income stream of $45,673 for the next 25 years, and the best part of all is that very little effort on your part will be required, because the new partner will be responsible for operating the apartments.

## Exchange of Properties

Another effective exit strategy involves the exchange of one property for another. The primary advantage of executing an exchange agreement is the ability to defer the tax liability that would result from any gain on sale. Exchanges do not have to be made between the same parties, meaning that you do not have to sell your property to Investor A and simultaneously purchase one of Investor A's properties. You can instead sell to Investor A and buy from Investor B through a 1031 exchange (see Chapter 5 for more information on exchanges). Exchanges can be fairly complex and should be facilitated by qualified attorneys familiar with this process. Take a moment to review the comparison of cash sale versus exchange of property in Table 13.4.

**Table 13.4**   Cash Sale versus Exchange of Property

| Original Assumptions | | | |
|---|---|---|---|
| Original purchase price | 2,000,000 | | |
| Equity at 20% | 400,000 | | |
| Amount to finance (80%) | 1,600,000 | | |

| Exit Strategy 1: Cash Sale | | Exit Strategy 2: Exchange | |
|---|---|---|---|
| Sales price | 2,600,000 | Sales price | 2,600,000 |
| Purchase price | 2,000,000 | Purchase price | 2,000,000 |
| Gain on sale before taxes | 600,000 | Gain on sale before taxes | 600,000 |
| Tax at 20% LT capital gains rate | 120,000 | Tax liability is deferred | 0 |
| Gain on sale after taxes | 480,000 | Gain on sale after taxes | 600,000 |
| Original down payment | 400,000 | Original down payment | 400,000 |
| Cash available at closing | 880,000 | Cash available at closing | 1,000,000 |
| Difference between methods | **(120,000)** | Difference between methods | **120,000** |

The principal difference between an outright cash sale and an exchange of property is the ability to defer the tax liability to some point in the future. The tax liability still exists, and the investor will eventually have to pay Uncle Sam, but at least the investor gets the use of the money for the time being for additional qualified investments. Assuming an 80 percent LTV rate, an investor using Exit Strategy 1 from Table 13.4 would be able to acquire an apartment building worth up to $4.4 million. The same investor implementing Exit Strategy 2 would be able to purchase a building worth up to $5.0 million. In this case, the deferred tax liability provides the investor with up to $600,000 of additional purchasing power.

## Combining Methods

The four exit strategies discussed thus far are all valid methods that can be adopted and subsequently implemented. While these methods can all be quite effective on a stand-alone basis, implemented independently of one another, they have the potential to be even more effective when they are combined.

The best way to illustrate this is by looking at an example. We have already discussed some of the advantages and disadvantages of each of the methods. Now let us examine the use of two techniques combined. Using the $2.6 million example from before, assume you decide to retain the property in your portfolio, but want to recoup your original investment, so you decide to refinance. Later you identify another investment opportunity for which you do not have the initial capital required. You know you have $520,000 of equity in your existing project, but the funds are not liquid. The seller of the property you want to acquire is not interested in accepting your equity as collateral. The seller needs the cash for still another opportunity.

A couple of options available to you under this scenario are to either find a buyer for your property or introduce an equity partner. Both of these are viable alternatives, and each can offer the buyer or partner of your property some advantages. Take a minute to study the combined exit strategies in Table 13.5.

The total cash proceeds under each scenario are the same as if Step 1, the refinancing, was omitted. The difference, however, lies in the ease with which the new buyer can assume the existing loan. By having the loan already in place, you have in effect created an investment opportunity that is now potentially more marketable than if the loan were not in place. If the new financing is less than a year old, there are usually no third-party reports required. Depending on the lender's specific requirements, the lender will already have a recent survey, appraisal, engineering, and environmental report; therefore, new ones should not be required. The benefit to your buyer is the ability to quickly acquire your property without having to expend the time, effort, and expense of ordering all of the reports. Rather than taking the usual 60 to 120 days to close, these types of loans can quite

**Table 13.5**   Combining Exit Strategies

| Original Assumptions | | | |
|---|---|---|---|
| Original purchase price | 2,000,000 | | |
| Equity at 20% | 400,000 | | |
| Amount to finance (80%) | 1,600,000 | | |

| Original Strategy: Refinancing Secondary Strategy: Sale | | Secondary Strategy: Equity Partnership | |
|---|---|---|---|
| Appraised value | 2,600,000 | Appraised value | 2,600,000 |
| New loan at 80% | 2,080,000 | New loan at 80% | 2,080,000 |
| Payoff of existing loan | 1,600,000 | Payoff of existing loan | 1,600,000 |
| Available cash proceeds | 480,000 | Available cash proceeds | 480,000 |
| Tax liability | 0 | Tax liability | 0 |
| Cash available at closing | 480,000 | Cash available at closing | 480,000 |
| Sales price | 2,600,000 | Appraised value | 2,600,000 |
| Buyer assumes new loan | 2,080,000 | Existing loan at 80% | 2,080,000 |
| Cash proceeds at closing | 520,000 | Equity partner at 20% | 520,000 |
| Tax liability | 120,000 | Tax liability | 0 |
| Remaining cash proceeds | 400,000 | Remaining cash proceeds | 520,000 |
| Total cash proceeds | 880,000 | Total cash proceeds | 1,000,000 |
| Difference between methods | **(120,000)** | Difference between methods | **120,000** |

often close within 30 to 45 days. One caveat is that when you refinance your property, you should be fully aware of all terms and conditions that may affect the assumption. Many conduit loans are easily assumable. Most financial institutions, however, will assess a 1 percent assumption fee.

An examination of the equity partnership secondary strategy in Table 13.5 reveals one key difference between this method and the method in which no refinancing exists (Table 13.3). In the original example, the seller agrees to accept a $520,000 capital infusion from the partner along with annual payments of $45,673. In Table 13.5, the seller receives $480,000 from refinancing along with an additional $520,000 from the new partner. The trade-off, of course, is that the seller is no longer entitled to receive the annual payments of $45,673. I personally would gladly accept $520,000 today in lieu of a stream of payments spread out over time, because I know I can take the $520,000 and put it to work immediately and earn far greater returns than the meager income alternatively provided by the partner. Keep in mind also that there are no related tax liabilities under this type of arrangement, because no sale has occurred. You are not selling your interest in the property; you are just agreeing to forgo any income derived from the operations in exchange for an investment of capital. Before entering into any agreement, however, I do encourage you to seek the advice and counsel of both your accountant and your attorney.

Another potential benefit to a prospective buyer is the possibility of buying the property with less than the normal 20 percent down. This would depend on your willingness to accept less than full market value for the property. If, for example, you had owned the property for 12 to 18 months and believed that you did not have to hold out for top dollar, you might be willing to take $500,000 for your efforts rather than $600,000. Refinancing the apartments at 80 percent of the appraised value still gives you a new loan of $2.08 million; subsequently divesting at a sales price of $2.5 million allows the buyer to acquire the property with only $420,000 in cash rather than $520,000. Look at how the two compare:

$$\frac{\$520,000}{\$2,600,000} = 0.200 = 20.00\% \quad \frac{\$420,000}{\$2,500,000} = 0.168 = 16.80\%$$

By being willing to accept $100,000 less for your property, you will certainly create an investment opportunity that will be highly attractive to prospective buyers. Much like yourself, investors are seeking to maximize the return on their invested capital. If they can acquire an apartment building with only 16.80 percent down rather than the normal 20.00 percent, they will do so, because this provides a greater yield on their invested dollars. Remember the five key ratios every investor should know that are discussed in Chapter 7? This concept applies to the cash return on investment. Investors want the greatest return on their invested capital. If you can provide an opportunity for them to achieve that when divesting your property, you will greatly increase its marketability.

As you can see, combining these exit strategies in various ways can provide both you and your buyer or equity investor advantages not available through more traditional means. I believe that if you spend some time experimenting with these combinations, you will surprise yourself with the possibilities.

In summary, there are many ways to capture the value you have created in your property. You can utilize any one of the four methods described in this chapter. Each has its own unique advantages and disadvantages. Or you can use your imagination and explore the various alternatives by combining these techniques. Whatever method you select, keep in mind the objectives previously outlined for the aggressive investor—to maximize the accumulation of wealth through the creation of value and subsequently to capture as much of that value as possible. We seek wealth to reward ourselves for our own efforts, to enjoy a higher quality of life, and, hopefully, to somehow enrich the lives of others along the way.

## CHAPTER 14

*I do not choose to be a common man. It is my right to be uncommon. I seek opportunity to develop whatever talents God gave me—not security. I do not wish to be a kept citizen, humbled and dulled by having the state look after me. I want to take the calculated risk; to dream, to fail, and to succeed. I refuse to barter incentive for a dole. I prefer the challenges of life to the guaranteed existence; the thrill of fulfillment to the stale calm of utopia. I will not trade freedom for beneficence nor my dignity for a handout. I will never cower before any earthly master nor bend to any threat. It is my heritage to stand erect, proud and unafraid; to think and act myself, enjoy the benefit of my creations and to face the world boldly and say, "This, with God's help, I have done."*
**—DEAN ALFANGE**

# Five Keys to Your Success

The central focus of this book is on arming you with the specific tools necessary to identify potential acquisition candidates, to acquire and manage those properties once you have identified them, to implement sound techniques for creating value, and, finally, to capture all of that value, or as much of it as possible, through various exit strategies. The process by which all of this can be accomplished rests, I believe, on five keys that are crucial to success. These keys do not deal with the mechanical processes involved in buying and selling apartment buildings, but are grounded in principles fundamental to life itself. These laws deal with the human psyche. They govern our thoughts, which, in turn, direct our actions. The failure to understand these keys—which can provide the foundation of happiness, and ultimately of success—will almost certainly guarantee your defeat.

**The Five Keys to Success**

1. Understanding risk.
2. Overcoming fear of failure.
3. Accepting responsibility.
4. Willingness to persevere.
5. Defining your sense of purpose.

# Understanding Risk

Many people today have misperceptions when it comes to risk. They do not understand that there is a difference between *risk* and *riskiness*. "Buy an apartment building? Never. Too risky. Buy a lottery ticket? Sure, why not? You can't win if you don't play." Unfortunately, this is the prevailing attitude among many people today. Even more unfortunate, this attitude is passed on from generation to generation. The pattern is learned by youth through observation of their parents and many other adults around them. Mom says, "Oh, don't do that. You might fail. Play it safe and get a job. That way you can grow up to be just like your father." Sound familiar?

I hear this from all sorts of people. The media are especially guilty of projecting this fear. Ever wonder why? It is because reporters are generally low-paid journalists with jobs. Anyone who has enjoyed any degree of success is often demonized by the press. Studies indicate many people believe that anyone who is wealthy either has somehow come by their wealth dishonestly, or has inherited it, or has won the lottery. What happened to good old-fashioned honest labor? Is it not possible that someone who enjoys a degree of affluence has come by that wealth through honesty and integrity?

I personally do not care what these types of people think of me. Let them think what they want. They are entitled to their opinions and belief systems, just as I am entitled to mine. If you are willing to risk just about everything to obtain wealth in your own right, then let others think what they want. I suppose what troubles me is that, unfortunately, many people who hold these prevailing attitudes end up as our elected officials. When misguided politicians hold offices of power, they somehow think it is their right to impose taxes on the wealthy. It is called the *redistribution of wealth.* Take from the "haves" and give to the "have nots." Yes, many arguments can be made for taxing the wealthy (after all, they can afford it), and an overabundance of ostensibly justifiable reasons are given for doing so. Each and every year the government takes a little more.

This seeming digression goes directly to the heart of the subject of risk. The majority of politicians are educated in law schools, where complexity and confusion are the norm. Political leaders have little or no concept of the true applications of risk, simply because they lack real-life experience in the business world. They do not understand the relationship between risk and reward. They do not understand that risk is a financial concept that can be quantified, and that the probability of a favorable or unfavorable outcome can be mathematically derived.

Sadly, some of these same misconceptions can be found in our own families. I recently attended a family reunion and was sitting at a table with several of my nieces, one of whom had just graduated from high school with a scholarship to a major university. She asked me something like, "So, Uncle Steve, I hear you do something with real estate or apartment buildings or something like that."

Without elaborating, I responded that I was involved in various real estate projects. Her very next question to me was, "Isn't that risky?"

I have to admit that I was not prepared for a question like that, but in retrospect, I suppose it should not have surprised me. After all, her question perfectly reflects the type of environment that most kids are exposed to.

I said to myself, as I sometimes do, "Ah ha! A teaching opportunity!" I firmly believe that adults have a duty and an obligation to teach their children, as well as other youth, at just such times.

After taking a brief moment to recover from her initial question, I immediately delved into a short explanation of the difference between *risk* and *riskiness*. I explained to my niece that *riskiness* applies to events over the outcome of which one has no control. Risky events include activities such as playing the lottery, spinning a roulette wheel, or playing the slot machines. Although the mathematical probability of each possible outcome of these events can be easily measured, the player has absolutely no control over the outcome. These are games of chance, nothing more and nothing less. *Risk,* conversely, applies to those activities or events over the outcome of which one has a very high degree of control. You can carefully examine all the internal and external factors, as well as analyze the micro- and macrofactors, which may impact the risk you assume. After completing a thorough analysis, you can map out a well-defined strategy that will allow you to guide and direct all of the activities related to the risk. It is this very process that allows you to control the outcome of your venture with great precision. These activities are far from games of chance. In fact, you enjoy a much higher probability of success by assuming risks associated with business ventures than you could ever hope to achieve in a risky game like the lottery. Unfortunately, it is our government bureaucrats who are the biggest offenders of duping citizens into willingly playing these games of chance.

"And this, my dear niece, is the difference between *risk* and *riskiness.*"

## Overcoming Fear of Failure

One of our greatest obstacles in life is that demon we call *Fear*. Just as surely as risk is introduced into the equation of success, so must failure be factored in. This is not to say that you will necessarily fail, but, rather, that the possibility for failure exists, and when that possibility is present, you must be prepared to properly deal with it. Failure is a natural part of learning. It is a completely natural process in most aspects of life. Just because you fail at something does not mean you are a failure. You become a failure only when you fail to continue failing. Many people are defeated by the *fear* of failure. They do not even make it to the failure stage because they are afraid to try. They are afraid of failing. They fear the unknown because it represents areas beyond the boundaries of their own comfort zone. They fear what others may think of them. They fear ridicule and derision by their friends, and sadly enough, even by their own families. They are told it cannot be done, so why bother trying?

Some friends or acquaintances act as a great weight placed about your shoulders. If you are not careful, this weight will act as an anchor, holding you steadfastly in place, keeping you from reaching your true potential. You must choose your friends wisely. You must choose friends who will act as buoys, lifting you up rather than weighing you down. And as for your family members, you can objectively consider their advice, and then choose the course of action you believe to be best for you, regardless of their opinions. As your family observes your own progress, their attitudes will change, and you may even discover that they will come to you for advice from time to time.

I know from my own personal experience that even though I have become more comfortable with risk over the years, there are still times when the little boy inside me says, "I'm afraid. I don't think I can do this." My lovely wife is attuned to the feelings and emotions of those around her, especially those of her family. She somehow always seems to be acutely aware of those who may be suffering, however trivial the matter may be. Even when I say nothing to her of my fears, she senses when something is not right. She will gently persuade me to share with her whatever it is that may be troubling me. My usual response is, "Oh, I'm okay, honey." She presses for an answer, "Are you sure nothing is bothering you?" It is at this point that I begin to open up to her. As I express my fears and concerns, we discuss viable solutions. My wife becomes, and has always been, my greatest supporter. While I am out slaying terrible, fire-breathing dragons, she is cheering me on from the sidelines, chanting, "Go, Steve, go!" This added emotional support gives me the courage to conquer all. I become formidable. I am invincible. I cannot be defeated and will surely prevail.

So you see, a supportive spouse can be a tremendous asset. Make your spouse your partner, not only in your business affairs, but in all aspects of your life. And be your spouse's greatest cheerleader. Encourage, praise, express your confidence, and then stand back and watch your spouse soar!

Napoleon Hill devotes an entire chapter of his classic book, *Think and Grow Rich* (New York: Fawcett Crest, 1960) to the subject of love and romance. Hill writes:

> Love, romance, and sex are all emotions capable of driving men to heights of super achievement. Love is the emotion which serves as a safety valve, and ensures balance, poise, and constructive effort. When combined, these three emotions may lift one to an altitude of a genius. . . . Love is, without question, life's greatest experience. It brings one into communion with Infinite Intelligence. When mixed with the emotions of romance and sex, it may lead one far up the ladder of creative effort. The emotions of love, sex, and romance are sides of the eternal triangle of achievement building genius. (p. 191)

Hill is a well-respected authority on the subject of successful people. His study of thousands of men and women over a period of more than 40 years led him to conclude that the elements of love, sex, and romance, when used in their proper balance, contribute greatly to an individual's success. In addition to Hill's conclusions regarding love, one must consider the proper application of these emotions. This precept can be summarized as follows: *Love is a verb which requires action. What you feel inside is the fruit of that love.* This principle represents a true cause-and-effect relationship. When you give service to your spouse, you are *loving* him or her. Giving selfless acts of service to your spouse will yield the fruit of love, which is the feeling you receive in your bosom. A proper understanding of this profound law of nature is fundamental to your happiness and will bring you more success in all aspects of your life than you ever thought possible. I issue this challenge and promise: if you and your spouse will apply this precept in your lives, you will experience a renewed sense of love and romance in your relationship. You will become each other's greatest allies, and as such, you will become an invincible team capable of overcoming any and all challenges you set your minds to. And finally, you will be able to draw tremendous strength from one another, which will allow you to defeat the great adversary, that demon we call Fear.

## Accepting Responsibility

The willingness to assume risk implies that we must also be willing to accept the responsibility associated with that risk. For some reason, we are led to believe that it is not okay to make mistakes and that when we do, it must be someone else's fault. Let me say here and now that it *is* okay to make mistakes. But when you do, you must be prepared to accept responsibility for those mistakes.

Just a few weeks ago, my wife and I were getting our van ready for summer vacation. Because we would be driving for 10 to 12 hours each way, we thought it would be nice if we could set up our 13-inch-screen videocassette player in the van so our boys could watch some of their tapes on the trip. Part of the process required plugging a power adapter into the cigarette lighter socket to convert the van's direct-current power to alternating-current power for the videocassette player. The adapter did not appear to be functioning properly, so I attempted to diagnose the problem. I started by plugging the cigarette lighter into its socket to determine whether the socket had power. When I removed the lighter from the socket, it was not red and therefore did not appear to be hot. Not thinking, I grasped the lighter with my left hand and gently placed it against the palm of my right hand. I was immediately impressed with two sensations. The first was a burning pain in my right hand, and the second was the pungent odor of burning flesh.

"Now that was stupid," I said aloud.

My wife, who was sitting next to me, looked at me as if I had lost my mind. And why not? After all, I had just taken a hot lighter and burned my hand, which was now beginning to blister.

By the way, the word *stupid,* along with several others, is a word we try not to use in our family. We refer to these words as *junk words* and make every effort to exclude them from our everyday vocabulary. I had gone and said it, though. And then, just for good measure, I said it again: "That was really stupid."

The natural thing for me to have done would have been to blame the lighter for burning me, or even to blame my wife. I could have just as easily turned to her and said, "Now look what you made me do."

The very next day, as I was putting on a dress shirt, I noticed a thread hanging from the back of the shirt. I asked my wife, who was busy, to use the scissors to clip the thread.

She replied, "Give me just a minute to finish, honey."

Not wanting to wait, I impatiently took the scissors from the drawer and clipped the thread myself. In the process, I cut a hole right through my shirt. Once again, I used the junk word. "That was really stupid," I exclaimed.

My wife just looked at me and laughed. And, yes, she agreed that it was really stupid.

Once again, it would have been easy to blame anyone but myself. After all, if she had cut the thread when I asked her to, I would not have cut a hole in my shirt, right? Wrong! If I had been even slightly more patient, my wife would gladly have clipped the thread for me, and she would have done it without putting a hole in my shirt.

So there you have it. Two stupid things two days in a row. First I burned my hand, then I cut a hole in one of my best dress shirts. It would have been easy for me to blame the lighter, or the scissors, or even my wife. While I am not proud of the fact that I used a junk word repeatedly, I am glad to report that I placed the blame for those careless acts squarely where it belonged, on myself. By accepting responsibility for my own thoughtless acts, I placed myself in a position to learn from my mistakes. If I had attempted to shift the responsibility elsewhere, I would not have learned anything and would therefore be likely to continue to make similar errors.

So it is for each of us. We will make many, many mistakes along the pathway we call life, and that is okay. You must be willing, however, to accept full responsibility for your errors. Refusing to do so is like being an alcoholic in denial. Until alcoholics acknowledge that a problem exists, they are in no position to overcome the illness. Accept responsibility for your actions, learn from your mistakes, and move on.

## Willingness to Persevere

The will to persevere is not only crucial to one's success in the apartment industry; it is crucial for success in all aspects of one's life. The ability to endure whatever challenges life has to offer is essential for personal development and growth. This is especially true for the attainment of wealth. If you are to accumulate wealth, you must be willing to dedicate your efforts to that end. Creating wealth and accumulating a fortune is like any other skill you choose to master. It takes persistence, patience, and the will to persevere.

Think of a skill or talent that you have now. You may be an expert musician, or perhaps you are an excellent athlete, or maybe you excelled in academics. If you are like most people, whatever level of skill or expertise you have achieved has likely been developed over a number of years and is most certainly the result of dedication and the will to excel in your chosen field. Nothing was handed to you. You did not win the lottery in academia and suddenly become a genius. If you are a star athlete, no one just gave you the first-place trophy because of your charm and good looks.

Nothing in life worth having is just handed over to you. Recall the Thomas Paine quote at the beginning of Chapter 12: "The harder the conflict, the more glorious the triumph. What we obtain too cheaply, we esteem too lightly." How true this is.

Think of some of the spoiled kids you know whose parents give them everything they want. Now think of the way those kids take care of their things. If they are anything like the kids I know, they leave their toys out or continually break them when they are little; they throw their bikes on the ground and trash their parents' cars as teenagers; and they eventually grow into irresponsible adults who lack crucial life-coping skills.

What does this teach children? It teaches them that everyone and everything owes them something. They are deprived of the opportunity and the privilege of coming to know and appreciate the value of hard work, and, as a result, they become self-centered, believing the world should be indebted to them.

One of the ways you can help your children to appreciate perseverance is through the value of hard work. This can best be accomplished by teaching them through your own example, and also by giving them greater and greater responsibility as they get older. These values can be instilled in them starting at a very early age. Do not make the mistake of waiting until they are teenagers to teach them to pick up their things. Children can begin learning at the age of one or two that when they are done playing with their toys, it is time to pick them up. If their parents get in the habit of picking up after them all the time, that is what they will learn, and that is what they will come to expect.

Perseverance is a conditioning process that is best learned in youth. Have you ever been to a circus and seen an elephant with a small steel band around its ankle, with a chain attached to the band at one end and to a wooden stake in the ground at the other? How is it possible that a chain so small relative to the size of a mighty 10,000-pound elephant could possibly restrain it? Surely the elephant is strong enough to simply pull the stake right out of the ground. So why doesn't it?

The answer lies in the way the elephant was trained since it was a baby. When the elephant was small, the same chain and wooden stake that holds it now could easily hold it then. As a baby, the elephant would tug and pull in an attempt to free itself. The harder it pulled, however, the more the metal band cut into the skin around the elephant's ankle. The elephant quickly began to associate pain with tugging at the chain. The way to alleviate the pain was to stop pulling. Although the elephant eventually grew much larger and stronger and could easily free itself from captivity, its mind is now conditioned to associate pain with any attempt to pull itself free from the chain.

Perhaps you, too, have been conditioned by your environment over the years. Family and friends tell you that you cannot do it. You cannot succeed. Like the elephant, this continual bombardment of negativity represents the chains of bondage that retard your progress. Past attempts to free yourself have resulted in failure and have been the source of much pain. To alleviate the pain, you stop trying. You simply give up. Under these conditions, it is difficult to realize that as you grope through the darkness toward your destination, there is radiant sunshine with bright, blue skies bursting forth just on the other side of the mountain. The nagging pain from years of improper conditioning, however, seem more than you can possibly bear. To push forward, to persevere, you must recognize that whatever short-term sacrifices you must endure now will be well worth the long-term benefits you will eventually enjoy.

Benjamin Franklin certainly understood the value of perseverance, for he applied this trait throughout much of his own life, making many significant contributions that have come to benefit mankind. In *Benjamin Franklin: The Autobiography and Other Writings,* edited by L. Jesse Lemisch (New York: New American Library, 1961), the immortal Franklin records his own thoughts about the virtues of perseverance:

> Like the man who in buying an ax of a smith my neighbor, desired to have the
> whole of its surface as bright as the edge; the smith consented to grind it bright

for him if he would turn the wheel. He turned while the smith pressed the broad face of the ax hard and heavily on the stone, which made the turning of it very fatiguing. The man came every now and then from the wheel to see how the work went on; and at length would take his ax as it was, without further grinding. "No," says the smith, "turn on, turn on; we shall have it bright by and by; as yet, tis' only speckled." "Yes," says the man, *"but I think I like a speckled ax best."* And I believe this may have been the case with many who having, for want of some such means as I employed, found the difficulty of obtaining good and breaking bad habits in other points of vice and virtue, have given up the struggle and concluded that "a speckled ax was best."

But on the whole, tho' I never arrived at the perfection I had been so ambitious of obtaining but fell far short of it, yet I was by the endeavor a better and a happier man than I otherwise would have been if I had not attempted it. (pp. 101–102)

I believe Franklin's example of the man grinding the ax is analogous to many of us who struggle each day only to find ourselves tired after a few turns of the grindstone. Since our muscles have not been properly conditioned, they quickly grow weary. Since our minds lack the discipline required to mentally persevere, they, too, quickly become fatigued. Let us commit to persevere by fully applying ourselves so that we may attain our goals, lest we find that we, too, "have given up the struggle and concluded that 'a speckled ax was best.' "

## Defining Your Sense of Purpose

Chapter 3 describes a captain of a ship who is about to embark on a journey across a great ocean. The captain not only has a specific destination in mind but also has a specific mission to accomplish upon arrival. As with the captain, it is just as important to know *why* you are going on the journey as it is to know *where* you are going on the journey. This poses the question, "What is our purpose in life?" What exactly is it you hope to achieve in this process of wealth accumulation?

Albert Einstein provides some insight into our purpose in life. He states, "The most important human endeavor is the striving for morality in our actions. Our inner balance and even our very existence depend on it. Only morality in our actions can give beauty and dignity to life."

This beauty and dignity in life that Einstein refers to can provide a sense of peace and happiness. Ultimately, I believe that is exactly what each of us is striving for. I know I am. I am seeking a higher quality of life, not only for me, but for those closest to me. The process of wealth accumulation challenges you to grow in ways you never thought possible. It provides a conduit to a higher plane in life by empowering you to reach your full potential. It is simply a means to an end. Wealth enables you to enrich the lives of those around you who may not be as fortunate for any number of reasons. Our purpose is much greater than to amass riches for the sake of serving only ourselves. I am not suggesting that you work hard all of your life to accumulate wealth only to turn around and give it all away. What I am suggesting, however, is that once you are fortunate enough to have achieved your objectives, much happiness lies in the giving of yourself and of that which you have attained through your labors.

Embodied within this sense of purpose is the underlying catalyst that can propel us to unimaginable heights. It gives us a reason to reach far beyond what we might otherwise be capable of. As we seek to bless the lives of others, doors are opened for us from which shine bright shafts of light illuminating the way. We learn to selflessly reach beyond the scope of our own needs so that we might lift up those around us. This sense of purpose gives us hope—hope for a higher quality of life, and hope to ease the burdens of those who are heavily laden.

The well-known author Og Mandino writes in his best-selling book *The Greatest Miracle in the World* (New York: Bantam Books, 1975) of a man named Simon Potter, whom he refers to as a ragpicker. The term *ragpicker* was used during the Depression of the 1930s to describe individuals who picked up rags and other waste materials from the streets to redeem for money, much as homeless people today scavenge for empty aluminum cans or pop bottles in order to reclaim the deposits. Potter, however, was a different sort of ragpicker. Rather than salvaging through materials such as rags or cans that had been discarded for one reason or another, Potter was a scavenger of human souls. He searched diligently each day for those individuals who had been discarded by society. He sought to give them hope, to restore their dignity, to give them another chance at life.

In one section of the book, Mr. Og (as Potter liked to refer to Mandino) and Potter are discussing miracles. Both agree that perhaps the greatest of all miracles is the ability to restore life to those who have already died. Mandino, referring to Potter's great collection of books, comments that he sees no connection between the books and how to perform a miracle such as restoring life to the dead. In reply, Potter states most emphatically:

Ah, but they do, Mr. Og. Most humans, in varying degrees, are already dead. In one way or another they have lost their dreams, their ambitions, their desire for a better life. They have surrendered their fight for self-esteem and they have compromised their great potential. They have settled for a life of mediocrity, days of despair and nights of tears. They are no more than living deaths confined to cemeteries of their choice. . . . Most of us build prisons for ourselves and after we occupy them for a period of time we become accustomed to their walls and accept the false premise that we are incarcerated for life. As soon as that belief takes hold of us we abandon hope of ever doing more with our lives and of ever giving our dreams a chance to be fulfilled. We become puppets and begin to suffer living deaths. It may be praiseworthy and noble to sacrifice your life to a cause or a business or the happiness of others, but if you are miserable and unfulfilled in that lifestyle, and know it, then to remain in it is a hypocrisy, a lie, and a rejection of the faith placed in you by your creator. . . . Yet they need not remain in that state. They can be resurrected from their sorry condition. They can perform the greatest miracle in the world. They can each come back from the dead. (p. 14)

The wisdom of Potter's words strikes a chord of truth in most of us. It is easy to allow the adversaries of Fear and Despair to overcome us. We have probably all been told at one time or another that "It cannot be done," or "You will fail, so why even bother?" A weak mind and a poor self-image will easily be defeated by these thoughts, and as Potter affirms, we become comfortable within the confines of the prison we have built with our own hands. We know how every bar of the prison feels, and how strong each one is, because we have allowed the walls to be erected around us, sometimes unknowingly, and other times fully cognizant as each block of the wall is built higher and higher, until, finally, it is no longer possible to escape, or so it seems.

A sense of purpose, however, can help us to defeat these demons we call Fear and Despair. A sense of purpose can act as a compass by showing us the way when we are confronted with these challenges. Like a compass, purpose gives us direction. Let us not allow ourselves to surrender our fight for self-esteem and thereby compromise our great potential. Let us not settle for a life of mediocrity, nor succumb to the adversary of Fear. Let us instead take Mandino's advice and be resurrected from our sorry condition, so that we, too, can come back from the dead.

If you believe that it is perhaps too late, that you are getting too old and that life has passed you by, I invite you to draw once again from the wisdom of Napoleon Hill's classic book, *Think and Grow Rich:*

Seldom does an individual enter upon highly creative effort in any field of endeavor before the age of forty. The average man reaches the period of his greatest capacity to create between forty and sixty. These statements are based upon analysis of thousands of men and women who have carefully been observed. They should be encouraging to those who become frightened at the approach of "old age," around the forty year mark. The years between forty and fifty are, as a rule, the most fruitful. Man should approach this age, not with fear and trembling, but with hope and eager anticipation. (p. 190)

If you are between 40 and 60, I am sure you take great comfort in Hill's remarks. This represents a period of time when you can fully apply yourself. As a pioneer and an explorer, it is a time when you can embark on the greatest journey of your life—the pursuit of a higher quality of life through the accumulation of wealth.

The laws for success are fully outlined in the pages of this book. This book discusses the merits of numerous financial concepts and principles that, when properly applied, will enable you to attain your goal of accumulating wealth. In addition, it provides you with the precepts necessary to master the human psyche, that element of our being that gives us the strength to persevere and to conquer our fears, gives us the wisdom to accept responsibility for our actions, and gives us direction in our lives by providing us with a sense of purpose. It is the culmination of these laws of success and emotional precepts that serves as a catalyst you can use to propel yourself to heights never before believed possible.

# www.thevalueplay.com

Current ordering information for The Value Play Rental House Analyzer, Rehab Analyzer, Income Analyzer, Refi Analyzer, and other real estate products can be found at www.thevalueplay.com.

# www.symphony-homes.com

Symphony Homes is one of Michigan's premier builders of high-quality new homes. We maintain a tradition of excellence by ensuring that each and every home we build meets our strict standards of quality. Symphony Homes is built on a foundation of three principals—quality, value, and service. From start to finish, we take care to ensure that only the best materials and the finest craftsmanship are utilized throughout the construction process. By partnering with key suppliers and efficiently managing our resources, we can effectively create value for home buyers by offering superior homes at competitive prices. Offering personal service to home buyers and fulfilling commitments to them allows us to provide each and every customer with an enjoyable building experience.

As a custom builder, Symphony Homes builds on home sites owned by individuals, or those owned by the company. We offer new home construction services in all of Genesee County, Lapeer County, and North Oakland County. For information regarding Symphony Homes, one of Michigan's premier builders, please log on to www.symphony-homes.com.

**Catch the Symphony Homes Vision!**

**Log on to www.symphony-homes.com!**

Real estate investors will find this glossary helpful for understanding words and terms used in real estate transactions. However, some factors may affect these definitions. Terms are defined as they are commonly understood in the mortgage and real estate industry. The same terms may have different meanings in another context. The definitions are intentionally general, nontechnical, and short. They do not encompass all possible meanings or nuances that a term may acquire in legal use. State laws, as well as custom and use in various states or regions of the country, may in fact modify or completely change the meanings of certain terms defined. Before signing any documents or depositing any money preparatory to entering into a real estate contract, the purchaser should consult with an attorney to ensure that his or her rights are properly protected.

**Abstract of Title**   A summary of the public records relating to the title to a particular piece of land. An attorney or title insurance company reviews an abstract of title to determine whether there are any title defects that must be cleared before a buyer can purchase clear, marketable, and insurable title.

**Acceleration Clause**   Condition in a mortgage that may require the balance of the loan to become due immediately in the event regular mortgage payments are not made or for breach of other conditions of the mortgage.

**Ad Valorem**   Designates an assessment of taxes against property in a literal sense according to its value.

**Adjustable Rate Mortgage Loans (ARM)**   Loans with interest rates that are adjusted periodically based on changes in a preselected index. As a result, the interest rate on your loan and the monthly payment will rise and fall with increases and decreases in overall interest rates. These mortgage loans must specify how their interest rate changes, usually in terms of a relation to a national index such as (but not always) Treasury bill rates. If interest rates rise, your monthly payments will rise. An interest rate cap limits the amount by which the interest rate can change; look for this feature when you consider an ARM loan.

**Adverse Possession**   A possession that is inconsistent with the right of possession and title of the true owner. It is the actual, open, notorious, exclusive, continuous, and hostile occupation and possession of the land of another under a claim of right or under color of title.

**Agency**   The relationship that exists by contract whereby one person is authorized to represent and act on behalf of another person in various business transactions.

**Agreement of Sale**   Known by various names, such as contract of purchase, purchase agreement, or sales agreement, according to location or jurisdiction. A contract in which a seller agrees to sell and a buyer agrees to buy, under certain specific terms and conditions spelled out in writing and signed by both parties.

**Amortization**   A payment plan that enables the borrower to reduce a debt gradually through monthly payments of principal, thereby liquidating or extinguishing the obligation through a series of installments.

**Annual Compounding**   The arithmetic process of determining the final value of a cash flow or series of cash flows when interest is added once a year.

**Annual Percentage Rate (APR)**   The cost of credit expressed as a yearly rate. The annual percentage rate is often not the same as the interest rate. It is a percentage that results from an equation considering the amount financed, the finance charges, and the term of the loan.

**Appraisal**   An expert judgment or estimate of the quality or value of real estate as of a given date. The process through which conclusions of property value are obtained. It is also refers to the formalized report that sets forth the estimate and conclusion of value.

**Appurtenance**   That which belongs to something else. In real estate law, an appurtenance is a right, privilege, or improvement, which passes as an incident to the land, such as a right of way.

**Assessed Value**   An official valuation of property most often used for tax purposes.

**Assignment**   The method or manner by which a right, a specialty, or contract is transferred from one person to another.

**Assumption of Mortgage**   An obligation undertaken by the purchaser of property to be personally liable for payment of an existing mortgage. In an assumption, the purchaser is substituted for the original mortgagor in the mortgage instrument and the original mortgagor is to be released from further liability in the assumption. The mortgagee's consent is usually required.

The original mortgagor should always obtain a written release from further liability to be fully released under the assumption. Failure to obtain such a release renders the original mortgagor liable if the person assuming the mortgage fails to make the monthly payments.

An assumption of mortgage is often confused with 'purchasing subject to a mortgage.' When one purchases subject to a mortgage, the purchaser agrees to make the monthly mortgage payments on an existing mortgage, but the original mortgagor remains personally liable if the purchaser fails to make the monthly payments. Since the original mortgagor remains liable in the event of default, the mortgagee's consent is not required for a sale subject to a mortgage.

Both assumption of mortgage and purchasing subject to a mortgage are used to finance the sale of property. They may also be used when a mortgagor is in financial difficulty and desires to sell the property to avoid foreclosure.

**Balance Statement**   A statement of the firm's financial position at a specific point in time.

**Balloon Mortgage**   Balloon mortgage loans are short-term fixed-rate loans with fixed monthly payments for a set number of years followed by one large final balloon payment ("the balloon") for the remainder of the principal. Typically, the balloon payment may be due at the end of 5, 7, or 10 years. Borrowers with balloon loans may have the right to refinance the loan when the balloon payment is due, but the right to refinance is not guaranteed.

**Bankruptcy**   A proceeding in a federal court to relieve certain debts of a person or a business unable to pay its debts.

**Bill of Sale**   A written document or instrument that provides evidence of the transfer of right, title, and interest in personal property from one person to another.

**Binder or Offer to Purchase**   A preliminary agreement, secured by the payment of earnest money, between a buyer and seller as an offer to purchase real estate. A binder secures the right to purchase real estate upon agreed terms for a limited period of time. If the buyer decides not to purchase, or is unable to purchase, the earnest money is forfeited unless the binder expressly provides that it is to be refunded.

**Blanket Mortgage**   A single mortgage that covers more than one piece of real estate. It is often used to purchase a large tract of land, which is later subdivided and sold as individual parcels.

**Bona fide**   Made in good faith; good, valid, without fraud; such as a *bona fide* offer.

**Bond**   Any obligation under seal. A real estate bond is a written obligation, usually issued on security of a mortgage or deed of trust.

**Breach**   The breaking of law, or failure of a duty, either by omission or commission; the failure to perform, without legal excuse, any promise that forms a part or the whole of a contract.

**Broker**   One who is engaged for others in a negotiation for contacts relative to property, with the custody of which they have no concern.

**Broker, Real Estate**   Any person, partnership, association, or corporation who, for a compensation or valuable consideration, sells or offers for sale, buys or offers to buy, or negotiates the purchase or sale or exchange of real estate, or rents or offers to rent, any real estate or the improvements thereon for others.

**Capital**   Accumulated wealth; a portion of wealth set aside for the production of additional wealth; specifically, the funds belonging to the partners or shareholders of a business, invested with the express purpose and intent of remaining in the business to generate profits.

**Capital Expenditures**   Investments of cash or other property, or the creation of a liability in exchange for property to remain permanently in the business; usually pertaining to land, buildings, machinery, and equipment.

**Capitalization**   The act or process of converting or obtaining the present value of future incomes into current equivalent capital value; also the amount so determined; commonly referring to the capital structure of a corporation or other such legal entity.

**Cash Out**   Any cash received when a new loan is obtained that is larger than the remaining balance of the current mortgage, based upon the equity already built up in the property. The cash out amount is calculated by subtracting the sum of the old loan and fees from the new mortgage loan.

**Caveat Emptor**   The phrase literally means "let the buyer beware." Under this doctrine, the buyer is duty bound to examine the property being purchased and assumes conditions that are readily ascertainable upon view.

**Certificate of Title**   A certificate issued by a title company or a written opinion rendered by an attorney that the seller has good marketable and insurable title to the property offered for sale. A certificate of title offers no protection against any hidden defects in the title that an examination of the records could not reveal. The issuer of a certificate of title is liable only for damages due to negligence. The protection offered a homeowner under a certificate of title is not as great as that offered in a title insurance policy.

**Chain of Title**   A history of conveyances and encumbrances affecting the title to a particular real property.

**Chattel**   Items of moveable personal property, such as animals, household furnishings, money, jewelry, motor vehicles, and all other items not permanently affixed to real property that can be transferred from one place to another.

**Closing Costs**   The numerous expenses that buyers and sellers normally incur to complete a transaction in the transfer of ownership of real estate. These costs are in addition to price of the property and are items prepaid at the closing day. The following is a common list of closing costs.

**BUYER'S EXPENSES:**

☑ Documentary Stamps on Notes
☑ Recording Deed and Mortgage
☑ Escrow Fees
☑ Attorney's Fee
☑ Title Insurance
☑ Appraisal and Inspection
☑ Survey Charge

**SELLER'S EXPENSES:**

☑ Cost of Abstract
☑ Documentary Stamps on Deed
☑ Real Estate Commission
☑ Recording Mortgage
☑ Survey Charge
☑ Escrow Fees
☑ Attorney's Fee

The agreement of sale negotiated previously between the buyer and the seller may state in writing who will pay each of the above costs.

**Closing Day**   The day on which the formalities of a real estate sale are concluded. The certificate of title, abstract, and deed are generally prepared for the closing by an attorney and this cost is charged to the buyer. The buyer signs the mortgage, and closing costs are paid. The final closing merely confirms the original agreement reached in the agreement of sale.

**Cloud on Title**   An outstanding claim or encumbrance that adversely affects the marketability of title.

**Collateral Security**   A separate obligation attached to a contract to guarantee its performance; the transfer of property or of other contracts or valuables to ensure the performance of a principal agreement or obligation.

**Commission**   Money paid to a real estate agent or broker by the seller as compensation for finding a buyer and completing the sale. Usually it is a percentage of the sale price ranging anywhere from 6 to 7 percent on single-family houses and 10 percent on land.

**Compound Interest**   Interest paid on the original principal of an indebtedness and also on the accrued and unpaid interest that has accumulated over time.

**Condominium**   Individual ownership of a dwelling unit and an individual interest in the common areas and facilities serving the multiunit project.

**Consideration**   Something of value, usually money, that is the inducement of a contract. Any right, interest, property, or benefit accruing to one party; any forbearance, detriment, loss or responsibility given, suffered or undertaken, may constitute a consideration that will sustain a contract.

**Contract of Purchase**   (*See* agreement of sale)

**Conventional Mortgage**   A mortgage loan not insured by HUD or guaranteed by the Veterans' Administration. It is subject to conditions established by the lending institution and state statutes. The mortgage rates may vary with different institutions and between states. (States have various interest limits.)

**Cooperative Housing**   An apartment building or a group of dwellings owned by a corporation, the stockholders of which are the residents of the dwellings. It is operated for their benefit by their elected board of directors. In a cooperative, the corporation or association owns title to the real estate. A resident purchases stock in the corporation, which entitles the resident to occupy a unit in the building or property owned by the cooperative. While the resident does not own the unit, the resident has an absolute right to occupy that unit for as long as he or she owns the stock.

**Covenant**  An agreement between two or more persons entered into by deed whereby one of the parties promises the performance of certain acts, or that a given state does or shall, or does not or shall not, exist.

**Debt**  An obligation to repay a specified amount at a specified time.

**Debt Service**  The portion of funds required to repay a financial obligation such as a mortgage, which includes interest and principal payments.

**Deed**  A formal written instrument by which title to real property is transferred from one owner to another. The deed should contain an accurate description of the property being conveyed, should be signed and witnessed according to the laws of the state where the property is located, and should be delivered to the purchaser on the day of closing. There are two parties to a deed—the grantor and the grantee. (*See also* deed of trust, general warranty deed, quitclaim deed, and special warranty deed.)

**Deed of Trust**  Like a mortgage, a security instrument whereby real property is given as security for a debt; however, in a deed of trust there are three parties to the instrument—the borrower, the trustee, and the lender (or beneficiary). In such a transaction, the borrower transfers the legal title for the property to the trustee, who holds the property in trust as security for the payment of the debt to the lender or beneficiary. If the borrower pays the debt as agreed, the deed of trust becomes void. If, however, the borrower defaults in the payment of the debt, the trustee may sell the property at a public sale, under the terms of the deed of trust. In most jurisdictions where the deed of trust is in force, the borrower is subject to having the property sold without benefit of legal proceedings. A few states have begun in recent years to treat the deed of trust like a mortgage.

**Default**  Failure to make mortgage payments as agreed to in a commitment based on the terms and at the designated time set forth in the mortgage or deed of trust. It is the mortgagor's responsibility to remember the due date and send the payment prior to the due date, not after. Generally, 30 days after the due date if payment is not received, the mortgage is in default. In the event of default, the mortgagor may give the lender the right to accelerate payments, take possession and receive rents, and start foreclosure. Defaults may also come about by the failure to observe other conditions in the mortgage or deed of trust.

**Depreciation**  Decline in value of a house due to wear and tear, adverse changes in the neighborhood, or any other reason. The term is most often applied for tax purposes.

**Down Payment**  The amount of money to be paid by the purchaser to the seller upon the signing of the agreement of sale. The agreement of sale will refer to the down payment amount and will acknowledge receipt of the down payment. Down payment is the difference between the sales price and maximum mortgage amount. The down payment may not be refundable if the purchaser fails to buy the property without good cause. If the purchaser wants the down payment to be refundable, a clause in the agreement of sale should be inserted, specifying the conditions under which the deposit will be refunded, if the agreement does not already contain such clause. If the seller cannot deliver good title, the agreement of sale usually requires the seller to return the down payment and to pay interest and expenses incurred by the purchaser.

**Duress**  Unlawful constraint exercised upon a person, whereby the person is forced to perform some act, or to sign an instrument or document against his or her will.

**Earnest Money**  The deposit money given to the seller or the seller's agent by the potential buyer upon the signing of the agreement of sale to show serious intent about buying a house or any other type of real property. If the sale goes through, the earnest money is applied against the down payment. If the sale does not go through, the earnest money will be forfeited or lost unless the binder or offer to purchase expressly provides that it is refundable.

**Easement Rights**  A right-of-way granted to a person or company authorizing access to or over the owner's land. An electric company obtaining a right-of-way across private property is a common example.

**Economic Life**  The period over which a property may be profitably utilized or the period over which a property will yield a return on the investment, over and above the economic or ground rent due to its land.

**Economic Obsolescence**  Impairment of desirability or useful life arising from economic forces, such as changes in optimum land use, legislative enactments that restrict or impair property rights, and changes in supply and demand relationships.

**Eminent Domain**   The superior right of property subsisting in every sovereign state to take private property for public use upon the payment of just compensation. This power is often conferred upon public service corporations that perform quasi-public functions, such as providing public utilities. In every case, the owner whose property is taken must be justly compensated according to fair market values in the prevailing area.

**Encroachment**   An obstruction, building, or part of a building that intrudes beyond a legal boundary onto neighboring private or public land, or a building extending beyond the building line.

**Encumbrance**   A legal right or interest in land that affects a good or clear title, and diminishes the land's value. It can take numerous forms, such as zoning ordinances, easement rights, claims, mortgages, liens, charges, a pending legal action, unpaid taxes, or restrictive covenants. An encumbrance does not legally prevent transfer of the property to another. A title search is all that is usually done to reveal the existence of such encumbrances, and it is up to the buyer to determine whether to purchase with the encumbrance, or what can be done to remove it.

**Equity**   The value of a homeowner's unencumbered interest in real estate. Equity is computed by subtracting from the property's fair market value the total of the unpaid mortgage balance and any outstanding liens or other debts against the property. A homeowner's equity increases as the mortgage is paid off, or as the property appreciates in value. When the mortgage and all other debts against the property are paid in full, the homeowner has 100% equity in the property.

**Escheat**   The reverting of property to the state by reason of failure of persons legally entitled to hold, or when heirs capable of inheriting are lacking the ability to do so.

**Escrow**   Funds paid by one party to another (the escrow agent) to hold until the occurrence of a specified event, after which the funds are released to a designated individual. In FHA mortgage transactions, an escrow account usually refers to the funds a mortgagor pays the lender at the time of the periodic mortgage payments. The money is held in a trust fund, provided by the lender for the buyer. Such funds should be adequate to cover yearly anticipated expenditures for mortgage insurance premiums, taxes, hazard insurance premiums, and special assessments.

**Estate**   The degree, quantum, nature, and extent of interest that one has in real property.

**Execute**  To perform what is required to give validity to a legal document. To execute a document, for example, means to sign it so that it becomes fully enforceable by law.

**Fee Simple**  The largest estate a person can have in real estate. Denotes totality of ownership, unlimited in point of time, as in perpetual.

**Fiduciary**  A person to whom property is entrusted; a trustee who holds, controls, or manages for another. A real estate agent is said to have a fiduciary responsibility and relationship with a client.

**Foreclosure**  A legal term applied to any of the various methods of enforcing payment of the debt secured by a mortgage, or deed of trust, by taking and selling the mortgaged property, and depriving the mortgagor of possession.

**Forfeiture Clause**  A clause in a lease enabling the landlord to terminate the lease and remove a tenant when the latter defaults in payment of rent or any other obligation under the lease.

**Functional Obsolescence**  An impairment of desirability of a property arising from its being out of date with respect to design and style, capacity and utility in relation to site, lack of modern facilities, and the like.

**General Warranty Deed**  A deed that conveys not only all the grantor's interests in and title to the property to the grantee, but also warrants that if the title is defective or has a "cloud" on it (such as mortgage claims, tax liens, title claims, judgments, or mechanic's liens against it) the grantee may hold the grantor liable.

**Generally Accepted Accounting Principles (GAAP)**  A standardized set of accounting principles and concepts by which financial statements are prepared.

**Grantee**  That party in the deed who is the buyer or recipient; the person to whom the real estate is conveyed.

**Grantor**  That party in the deed who is the seller or giver; the person who conveys the real estate.

**Hazard Insurance**  Protects against damages caused to property by fire, windstorms, and other common hazards.

**Highest and Best Use**   That use of, or program of utilization of, a site that will produce the maximum net land returns over the total period comprising the future; the optimum use for a site.

**Implied Warranty or Covenant**   A guaranty of assurance the law supplies in an agreement, even though the agreement itself does not express the guaranty or assurance.

**Income Statement**   The financial report that summarizes a business's performance over a specific period of time.

**Injunction**   A writ or order of the court to restrain one or more parties to a suit from committing an inequitable or unjust act in regard to the rights of some other party in the suit or proceeding.

**Interest**   A charge paid for borrowing money.

**Internal Rate of Return (IRR) Method**   A method of ranking an investment proposal using the rate of return on an investment, calculated by finding the discount rate that equates the present value of future cash inflows to the project's cost.

**Joint Tenancy**   Property held by two or more persons together with the right of survivorship. While the doctrine of survivorship has been abolished with respect to most joint tenancies, the tenancy by the entirety retains the doctrine of survivorship in content.

**Judgment**   The decision or sentence of a court of law as the result of proceedings instituted therein for the redress of an injury. A judgment declaring that one individual is indebted to another individual when properly docketed creates a lien on the real property of the judgment debtor.

**Lease**   A species of contract, written or oral, between the owner of real estate, the landlord, and another person, the tenant, covering the conditions upon which the tenant may possess, occupy, and use the real estate.

**Lessee**   A person who leases property from another person, usually the landlord.

**Lessor**   The owner or person who rents or leases property to a tenant or lessee; the landlord.

**Liabilities**   The debts of a business or entity in the form of financial claims on its assets.

**LIBOR (London Interbank Offered Rate)**   The interest rate charged among banks in the foreign market for short-term loans to one another. A common index for ARM loans.

**Lien**   A claim by one person on the property of another as security for money owed. Such claims may include obligations not met or satisfied, judgments, unpaid taxes, materials, or labor.

**Limited Liability Partnership (Limited Liability Company)**   A hybrid form of organization in which all partners enjoy limited liability for the business's debts. It combines the limited liability advantage of a corporation with the tax advantages of a partnership.

**Limited Partnership**   A hybrid form of organization consisting of general partners who have unlimited liability for the partnership's debts, and limited partners, whose liability is limited to the amount of their investment.

**Loan Application**   An initial statement of personal and financial information required to apply for a loan.

**Loan Application Fee**   Fee charged by a lender to cover the initial costs of processing a loan application. The fee may include the cost of obtaining a property appraisal, a credit report, and a lock-in fee or other closing costs incurred during the process, or the fee may be in addition to these charges.

**Loan Origination Fee**   Fee charged by a lender to cover administrative costs of processing a loan.

**Loan-to-Value Ratio (LTV)**   The percentage of the loan amount to the appraised value (or the sales price, whichever is less) of the property.

**Lock or Lock-In**   A lender's guarantee of an interest rate for a set period of time. The time period is usually that between loan application approval and loan closing. The lock-in protects you against rate increases during that time.

**Market Value**   The amount a property would sell for if put on the open market and sold in the manner property is ordinarily sold in the community in which the property is situated. The highest price estimated in terms of money that a buyer would be warranted in paying and a seller would be justified in accepting, provided both parties were fully informed, acted intelligently and voluntarily, and furthermore that all the rights and benefits inherent in or attributable to the property were included in the transfer.

**Marketable Title**  A title that is free and clear of objectionable liens, clouds, or other title defects. A title that enables an owner to sell the property freely to others, and which others will accept without objection.

**Meeting of Minds**  A mutual intention of two persons to enter into a contract affecting their legal status based on agreed upon terms.

**Metes and Bounds**  A term that comes from the old English words "metes," meaning measurements, and "bounds," meaning boundaries. It is generally applied to any description of real estate; describes the boundaries by distance and angles.

**Mortgage**  A lien or claim against real property given by the buyer to the lender as security for money borrowed. Under government-insured or loan guarantee provisions, the payments may include escrow amounts covering taxes, hazard insurance, water charges, and special assessments. Mortgages generally run from 10 to 30 years, during which the loan is to be paid in full.

**Mortgage Commitment**  A written notice from the bank or other lending institution saying it will advance mortgage funds in a specified amount to enable a buyer to purchase a house.

**Mortgage Note**  A written agreement to repay a loan. The agreement is secured by a mortgage, serves as proof of an indebtedness, and states the manner in which it shall be paid. The note states the actual amount of the debt that the mortgage secures and renders the mortgagor personally responsible for repayment.

**Mortgage (Open End)**  A mortgage with a provision that permits borrowing additional money in the future without refinancing the loan or paying additional financing charges. Open-end provisions often limit such borrowing to no more than would raise the balance to the original loan figure.

**Mortgagee**  The lender in a mortgage agreement.

**Mortgagor**  The borrower in a mortgage agreement.

**Net Cash Flow**  The actual net cash, as opposed to accounting net income, that a firm generates during some specified period.

**Net Income**  In general, synonymous with net earnings, but considered a broader and better term; the balance remaining after deducting from the gross income all expenses, maintenance, taxes, and losses pertaining to operating properties except for interest or other financial charges on borrowed or other forms of capital.

**Net Lease**  A lease where, in addition to the rent stipulated, the lessee assumes payment of all property charges such as taxes, insurance, and maintenance.

**Nonconforming Use**  A use of land that predates zoning, but is not in accordance with the uses prescribed for the area by the zoning ordinance. Because it was there first, it may be continued, subject to certain limitations.

**Note**  An instrument of credit given to attest a debt; a written promise to pay money, which may or may not accompany a mortgage or other security agreement.

**Offer**  A proposal, oral or written, to buy a piece of property at a specified price under specified terms and conditions.

**Option**  The exclusive right to purchase or lease a property at a stipulated price or rent within a specified period of time.

**Percentage Lease**  A lease of commercial property in which the rent is computed as a percentage of the receipts, either gross or net, from the business being conducted by the lessee, sometimes with a guaranteed minimum rental.

**Personal Property**  Moveable property that is not by definition real property, including tangible property such as moneys, goods, chattel, as well as debts and claims.

**Planned Unit Development (PUD)**  Residential complex of mixed housing types. Offers greater design flexibility than traditional developments. PUDs permit clustering of homes, sometimes not allowed under standard zoning ordinances, utilization of open space, and a project harmonious with the natural topography of the land.

**Points**  Sometimes referred to as 'discount points.' A point is one percent of the amount of the mortgage loan. For example, if a loan is for $250,000, one point is $2,500. Points are charged by a lender to raise the yield on a loan at a time when money is tight, interest rates are high, and there is a legal limit to the interest rate that can be charged on a mortgage. Buyers are prohibited from paying points on HUD or Veterans' Administration guaranteed loans (sellers can pay them, however). On a conventional mortgage, points may be paid by either buyer or seller or split between them.

**Portfolio**    The combined holdings of more than one stock, bond, real estate asset, or other asset by an investor.

**Prepayment**    Payment of mortgage loan, or part of it, before due date. Mortgage agreements often restrict the right of prepayment either by limiting the amount that can be prepaid in any one year or charging a penalty for prepayment. The Federal Housing Administration does not permit such restrictions in FHA insured mortgages.

**Principal**    The basic element of the loan as distinguished from interest and mortgage insurance premium. In other words, principal is the amount upon which interest is paid. The word also means one who appoints an agent to act for, and in behalf of, the person bound by an agent's authorized contract.

**Property**    The term used to describe the rights and interests a person has in lands, chattel, and other determinate things.

**Purchase Agreement**    An offer to purchase that has been accepted by the seller and has become a binding contract.

**Quiet Enjoyment**    The right of an owner of an interest in land, whether an owner or a tenant, to protection against disturbance or interference with possession of the land.

**Quitclaim Deed**    A deed that transfers whatever interest the maker of the deed may have in the particular parcel of land. A quitclaim deed is often given to clear the title when the grantor's interest in a property is questionable. By accepting such a deed the buyer assumes all the risks. Such a deed makes no warranties as to the title, but simply transfers to the buyer whatever interest the grantor has. (*See* deed.)

**Real Estate Agent**    An intermediary who buys and sells real estate for a company, firm, or individual and is compensated on a commission basis. The agent does not have title to the property, but generally represents the owner.

**Real Estate Investment Trust (REIT)**    An entity that allows a very large number of investors to participate in the purchase of real estate, but as passive investors. The investors do not buy directly, but instead purchase shares in the REIT that owns the real estate investment. REITs are fairly common with the advent of mutual funds and can be purchased for as little as $10 per share and sometimes less.

**Real Property** Land and buildings and anything that may be permanently attached to them.

**Recording** The placing of a copy of a document in the proper books in the office of the Register of Deeds so that a public record will be made of it.

**Redemption** The right that an owner-mortgagor, or one claiming under him or her, has after execution of the mortgage to recover back the title to the mortgaged property by paying the mortgage debt, plus interest and any other costs or penalties imposed, prior to the occurrence of a valid foreclosure. The payment discharges the mortgage and places the title back as it was at the time the mortgage was executed.

**Refinancing** The process of the same mortgagor paying off one loan with the proceeds from another loan.

**Reformation** The correction of a deed or other instrument by reason of a mutual mistake of the parties involved or because of the mistake of one party caused by the fraud or inequitable conduct of the other party.

**Release** The giving up or abandoning of a claim or right to the person against whom the claim exists or against whom the right is to be exercised or enforced.

**Release of Lien** The discharge of certain property from the lien of a judgment, mortgage, or claim.

**Renewal** Taking a new lease after an existing lease expires.

**Rent** A compensation, either in money, provisions, chattel, or labor, received by the owner from a tenant for the occupancy of the premises.

**Rescission of Contract** The abrogating or annulling of a contract; the revocation or repealing of a contract by mutual consent of the parties to the contract, or for other causes as recognized by law.

**Restrictive Covenants** Private restrictions limiting the use of real property. Restrictive covenants are created by deed and may run with the land, thereby binding all subsequent purchasers of the land, or may be deemed personal and binding only between the original seller and buyer. The determination whether a covenant runs with the land or is personal is governed by the language of the covenant, the intent of the parties, and the law in the state where the land is situated. Restrictive covenants that run with the land are encumbrances and may affect the value and marketability of title. Restrictive covenants may limit the density of buildings per acre, regulate size, style, or price range of buildings to be erected, or prevent particular businesses from operating or minority groups from owning or occupying homes in a given area. This latter discriminatory covenant is unconstitutional and has been declared unenforceable by the U.S. Supreme Court.

**Retained Earnings**   That portion of the firm's earnings that has been saved rather than paid out as dividends.

**Return on Assets (ROA)**   The ratio of net income to total assets.

**Return on Equity (ROE)**   The ratio of net income to equity; measures the rate of return on common stockholders' investment.

**Revocation**   The recall of a power or authority conferred, or the vacating of an instrument previously made.

**Right of Survivorship**   Granted to two joint owners who purchase using that particular buying method. Stipulates that one gets full rights and becomes the sole owner of the property upon the death of the other. Right of survivorship is the fundamental difference between acquiring property as joint owners and as tenants in common.

**Sales Agreement**   (*See* agreement of sale)

**Security Deposit**   Money or things of value received by or for a property owner to ensure payment of rent and the satisfactory condition of the rented premises upon termination of the written or oral lease.

**Security Interest**   An interest in property that secures payment or performance of an obligation.

**Special Assessment**   A legal charge against real estate by a public authority to pay the cost of public improvements, such as for the opening, grading, and guttering of streets, the construction of sidewalks and sewers, or the installation of street lights or other such items to be used for public purposes.

**Special Assessments**   A special tax imposed on property, individual lots, or all property in the immediate area, for road construction, sidewalks, sewers, street lights, etc.

**Special Lien**   A lien that binds a specified piece of property, unlike a general lien, which is levied against all one's assets. It creates a right to retain something of value belonging to another person as compensation for labor, material, or money expended in that person's behalf. In some localities it is called 'particular' lien or 'specific' lien. (*See* lien.)

**Special Warranty Deed**   A deed in which the grantor conveys title to the grantee and agrees to protect the grantee against title defects or claims asserted by the grantor and those persons whose right to assert a claim against the title arose during the period the grantor held title to the property. In a special warranty deed, the grantor guarantees to the grantee that nothing has been done during the time title to the property was held that has, or which might in the future, impair the grantee's title.

**Specific Performance**   A remedy in court of equity whereby the defendant may be compelled to do whatever was agreed to in a contract executed by the defendant.

**Statute**   A law established by the act of the legislative powers; an act of the legislature; the written will of the legislature solemnly expressed according to the forms necessary to constitute it as the law provides.

**Subdivision**   A tract of land divided into smaller parcels of land, or lots, usually for the purpose of constructing new houses.

**Sublease**   An agreement whereby one person who has leased land from the owner rents out all or a portion of the premises for a period ending prior to the expiration of the original lease.

**Subordination Clause**   A clause in a mortgage or lease stating that one who has a prior claim or interest agrees that this interest or claim shall be secondary or subordinate to a subsequent claim, encumbrance, or interest.

**Survey**   A map or plat made by a licensed surveyor showing the results of measuring the land with its elevations, improvements, boundaries, and its relationship to surrounding tracts of land. A survey is often required by the lender to assure that a building is actually sited on the land according to its legal description.

**Survivorship**   The distinguishing feature of a tenancy by the entirety, by which on the death of one spouse, the surviving spouse acquires full ownership.

**Tax**   As applied to real estate, an enforced charge imposed on persons, property, or income, to be used to support the State. The governing body in turn utilizes the funds in the best interest of the general public.

**Tax Deed**   A deed given where property has been purchased at public sale because of the owner's nonpayment of taxes.

**Tax Sale**   A sale of property for nonpayment of taxes assessed against it.

**Tenancy at Will**  An arrangement under which a tenant occupies land with the consent of the owner, but without a definite termination date and without any definite agreement for regular payment of rent.

**Tenancy in Common**  Style of ownership in which two or more persons purchase a property jointly, but with no right of survivorship. Each tenant in common is the owner of an undivided fractional interest in the whole property. They are free to will their share to anyone they choose, a primary difference between that form of ownership and joint tenancy.

**Tenant**  One who holds or possesses land or tenements by any kind of title, either in fee, for life, for years, or at will. The term is most commonly used as one who has under lease the temporary use and occupation of real property that belongs to another person or persons. The tenant is the lessee.

**Time is of the Essence**  A phrase meaning that time is of crucial value and vital importance and that failure to fulfill time deadlines will be considered a failure to perform the contract.

**Title**  As generally used, the rights of ownership and possession of a particular property. In real estate usage, title may refer to the instruments or documents by which a right of ownership is established (title documents), or it may refer to the ownership interest one has in the real estate.

**Title Insurance**  Protects lenders or homeowners against loss of their interest in property due to legal defects in title. Title insurance may be issued to a mortgagee's title policy. Insurance benefits will be paid only to the 'named insured' in the title policy, so it is important that an owner purchase an 'owner's title policy' if he or she desires the protection of title insurance.

**Title Search or Examination**  A check of the title records, generally at the local courthouse, to make sure the buyer is purchasing a house from the legal owner and there are no liens, overdue special assessments, or other claims or outstanding restrictive covenants filed in the record that would adversely affect the marketability or value of title.

**Trust**  A relationship under which one person, the trustee, holds legal title to property for the benefit of another person, the trust beneficiary.

**Trustee**  A party who is given legal responsibility to hold property in the best interest of or 'for the benefit of' another. The trustee is one placed in a position of responsibility for another, a responsibility enforceable in a court of law. (*See* deed of trust.)

**Truth-in-lending Act**   Federal law requiring written disclosure of the terms of a mortgage (including the APR and other charges) by a lender to a borrower after application. Also requires the right to rescission period.

**Underwriting**   In mortgage lending, the process of determining the risks involved in a particular loan and establishing suitable terms and conditions for the loan.

**Unimproved**   As relating to land, vacant or lacking in essential appurtenant improvements required to serve a useful purpose.

**Useful Life**   The period of time over which a commercial property can be depreciated for tax purposes. A property's useful life is also referred to as its economic life.

**Usury**   Charging a higher rate of interest on a loan than is allowed by law.

**Valid**   Having force, or binding forces; legally sufficient and authorized by law.

**Valuation**   The act or process of estimating value; the amount of estimated value.

**Value**   Ability to command goods, including money, in exchange; the quantity of goods, including money, that should be commanded or received in exchange for the item valued. As applied to real estate, value is the present worth of all the rights to future benefits arising from ownership.

**Variance**   An exception to a zoning ordinance granted to meet certain specific needs, usually given on an individual case-by-case basis.

**Void**   That which is unenforceable; having no force or effect.

**Waiver**   Renunciation, disclaiming, or surrender of some claim, right, or prerogative.

**Warranty Deed**   A deed that transfers ownership of real property and in which the grantor guarantees that the title is free and clear of any and all encumbrances.

**Zoning Ordinances**   The acts of an authorized local government establishing building codes and setting forth regulations for property land usage.

# A

Abstract of title, 216

Acquisition, efficiency of, 14–15

Advertisements, classified, 85, 87

Air conditioning, 62–63, 185–186

Alfange, Dean, 255

Aluminum wiring, 78, 207

Amortization, loan, 197

Apartment buildings:
consolidation of complexes, 40–41
specialty financing for, 194–195, 208

Aspiration, degree of, 31–33

Assessment, one-minute, 124–125

Assets, 109

Attorney opinion letter, 213

# B

Balance sheet, 108–109, 111, 126

Banks. *See also* Real estate owned (REO) portfolios, of banks
conventional financing by, 192–195, 196–197
credit scores and, 208
as property sources, 85–86, 89–90
small local, 192–193
third-party reports and, 162–163

Beaumont case study, 151–162

Belongingness, 28

*Benjamin Franklin: The Autobiography and Other Writings* (Lemisch, ed.), 266

Brokers, 86–87
apartment, 86–87
as intermediaries, 176–180
mortgage, 206–207

Business plan:
components of, 52–53
importance of, 24–25

Butler Burgher, LLC, 95, 98, 99–100, 101–102

Buy-and-hold approach, 22, 36–37, 143–144
    versus value play, 35–36, 141–151

## C

Cable TV services, 40–41, 43
Capital gains, 79, 150, 234
    *See also* Taxes, capital gains
Capital improvements, 53–55, 106, 167–173
    cost of, 48
    Houston case study, 162–173
Capitalization rate, 117–119, 127, 163, 236–237
Case studies, 129–173
    Beaumont example, 151–162
    Houston example, 162–173
    Saginaw example, 142–151
Cash flow, 197–198
    discounted, 82
    reduction of, 244–245
Cash on cash return. *See* Return on investment (ROI)

Cash return on investment (cash ROI). *See* Return on investment (ROI)
Cellular telephone companies, 40
Closing, 215–223
    credits, 219–223
    documentation for, 216–219
Comfort zone, 35. *See also* Fear
Community, evaluation of, 151. *See also* Due diligence
Compensating incentive, 183–184
Competitor analysis, 40, 53
Concentration of units, 16–17, 162–173
Conditioning, psychological, 265–266
Conduit loans, 194–195, 197, 243, 250
    credit scores and, 207–208
    lockout period and, 201–202
    third-party reports and, 199
Corporations, use of, 244
Cost approach, 127

Cost-benefit analysis, 48–51
  personal example, 61–67
Credits, closing, 217–223
Credit scores, 207–208,
  212–213

# D

Damage. *See* Unexpected
  incidents
Debt service, 104–106
Debt service coverage ratio
  (DSCR), 117, 120–121,
  126, 208, 238–240
Debt-to-equity ratio, 108
Declining neighborhoods, 98
Deed of trust, 217–218
Demographics, 53
Depreciation expenses, 105
Despair, 269–270
Deterioration, assessing level of,
  47–48
Discounted cash-flow analysis,
  100–101
Documentation:
  closing, 215–219
  insurance, 212–213
  for loans, 209–214

DSCR. *See* Debt service coverage
  ratio (DSCR)
Due diligence, 175–190
  checklist, 189–190

# E

Economy of scale, 71–72
Einstein, Albert, 267–269,
  233
Elephant, training of,
  265–266
Entry strategy, 26, 54, 162,
  167–177
Environmental issues, 189
Equity, 19–21, 109–110. *See
  also* Refinancing
  accessing, 27, 204–205
  financing, 204–205
  owner's, 110
  partnership (*see* Partnerships,
    equity)
Equity agreement, 204
Esteem, 28
Exit strategy, 26, 55, 57, 162,
  167–171
  combining methods, 249–253
  effective, 233

Expenses:
  cutting, 44–47
  general and administrative,
    105
  and income, relative, 125
  interest, 105
  payroll, 45, 104–105

## F

Failure, fear of, 256, 259–261
Fair, Isaac and Company scores
  (FICO), 207, 213
FASB. *See* Financial
  Accounting Standards
  Board (FASB)
Fear, 29–33, 36, 269–270
  of failure, overcoming, 213,
    259–261
Feasibility period, 183–184
Fees. *See also* Transaction
  costs, 44
FICO. *See* Fair, Isaac and
  Company scores (FICO)
Financial Accounting Standards
  Board (FASB), 103
Financial analysis, 53
  principles of, 91–127

Financial statement, 53, 102,
  126
  analysis of, 125–127
  for multifamily properties,
    102
  personal, 212
Financing, 51–52, 192,
  204–206
  conduit loans, 194–195
  secondary alternatives, 203
  specialty apartment lending
    programs, 194–195
  summary of considerations,
    213–214
Fixer-upper, 48–49
Franklin, Benjamin, 266–267
Free look. *See* Feasibility period

## G

GAAP. *See* Generally accepted
  accounting principles
  (GAAP)
Gates, Bill, 29
Generally accepted accounting
  principles (GAAP), 102
*Greatest Miracle in the World,*
  *The* (Mandino), 269

# H

Heat, 186
  lack of, 63
Hill, Napoleon, 60, 270–271
Holding period, 70, 79
  tax implications of, 79
  Houston case study, 151–162

# I

Income:
  enhancement of, 40
  and expenses, relative, 126
  gross scheduled, 104
  net operating, 104, 106
*Income and Expense
  Analysis: Conventional
  Apartments* (National
  Association of Realtors),
  125–127
Income capitalization approach,
  99–102, 126, 236
Income statement, 105–106,
  126
  Beaumont case study,
  156–157

essential components of, 104
Houston case study, 164–165,
  168–170
purchase price and, 178
Saginaw case study,
  146–149
Inspection, physical, 62–64,
  186, 216
  checklist, 187–188
  before closing, 219
Installment sales, 82
Institute of Real Estate
  Management (IREM),
  126
Insurance, 105
  cost of, 47
  documentation of, 213
  exchanges and, 81
Interest, prepaid, 221
Interest rates, 193–195, 198
  borrower rating and, 210
Inventory, availability of,
  15–16
Investment summary, case
  study, 154
Investors associations, 86, 89,
IREM. *See* Institute of Real
  Estate Management
  (IREM)

**J**

Jeffery, R. Dale, 85

**K**

Keller, Helen, 21
Kessler, A. D., 273, 286
Kiyosake, Robert, 182

**L**

Laundromat services, 42–43
Lease agreements, 189,
    211–212
Lemisch, L. Jesse, 266
Leverage, 23
Liabilities, 108–110
Life-changing events,
    182–183
Like-kind exchange. *See* 1031
    exchange
Litigation, pending, 189
*Little Engine That Could, The,*
    31
Loans:
    amortization period of, 197
    assumability of, 200–201

conduit (*see* Conduit loans)
documentation required for,
    210–214
fees for, 197–199
long-term, 192
nonrecourse, 196, 209
recourse, 195–196
term of, 196–197
underwriting guidelines for,
    209–210
Loan-to-value ratio (LTV), 121,
    209, 239
Lockout period, 201–202
LoopNet, 88–89
LTV. *See* Loan-to-value ratio
    (LTV)

**M**

Mahoney, Don, 129
Maintenance:
    contracts, 189, 213
    expenses, 45, 104
    staff, 17–18
Management, poor, 181
Management agreement,
    225–226
Manager:
    owner as, 72–73

property (*see* Property
manager)
strategic, 223
Mandino, Og, 269–271
Market analysis, 40–41
Marketing strategy, 53
Maslow, Abraham, 27–29, 36
Maslow's hierarchy of needs,
27–29
McKay, David O., 31
Microsoft Corporation, 29
Mission statement, 52
Mistakes, accepting
responsibility for,
261–264
MLS. *See* Multiple Listing
Service (MLS)
*Money Income Tax Handbook*
(Sprouse), 80–83
Mortgage:
brokers, 206–207, 240–241
wraparound (*see* Wraparound
mortgage)
Motivation:
behavioral, 27
of seller, 178–183
*Motivation and Personality*
(Maslow), 27
Multifamily property:
analysis of, 117

financial statement for,
102–103
versus single family, 13, 15
Multiple Listing Service (MLS),
87–89

**N**

Negotiation, strategies for,
175–176
Net operating income (NOI), 48,
117–119, 174, 237
Niche, establishing, 70
NOI. *See* Net operating income
(NOI)
Nonrecourse loans, 196, 209

**O**

Objectives, 24, 52, 162, 255,
267–271
Occupancy rates, 40, 47–48,
112. *See also* Turnover,
tenant
high, 113–116
lenders' minimum, 48
Office buildings, 81
Oil leasehold, 81

One-minute assessment, 124–125

Operating expenses, 104

Operating revenues, 104

OPM. *See* Other people's money (OPM) principle

Origination fees, 244

Other people's money (OPM) principle, 23

Owner:
  as manager, 73
  role, defining, 223, 227

Owner financing, 203–204

# P

Paine, Thomas, 264

Partnerships, 205–206
  advantages of, 246–247
  disadvantages of, 247–248
  equity, 245–248, 251–252
  financial assumptions, 246
  taxes and, 251–252

Perseverance, 256, 264–267

Personal liability, financial, 195–196, 243–244

Physiological needs, 28

Playground, 56

Politicians, 257

Postentry strategy, 26, 54, 162, 170, 171, 223

Potter, Simon, 269–270

Prepayment penalties, 202–203

Problems. *See* Unexpected incidents

Profitability, level of, 181

Promissory note, 217

Properties:
  advantages of types, 13, 18
  age of, 74–79, 90
  Class A, 74–75, 113
  Class B, 75–76, 113
  Class C, 61, 76–77, 93, 113
  Class D, 78–79
  disposition of, 18–19, 234
    (*see also* Exit strategy)
  exchange of (*see* 1031 exchange)
  inspection of, 62–64, 186–189, 216, 219
    (*see also* Cost-benefit analysis)
  locating, 85–86
  profitability level of, 181
  replacement, types of, 81–82
  size of, 70–73

Property assessments. *See* Taxes, real estate

Property manager, 17–18, 113,
238
full-time, 45
hiring, 224–228
owner as, 73
professional, 71–73, 224–228,
232
responsibilities of, 225
Public speaking, fear of,
29–30
Purchase agreement, 53
Purchase price, negotiating,
176–178. *See also*
Negotiation, strategies for
Purpose, defining sense of,
24–26, 162, 173, 255,
267–271


# R


Ragpicker, 269
Ratios, key, 117, 121–122,
126–127
Real estate:
investment clubs, 86–87, 89
publications, 86, 88
Web sites, 88–89
Real estate investment trust
(REIT), 74

Real estate owned (REO)
portfolios, of banks, 89,
151–162
Record keeping, 18
Recourse loans, 195–196
Refinancing, 235–245
advantages of, 241–242
versus cash sale, 243
disadvantages of, 242–243
model, 241
REIT. *See* Real estate investment
trust (REIT)
Rent:
average per square foot, 41
below-market, case study,
142–151
decreasing, 41
Houston case study, 170
increasing, 39–41, 56–57
schedule (*see* Rent roll)
Rental market, tight, 113–116
Rent roll, 110, 112–116,
126–127
purchase price and, 178
REO. *See* Real estate owned
(REO) portfolios, of
banks
Repairs, cost of, 45, 66–67.
*See also* Capital
improvements

Replacement cost approach, 98–99, 236

Reserve requirements, 104, 106

Resources, level of, 19, 70–71
  maximizing, 22

Responsibility, accepting, 256, 261–264

Retained earnings, 110

Retirement, 183

Return, maximization of, 73

Return on investment (ROI), 23, 60, 117, 119–121, 126–127

*Rich Dad Secrets to Money, Business and Investing* (Kiyosake), 182

Risk:
  comfort level and, 30–31
  versus riskiness, 256–258
  understanding, 255–258

Risk-free rate, 101

ROI. *See* Return on investment (ROI)

## S

Safety, 28

Saginaw case study, 142–151

Salaries, 45. *See also* Expenses, payroll

Sale, outright, 234
  versus refinancing, 243
  versus 1031 exchange, 249

Sales, installment, 82

Sales comparison, 95–98, 126–127, 159, 236–237

Satellite services, 40, 43

Seasoning period, 58, 235, 239

Second-lien positions, 203–204

*Secrets of a Happy Life* (McKay), 31

Security deposits, 221–222

Self-actualization, 28–29, 36

Seller, motivation of, 178–183

Settlement statements, 216

Setup sheet, 124–125

Single-family units:
  disposition of, 18–19
  versus multifamily property, 21–23

Site location, 52

Spouse, supportive, 259–260

Sprouse, Mary L., 80

Stable property, 112

Staff, maintenance, 17–18, 71–72

Storage space, excess, 40, 44
Stupid, use of term, 261–264
Submetering, of utilities, 40, 41–42, 45–46, 163–167, 172
Subsidies, government, 116
Substitution, principle of, 95
Success, keys to, 255–271

**T**

Taxes, 18, 105
 capital gains, 26, 79–80, 83, 234
 closing costs and, 221–222
 documentation for loans, 213
 partnerships and, 247, 251
 real estate, 40, 46–47
 seller's considerations, 182
 1031 exchange and, 248
 on wealth, 257
1031 exchange, 80–83, 248–249
 versus cash sale, 249
 rules governing, 81–82
thevalueplay.com, 151, 296
*Think and Grow Rich* (Hill), 260–261, 270–271

Third-party reports, 199–200, 213
 expenses for, 199
Time, efficient use of, 14–15, 17
Title report. *See* Abstract of title
Total cash return on investment (total ROI). *See* Return on investment (ROI)
Trailing 12-month period, 103
Transaction costs, 16–17, 242–243
Turnaround time, 79
Turnover, tenant, 41–42, 66, 171
 calculating rate of, 112–113

**U**

Underwriting guidelines, 209–210, 239
 additional compensating factors, 210
Unexpected incidents, 228–232
Unrealized gain, 242
Utilities:
 cutting costs of, 45–46
 expenses for, 105
 submetering of, 40, 41–42, 45, 163–164, 171

# V

Vacancy loss, 104
Valuation analysis, 47–48,
    92–93, 236, 238
  illustration of, 93
  methodologies for, 95
Value, creating, 39–40, 158
Value play, 22, 35, 38–39, 59–60
  versus buy-and-hold approach,
    35–39, 142–151
  example of, 78–79
  finding opportunities for,
    66–67
  length of loan and, 196–197
Vehicle, business, 81
Vending services, 40, 42–43

# W

Water-saving devices, 40, 45–46
Wealth:
  accumulation of, long-term,
    27, 264, 268
  redistribution of, 257
Weather-related incidents, 228
Work, value of, 265
Wraparound mortgage, 204,
    245

# Z

Ziglar, Zig, 35
Zoning ordinances, 189